THE POLITICS OF MISRECOGNITION

This edited volume offers a timely intervention since it is the first that explicitly shifts the theoretical focus from recognition to misrecognition as a distinctive and fruitful concept for critical theory. Several of the individual contributions demonstrate how a focus on misrecognition can generate new insights into a range of social phenomena including crime, disability and the unequal division of labour.

Shane O'Neill, Queen's University Belfast, UK

Rethinking Political and International Theory

Series Editors:
Keith Breen, Dan Bulley and Susan McManus,
all at Queens University Belfast, UK

Committed to a critical and creative exploration of the ways that canonical approaches in political and international theory may be applied to 21st century politics, this series presents pioneering theoretical work on contemporary political issues that both furthers our understanding and shapes exciting new agendas for research. The works featured will advance our appreciation of the relevance of seminal thinkers to the current socio-political context, as well as problematize, and offer new insights into, key political concepts and phenomena within the arena of politics and international relations.

Also in the series

Institutionalizing Agonistic Democracy
Post-Foundationalism and Political Liberalism
Ed Wingenbach
ISBN 978 1 4094 0353 1

Power, Judgment and Political Evil
In Conversation with Hannah Arendt
Edited by Andrew Schaap, Danielle Celermajer and Vrasidas Karalis
ISBN 978 1 4094 0350 0

The Politics of Misrecognition

Edited by

SIMON THOMPSON
University of the West of England, UK

MAJID YAR
University of Hull, UK

Routledge
Taylor & Francis Group
LONDON AND NEW YORK

First published 2011 by Ashgate Publishing

2 Park Square, Milton Park, Abingdon, Oxfordshire OX14 4RN
711 Third Avenue, New York, NY 10017

Routledge is an imprint of the Taylor & Francis Group, an informa business

First issued in paperback 2018

British Library Cataloguing in Publication Data
The politics of misrecognition. -- (Rethinking political
and international theory)
1. Identity politics. 2. Minorities--Social conditions.
3. Minorities--Legal status, laws, etc. 4. Politics and
culture. 5. Social ethics.
I. Series II. Thompson, Simon, D. Phil. III. Yar, Majid.
306.2-dc22

Library of Congress Cataloging-in-Publication Data
The politics of misrecognition / [edited] by Simon Thompson and Majid Yar.
p. cm. -- (Rethinking political and international theory)
Includes bibliographical references and index.
ISBN 978-1-4094-0169-8 (hbk) 1. Marginality, Social. 2. Minorities--Social conditions.
I. Thompson, Simon, 1962- II. Yar, Majid.

HM1136.P65 2011
305.5'6--dc23

2011015945

ISBN 978-1-4094-0169-8 (hbk)
ISBN 978-1-138-38394-4 (pbk)

Contents

List of Contributors

Laura Brace: Senior Lecturer, Department of Politics and International Relations, University of Leicester, UK.

Gideon Calder: Reader in Ethics and Social Philosophy, School of Health and Social Sciences, University of Wales, Newport, UK.

Estelle Ferrarese: Associate Professor, University of Strasbourg, France.

Paul Hoggett: Professor of Politics and Director of the Centre for Psycho-Social Studies, University of the West of England, Bristol, UK.

Nasar Meer: Research Fellow, The Centre for the Study of Ethnicity and Citizenship, University of Bristol, UK.

Ricardo Fabrino Mendonça: Assistant Professor, Political Science Department, Federal University of Minas Gerais, Brazil.

Andrew Sayer: Professor of Sociology, University of Lancaster, UK.

Simon Thompson: Reader in Politics, University of the West of England, Bristol, UK.

Majid Yar: Professor of Sociology, University of Hull, UK.

Introduction

Simon Thompson and Majid Yar

Opening Remarks

Over the last two decades, there has been a strong revival of interest in the politics of recognition. Although it is sometimes conflated with other ideas, especially the politics of identity and difference, it can be argued that the politics of recognition offers a distinctive and valuable perspective on contemporary politics. This is because the idea of recognition has been deployed not only as a normative conception of justice, but also as a way of understanding a wide range of phenomena, from the formation of individual psyches, through the dynamics of political struggles, to the nature of moral progress. The idea of recognition also invites investigation of the complementary idea of misrecognition. This latter idea should not be understood simply as the opposite of a normative conception of recognition, and therefore as a synonym for injustice. Misrecognition has also been used as the basis for explanations of a variety of phenomena, including the malformation of individual psyches, and the dynamics of struggles for justice. For some thinkers, indeed, the idea of misrecognition has a certain priority over that of recognition since, so they argue, it is the experience of such misrecognition which is the impetus behind struggles for recognition.

Our aim in this book is to place the spotlight on misrecognition. We would argue that, although debates about the politics of recognition have yielded significant theoretical insights into the nature of recognition, its logical and necessary counterpart, misrecognition, has been relatively neglected. While in debates about the politics of recognition, recurrent and almost ritualistic references are made to harms that misrecognition may do to individual and collective autonomy, individuals' and groups' self-conceptions, self-respect and self-esteem, the precise dynamics of misrecognition and their broader political significance have been for the most part only mentioned in passing. We intend this book to serve as an important corrective to this situation, bringing concerted attention to bear both on the idea of misrecognition and on the dynamics of the struggles which it inspires. In order to do so, this book brings together scholars writing about misrecognition in a number of different intellectual disciplines, including philosophy, political theory, sociology, psychoanalysis, history, moral economy and criminology. These authors explore the politics of misrecognition in relation to a wide array of types of social, political and personal experience, including those of class identity, disability, slavery, criminal victimization and domestic abuse. Through a mediation of theoretical and empirical insights, they offer the most systematic reflection to date on the importance of misrecognition for our understandings of personal and political experience and, indeed, of the 'moral grammar of social conflicts' (Honneth 1995).

The rest of this introduction falls into three sections. We begin by explaining the idea of a politics of recognition, and then trace the development of political theories of recognition up to the present day. We also give a brief account of the broad range of fields in which this idea is now being productively employed. We then outline several important conceptions of recognition, and explicate their corresponding notions of misrecognition, and focusing in particular on the tensions between these conceptions. Finally, by providing a brief account of each of the chapters that follow, we explain the significance of the politics of misrecognition, and suggest the rich variety of ways in which this idea can be deployed. Here we seek both to highlight significant shared themes, and to draw attention to some important areas of disagreement between the authors included in this volume.

Political Struggles and Political Theories

It is important to understand that the phrase 'the politics of recognition' – and therefore 'the politics of misrecognition' – can be used in two distinct ways. First, it can describe a range of empirical phenomena, and, second, it can denote a certain sort of normative response to such phenomena. For reasons of clarity, we shall refer to the empirical phenomena as 'the politics of recognition', and to the normative responses as 'political theories of recognition'. In this section, we provide a brief sketch of the politics of recognition, including comments on tensions between various aspects of such a politics, and then give an account of the history of the idea of recognition which leads up to a sketch of the state of current debates about the political theory of recognition. Here we focus in particular on the work of three prominent contemporary theorists: Charles Taylor, Axel Honneth and Nancy Fraser.

With regard to the politics of recognition, it has been argued that it encompasses a broad range of political phenomena. Taylor – the renowned Canadian philosopher – mentions a number of cases, from the relations between Canada and Quebec, to the 'campus wars' which have sporadically broken out in North American universities (1995). Honneth – the leading representative of German critical theory today – suggests that 'a great many contemporary social movements can only be properly understood from a normative point of view if their motivating demands are interpreted along the lines of a "politics of identity" – a demand for the cultural recognition of their collective identity'. He gives the examples of 'feminism, ethnic minorities, gay and lesbian subcultures' (2003: 111). In a similar vein, Fraser – the American feminist and critical theorist – cites examples 'from battles around multiculturalism to struggles over gender and sexuality, from campaigns for national sovereignty and subnational autonomy to newly energized movements for international human rights' (2003: 88-9). Bringing these three accounts together, it is clear that the politics of recognition has been used to describe a wide array of political movements and formations. Indeed, some have argued that the net has been cast too widely, and that as a consequence vital differences between different sorts of political struggles have been overlooked. Thus Jürgen Habermas contends that Taylor has squeezed too many different political phenomena into a single, overextended theoretical framework (Habermas 1994).

However, while acknowledging that there are a number of very important differences between the various political forms just mentioned, we would suggest that there are also a number of features that they have in common. Three in particular are worth highlighting. First, there is a focus on ideas of identity and difference. The conceptions of ethnicity, nationality, sexuality and gender invoked here are all markers of identity: they point to certain features which make some people different from others.[1] Second, there is a concern with inclusion and equality. Often the groups demanding recognition feel invisible and inaudible, and hence they demand to be seen and heard, to be included, to be regarded as each others' equals.[2] The example of Martin Luther King and the American civil rights movement would exemplify this aspect of the politics of recognition (Williams 1987). Third, there is also a concern – which can be in tension with the previous feature – with distinctiveness. A group seeking recognition may feel overlooked and unvalued. However, rather than wanting to be treated the same as others, it may demand that its distinctive contribution be valued or its unique identity affirmed. Stokeley Carmichael (later Kwame Ture) and the black power movement would provide a good illustration of this aspect of the politics of recognition (Ogbar 2004).

It is worth emphasizing that these three features of the politics of recognition do not always co-exist in perfect harmony. In the first place, the identity of the group in question may be hotly contested, both by members of this group and by others outside of it. For example, in British politics the terms 'Black' and 'Asian' have long been the subject of considerable dispute, as various parties disagree about the extension and intension of these terms. Different accounts of who should be included in the group, and of what properties they must possess in order to be included, will lead to different sorts of demands for recognition being made. Furthermore, as we have just suggested, there may also be a tension between these demands themselves. Some members of a group which is struggling for recognition may want to be treated no differently to other people. Indeed, they may believe that it is unfair that they are singled out for special attention. For example, Turkish Germans may demand the same rights of citizenship that 'ethnic' Germans already enjoy. Other members of a group may believe that it is in light of their unique

1 Other possible markers include 'race', culture, language and religion.

2 Honneth's focus on the idea of 'invisibility' as the key to understanding the epistemology of recognition is of particular importance in this regard (Honneth 2001).

identity that they deserve different treatment. Thus Rastafarians may demand exemption for a general law which make the smoking of marijuana illegal.

With these images of struggles of recognition in mind, we can now turn to the normative response to such struggles. The first – and still the most important – philosopher of recognition was G.W.F. Hegel. The short section in his *Phenomenology of Spirit* (1807), most often translated as 'the dialectic of master and slave', has been the locus classicus for a great many of the philosophers of recognition who have followed him. In this passage, Hegel seeks to demonstrate how a subject's acquisition of self-consciousness necessarily requires the presence of another subject who recognizes the first. Since Hegel's vignette depicts two subjects who are engaged in a struggle to the death, as each seeks to win recognition from another, it has not been difficult for later theorists to translate this account into more overtly political contexts. In the last century, the revival of interest in this aspect of Hegel's philosophy was sparked by the publication of Alexandre Kojève's *Introduction to the Reading of Hegel*, first published in French – as *Introduction à la lecture de Hegel* – in 1947. His influence can be seen in Sartre's analysis of anti-Semitism (1947), in de Beauvoir's analysis of the *Second Sex* (1949), and in Fanon's analysis of colonialism (1952; 1961). Although very different in many ways, all of these works depict struggles for recognition, whether these are between anti-Semite and Jew, men and women, or colonizers and the colonized.

It is possible to date the turn to recognition in contemporary political philosophy to the first half of the 1990s. In 1992, Taylor's extended essay 'The Politics of Recognition' (reprinted in Taylor 1995) was published in a volume which also included comments by a number of critics. Arguably this essay remains the single most influential work on recognition in modern political theory. In the same year, Honneth published *Kampf um Anerkennung*, which was published in English as *The Struggle for Recognition* in 1995 (as we shall see, Honneth's theoretical framework provides the starting point for a number of the chapters in this volume). Three years later, Fraser published her influential essay 'From Redistribution to Recognition?' in which she began to develop her own distinctive political theory of recognition. Since 1992, Taylor has not had much more to say directly about recognition, although his essays on democracy and inclusion have added considerably to our understanding of this important aspect of the political theory of recognition (Taylor 1998; 1999). In the meantime – although not simply by default we should add – Honneth and Fraser have become two of the most important contemporary theorists of recognition. Indeed, we would argue that between them, their rival accounts cover much of the intellectual field. The terms of their debate (aspects of which we shall summarize very briefly below) are laid out very clearly in their jointly authored book *Redistribution or Recognition?* (2003). Although their subsequent work of recognition has to some degree gone off in different directions, it is interesting to note that both thinkers are now attempting to apply their theories of recognition to issues of global justice (Fraser 2005; Honneth 2010).

It would, of course, be quite wrong to give the impression that Taylor, Honneth and Fraser are the only theorists who have anything worthwhile to say about the politics of recognition today. In the rest of this section, then, we provide a very brief indication of the wide range of other work to be found in this rapidly developing field. For one thing, there are a number of other important philosophers who have given considerable attention to the idea of recognition. Let us mention just three. Robert Brandom, the American analytical philosopher, who is perhaps best known for his work on semantics, has also engaged very seriously with Hegel on recognition (Brandom 2002; 2007). Brandom seeks to rehabilitate Hegel from his detractors in both analytic and post-structuralist philosophy, recovering what he sees as the innate connections between rationality, freedom, and norm-based communities of mutual recognition. In Paul Ricoeur's last book, *The Course of Recognition* (2005), the French hermeneutical philosopher presents his account of a quest for mutual esteem which he believes is based on the unity of humanity. In 1995 James Tully, the Canadian political philosopher, published his *Strange Multiplicity*, which can be regarded as the first stage in the development of his own distinctive quasi-Nietzschean account of recognition.[3] By reworking the concept in this way, Tully seeks to resolve the problems faced by modern political constitutions in dealing with cultural difference and the demands and conflicts it generates.

In addition, the political theory of recognition is now a sufficiently developed academic field to have attracted a number of book-length critiques. Again we shall mention just a few. Patchen Markell, drawing on the ideas of Hannah Arendt, argues that the practice of recognition, as it is conventionally understood, is always bound up with a deeper layer of misrecognition 'of one's own fundamental situation or circumstances' (2003: 5). He holds that recognition theory (with its desire for transparency, invulnerability and reconciliation) suppresses the innate fragility of human existence, the fact that it is inevitably conditioned by finitude and tragedy. It is for this reason that he proposes a 'politics of acknowledgement' as a distinct alternative to the politics of recognition (2003: 35-8). Kelly Oliver, in her 2001 book *Witnessing*, argues that the struggle for recognition, far from offering a resolution to the experience of oppression, actually reproduces and sustains the pathological dynamic of contestation and domination. She therefore seeks to go 'beyond recognition' in order to defend an account of ethical relations in which subjects are infinitely responsive to one another, a responsiveness based upon an openness to difference. Lois McNay is firmly 'against recognition' (2008). She deploys Pierre Bourdieu's notion of habitus in order to point out what she regards as the failings of contemporary accounts of recognition, and also to suggest a way beyond them. In particular, she holds that recognition-based perspectives are undermined by their reliance upon a reductive notion of power (viewed as, in essence, a dyadic relationship). For McNay, this crucially misses the ways in which abstract social structures mediate and condition human experience, and

3 For an overview of his current position, see his collected papers in Tully (2009).

hence the ways in which inequality, suffering and disadvantage are shaped by forces residing outside the sphere in inter-subjective interaction.

Thus far we may have given the impression that debates about the politics of recognition have been conducted at a very rarefied theoretical level. If so, then it is important to end this part of our introduction by pointing out that the idea of such a politics has also been utilized to illuminate a wide range of economic, social and political phenomena. For instance, in the field of economics, there is now a rapidly growing literature on recognition and work. Emphasizing the importance of work for individuals' sense of self-worth, this literature provides an important corrective to accounts of recognition which focus exclusively on cultural identity (Dejours 2007; Sayer 2005; Smith 2009; Voswinkel 2005). It also serves, *inter alia*, as a response to criticisms (such as those of McNay, noted above) that the theory of recognition fails to give adequate attention to the structural forces that situate and shape individual life experiences. In social studies, ideas of recognition have been used to explain aspects of the formation of identity in schools (Bingham 2001; Jenlink 2009). Bingham, for example, seeks to chart the ways in which various pedagogic practices can contribute to the fostering of recognition. Theorists of social movements have deployed the idea of struggles for recognition to illuminate important features of such movements. For example, Hobson (2003) aims to show how the dynamics of recognition struggles figure in the emergence of emancipatory social movements worldwide, ranging from those associated with the assertion of cultural identity and difference to those oriented by claims to economic justice in situations of extreme disadvantage. Other authors have placed the idea of recognition at the centre of their accounts of particular dimensions of contemporary multiculturalism (Banting and Kymlicka 2006; Povinelli 2002). Finally, in the area of political studies, the idea of recognition has been used a wide range of contexts, from Ireland to Cameroon (De Wispelaere, McBride and O'Neill 2008; Konings and Nyamnjoh 2003).[4] Here, the concept has been mobilized so as to better grasp what is at stake in the emergence, and potential resolution, of specific political conflicts and processes.

Ideas of Recognition and Misrecognition

Given the quantity and diversity of the literature to which we have just referred, it would be very difficult to give anything like a comprehensive account of the variety of conceptions of recognition and misrecognition to be found there. In this case, we begin this section by focusing once again on Taylor, Honneth and Fraser. We do so for two closely related reasons. First, these three are arguably the most influential political theorists of recognition at work today, and, second, the authors in this volume refer to these three theorists more than any others. We

4 The website recognitionforum.com.au 'provides links to key references in the philosophy and politics of recognition'.

start by analysing each thinker's conceptions of recognition, before drawing out the implications for their conceptions of misrecognition. We end this section by focusing on the significance of the differences between these accounts for theorists wanting to understand particular aspects of misrecognition.

Beginning with Taylor, it is important to understand that he is deeply indebted to Hegel. This debt can be seen in the most frequently cited passage from his essay on the politics of recognition which concerns the psychic damage which individuals can suffer if they are the victims of misrecognition. As he says, failures of recognition or acts of misrecognition by others 'can inflict harm, can be a form of oppression, imprisoning someone in a false, distorted, and reduced mode of being' (1995: 225). It is important to note, however, that Taylor puts aside this sort of harm when discussing the politics of misrecognition. Making a distinction between the intimate and public spheres of society, he places psychic harms in the former sphere, and does not consider them when discussing the latter (1995: 233). In the case of the politics of recognition, Taylor's analysis is based on a contrast between what he calls the 'politics of universalism' and the 'politics of difference' (1995: 233). These, he argues, are two distinct interpretations of a politics of equal dignity. According to the first, we enjoy equal respect if our individual capacity for rational autonomy receives recognition. In the modern world, the usual mechanism for doing so is by instituting systems of individual rights. By contrast, according to the second way of understanding the politics of equal dignity, we enjoy such dignity if our capacity for creating distinctive identities is appropriately acknowledged. Today, this goal may be achieved in a variety of ways. On one popular reading of Taylor's essay, it is suggested that he endorses the idea of a right to cultural survival. On an alternative reading, his proposal is that people should have fair opportunities to defend their cultures.[5] Seeking a middle path between these rival accounts of the politics of equal dignity, Taylor defends a system of recognition in which individuals' most fundamental rights are protected, but other rights that they may lay claim to can legitimately be overridden in the interests of cultural protection. It follows that, for Taylor, there are two principal forms of misrecognition which individuals may experience in the sphere of politics. First, if they are denied basic rights, then their capacity for rational autonomy is not appropriately acknowledged. Second, if they lack a reasonable opportunity to defend their cultures, then their capacity to cultivate distinctive collective identities is not adequately recognized.

Honneth also owes a large debt to Hegel, and his *Struggle for Recognition* opens with a detailed analysis of the idealist philosopher's Jena writings. Following Hegel, Honneth believes that humans need recognition in order to form integrated identities, and having such identities makes it possible for them to achieve self-realization. Hence he argues that justice is achieved to the extent to which the relations of recognition necessary for such self-realization are in place. It is important to understand that, for Honneth, recognition takes three distinct forms.

5 On these different interpretations, see Thompson 2006: Section 4.2.

First, love is a relationship of strong affective attachment between significant others, a relationship in which each is responsive to the other's unique needs. Second, respect is a relationship in which all others, since they are capable of acting autonomously, are treated as morally responsible for their actions. Third, esteem is a relationship in which particular others are valued for their achievements, and in particular for the contribution that they make to societal goals. In practice, these three forms of recognition are realized in distinctive ways: love through relations of care between significant others, respect in the form of a system of individual rights, and esteem within the framework of a horizon of shared values. If suitable relations of care, the right sort of system of rights, and an appropriate value-horizon are all in place, then individuals may form integrated identities and hence be able to achieve self-realization. It follows from Honneth's account of recognition that there are also three distinctive forms of misrecognition. First, individuals' body-related self-confidence may be damaged by attacks on their physical integrity (Honneth 1992: 193; 1995: 132). We would broaden this analysis in order to argue that harm to individuals' self-confidence may also result from significant others' insensitivity to their expressions of need. Second, individuals are misrecognized if they do not enjoy rights equal to those of their fellow citizens. As a result, their self-respect is likely to be undermined. Third, individuals – as members of various sorts of collective bodies – are misrecognized if the value of their way of life to society at large is overlooked. Such inattention is likely to harm the self-esteem of members of the collectivities in question.

In sharp contrast to Taylor and Honneth, Fraser's account of recognition is strongly anti-Hegelian, making no reference to individual identity or self-realization. She thinks that justice is a matter of parity of participation, which is achieved when all citizens can participate on a par with their peers in the life of their society. To achieve such parity, it is necessary to attend to three analytically distinct dimensions of the social order which are – or should be – governed by three mutually irreducible principles of justice. First, the cultural dimension of justice pertains to a society's 'status order'. Here the principle of recognition is realized if there are no status inequalities – such as sexism or racism – which stand in the way of participatory parity. Second, the economic dimension of justice unsurprisingly concerns the 'economic structure' of society. Here the principle of redistribution is realized if citizens have the resources that they need in order to enjoy parity with their peers. Third, the political dimension of justice relates to what Fraser calls the 'political constitution' of society. Here the principle of representation is met if political decision rules and political boundaries facilitate parity of participation (2005: 73-6). It follows from Fraser's analysis that individuals can suffer from three distinctive forms of injustice, although only one of these is properly called misrecognition. If individuals are unable to participate on a par with their peers since they lack the necessary resources, then they are the victims of maldistribution. If they are cannot participate on a par since they do not enjoy political voice, then they suffer from misrepresentation. But individuals only suffer from misrecognition proper if their lack of participatory parity is the result of their poor social standing.

So what are the decisive differences between the three thinkers? And how do these differences impact upon the theorization of misrecognition? The first important point to make about these three philosophers is that, contrary to the impression often given of their work, none of them regard identity or difference as the direct object of recognition or misrecognition. For Taylor, members of a group may justly claim rights or the opportunity to defend what they regard as their culture. For Honneth, individuals may deserve to be cared for by others, they may justly demand rights, and they may insist that the achievements of their group receive appropriate acknowledgement. And for Fraser, individuals enjoy due recognition if no cultural values prevent them from participating on a par with their peers. Hence individuals' vulnerability, their capacity for autonomy, their interests in defending their culture, and their right to parity can all be the basis of a claim to recognition, but their identity, *per se*, cannot.

After this point of agreement, however, significant differences between these three thinkers can be seen. The principal dividing line separates the Hegelians Taylor and Honneth from the explicitly anti-Hegelian Fraser. Three differences are worth particular attention. First, both Taylor and Honneth believe that recognition plays a key role in the formation of individual identity – although the former does not think that this fact should play a role in a *politics* of recognition. By contrast, Fraser seeks to drive a wedge between recognition and identity. Second, while both Taylor and Honneth think that rights are one important mode of recognition, Fraser regards rights merely as a means which may be appropriate in the achievement of justice. Third, Taylor and Honneth believe that individuals should have a chance to have the achievements of their cultures acknowledged, while for Fraser culture plays a merely negative role in the sense that patterns of cultural values may undermine particular sets of individuals' parity of participation.

The differences between these three thinkers' views on recognition correspond to differences in their views on misrecognition. For Taylor and Honneth, injuries of misrecognition can reach deep in the individual psyche. Fraser does not in fact deny that such injuries can occur, but she denies that they are in themselves an injustice. The two Hegelians agree that individuals are misrecognized if they are denied rights to which they have a legitimate claim. By contrast, their anti-Hegelian critic does not regard the granting of rights as the direct expression of a type of recognition, but simply as one way in which aspects of injustice may be rectified. Finally, Taylor thinks that misrecognition may occur if individuals lack the opportunity to defend what they regard as their culture, while Honneth thinks that individuals may be misrecognized if the distinctive contributions of their culture are not acknowledged. Unlike either of them, Fraser gives culture – or more specifically sets of cultural values – an exclusively negative role: it may be an obstacle to parity of participation, but cannot in itself be a reason for recognition.

Summaries of Chapters

As we can see, debates about the politics of recognition have produced a number of distinctive accounts of misrecognition. This book aims to make an original contribution to these debates. It begins with three chapters which suggest different theoretical frameworks in which the politics of misrecognition may be understood. These are followed by five more applied chapters in which the idea of misrecognition is put to work in a variety of contexts and to a variety of ends.

In their chapter, Thompson and Hoggett consider a range of cases in which good reasons to recognize do not lead to practical acts of recognition. They focus in particular on cases in which certain psychic structures inhibit individuals' and groups' ability to give others the recognition that is their due. In order to understand this sort of reason for misrecognition, Thompson and Hoggett refer to the work of a number of psychoanalytical thinkers. Drawing on their work, Thompson and Hoggett place the notion of ambivalence at the heart of their account of the psychological reasons for misrecognition. Ambivalence, according to their interpretation, is the constant conjunction of conflicting affects which a subject has toward its object. Put in these terms, their central thesis is that an appreciation of the significance of such ambivalence will make it possible to spell out the circumstances in which psychological factors do not present obstacles to recognition. In order to justify this thesis, Thompson and Hoggett discuss each of Honneth's three modes of recognition in turn. In each case, they suggest how certain affective forces may derail recognition, and how it may be possible for them not to do so. To put it very briefly, they contend that love is hate thwarted, respect is narcissism conquered, and esteem is envy overcome. Their conclusion is that for recognition to succeed, the ambivalence of affect must be taken into account. By doing so, they believe, it will be possible to transform and utilize the energy of negative affects so that misrecognition can be overcome.

In the following chapter, Estelle Ferrarese observes that in Axel Honneth's theory, the motif of recognition rarely appears without that of struggle, implying that my expectations or even my demands for recognition are often resisted. But why, in spite of the fact that Honneth does not see it as the result of any sort of logical constraint, does struggle play such a prominent role in his account? Why is misrecognition to be defeated, as opposed simply to coming to an end? What is lost, on a theoretical level, if we speak of recognition without speaking of struggle? Ferrarese first shows that the Hegelian background from which Honneth extracts the theme of recognition does not suffice to explain the centrality attributed to struggle. She then turns her attention to the attributes which struggle assumes in its material expression, considering three possible effects specific to struggle: it transforms the party which demands recognition; it transforms the party which resists recognition; or else it modifies their interaction and thus the world that gives shape to it. It turns out, Ferrarese contends, that the resistance to demands for recognition is necessary because it is the sign – being defeated during the struggle – of one's ability to alter the world: the status of world-changer can only result from a struggle against an enemy that resists. If instead the enemy anticipates the request or even the demand for recognition, it maintains its monopoly over this status.

Nasar Meer's chapter focuses on the renewed interest in W.E.B. Du Bois' idea of double consciousness. This refers to the paradox of being intimately part of a polity while being excluded from its public culture – or, as Du Bois put it, 'being an outcast and stranger in mine own house'. Meer suggests that there are a number of issues of misrecognition that inform the idea of double consciousness, which are loosely grouped into two sets, which mediate between agency and structure, individual and society, and between minority and majority subjectivities. He argues that these comprise, firstly, the internalization by minorities of the contempt majorities may direct toward them. Secondly, the creation of an additional perspective or standpoint, in the form of a 'gifted second sight', which this experience cultivates. Thirdly, a conception of minorities as having fewer civic rights but no fewer duties or responsibilities of an ideal of formal citizenship. Finally, diverging sets of un-reconciled ideals or 'strivings' held by minorities which are objected to by majorities. It is argued that Du Bois' concept of 'double consciousness' provides a schema which becomes progressively thicker in capturing the political dimension in which minority subjectivity may be formed, the nature and form of this subjectivity in and for itself, alongside the transformative potential it heralds for society as a whole. Through an original reading of this concept, Meer presents Du Bois as a precursor to later advocates of 'difference', 'cultural diversity', and especially 'recognition'. Significant here is that if we take 'double consciousness' as a potentially positive resource for enriching society and culture as a whole, then misrecognition is to be welcomes insofar as it fuels the development of such a consciousness. As with Ferrarese's analysis of struggle, Meer's account of double consciousness requires us to rethink misrecognition as a positive potentiality in its own right.

In her chapter, Laura Brace focuses on the status of a slave as an outsider, and on slavery as the ultimate wound inflicted by misrecognition. She draws in particular on the work of Orlando Patterson, and his concepts of social death and natal alienation, to explore the permanent dishonour of slavery. While these dimensions of slavery are important, Brace's chapter brings out the risks of focusing on slavery as a denial of identity and authenticity. Understanding slaves as the prototype of outsiders and others can tempt us to naturalize their status and recognize them only as victims. This in turn can lead to forms of incorporation that reinforce their exploitation and the absence of their liberty. Brace uses the complexities of slavery and the layers of power, adaptability, variety, compromise and struggle within it to explore the possibilities and the limits of a politics of recognition.

In the following chapter, Andrew Sayer argues that in the context of enduring, structural inequalities such as those of class, attempts at recognition between individuals or groups who are differently placed are likely to be unsatisfactory or tokenistic, inviting suspicions of condescension or disrespect and resentment.

To appreciate why, Sayer argues, we need to look beyond inequalities of distribution to inequalities of contribution, particularly in terms of the kinds of work that individuals are allowed or required to do. An unequal social division of labour which concentrates the best quality kinds of work into a subset of jobs, leaving low quality work concentrated in other jobs, prevents some individuals from being able to do the kinds of work that tend to bring respect and esteem. The resulting inequalities tend to be passed on to the next generation through socialization. In the course of his argument, Sayer shows that 'misrecognition' actually covers a number of different possible cases, some well-intentioned, some not. Acknowledgement of class may be avoided for 'ethical' reasons (to avoid humiliating the subordinate classes) or instrumental ones (to hide the privilege of the dominant), but such evasions may be mutually supportive and allow an individualistic explanation of class inequalities.

Gideon Calder's chapter relates the politics of disability to wider questions about the nature and scope of misrecognition. The influence of the disability rights movement has led, in the UK and elsewhere, to formal acknowledgement that disablement arises from social environments, rather than simply from individual deficits or failings. Yet rather glaringly, disability is not addressed at any length (indeed, hardly at all) in the mainstream of the literature on recognition itself. Calder explores the extent to which disability highlights strengths and weaknesses of recognition politics – and specifically, the location of mis- or non-recognition at the heart of injustice. He argues that the 'social model' of disability can indeed be seen as a critique of misrecognition. But the model itself raises sticking points, particularly around the relative roles of (physical) impairments and social factors as barriers. These provide a kind of parallel with the debates among recognition theorists – and particularly around Nancy Fraser's work – on the place of recognition vis-à-vis other conditions of social justice. Looking at Fraser's notion of 'participatory parity', Calder suggests that the implications of recent disability politics support Fraser's well-known contention that when it comes to social justice, misrecognition is not the only game in town. Exclusive attention to it risks an overemphasis on culture at the expense of other dimensions of oppression and disadvantage. But departing from Fraser, he argues that 'participatory parity' is less well equipped than a capabilities-based approach to tackle the particular political-theoretical challenges which emerge with the new politics of disability.

In the following chapter, Majid Yar focuses on criminology. He begins from Honneth's account of moral development that links the formative experience of love to the acquisition of moral capacities enabling relations of recognition in the political sphere. Yar attempts, firstly, to offer an analytical reconstruction of this developmental hypothesis by drawing upon psychoanalytic theory. He goes on to offer empirical support for an 'ontogenetic' link between love, rights and solidarity by drawing upon a range of criminological research, especially recent contributions from the psychosocial perspective. Specifically, Yar seeks to demonstrate how the absence of 'love' (through neglect, abuse, and other similar harms) manifests itself in later dispositions to harm others, thereby empirically connecting non-recognition across the spheres of love, solidarity and rights. He therefore argues that misrecognition reproduces itself socially and temporally, with the misrecognized themselves becoming agents of further acts of misrecognition.

The penultimate chapter, by Ricardo Fabrino Mendonça, considers the dynamics of misrecognition as experienced by sufferers of Hansen's Disease (leprosy) in contemporary Brazil. His focus falls upon the struggle for social esteem amongst a group of persons who continue to suffer from symbolic as well as economic marginalization arising from societal stigmatization. In addition to empirically uncovering the importance of social esteem for self-realization amongst sufferers of the disease, Mendonça uses his case study to defend Honneth's theorization of esteem-oriented struggles against some of its critics. In particular, he takes issue with suggestions that endorsing such struggles entails either the reification of collective identities and difference, or fosters a social competition in which some assert their claims for esteem at the expense of others (see in particular the critiques offered by Markell 2003, Fraser 2003 and Seglow 2009). Such problematic outcomes are not, he argues, an inevitable corollary of esteem-oriented responses to misrecognition, and in the case of Hansen's patients he aims to show how their own struggles are in fact compatible with the societal pursuit of a reciprocal and inclusive form of solidarity.

In a brief conclusion, our aim is to draw the main threads together. We highlight themes common to the preceding chapters, and then use these themes to reach some conclusions about how best to understand the idea of misrecognition, and how to deploy the idea of a politics of misrecognition to illuminate a range of important issues, from the tension between individual freedom and equality in multicultural societies, to the intersections between the multiple inequalities by which such societies are scarred. In this way, our hope is to set the agenda for further investigations of the politics of misrecognition.

References

Banting, K. and Kymlicka, W. (eds). 2006. *Multiculturalism and the Welfare State: Recognition and Redistribution in Contemporary Democracies*. Oxford: Oxford University Press.

Bingham, C. 2001. *Schools of Recognition: Identity Politics and Classroom Practices*. Lanham, MD: Rowman & Littlefield.

Brandom, R. 2002. *Tales of the Mighty Dead*. Cambridge, MA: Harvard University Press.

Brandom, R. 2007. The Structure of Desire and Recognition. *Philosophy and Social Criticism*, 33(1), 127-50.

Dejours, C. 2007. Subjectivity, Work, and Action, in *Recognition, Work, Politics: New Directions in French Critical Theory*, edited by J-P. Deranty et al. Leiden: Brill.

De Beauvoir, S. 1997. *The Second Sex*. New York: Vintage (French original 1949).

De Wispelaere, J., McBride, C. and O'Neill, S. (eds). 2008. *Recognition, Equality and Democracy: Theoretical Perspectives on Irish Politics*. London: Routledge.

Fanon, F. 1967. *The Wretched of the Earth*. Harmondsworth: Penguin (French original 1961).

Fanon, F. 2008. *Black Skin, White Masks*. London: Pluto (French original 1952).

Fraser, N. 1995. From Redistribution to Recognition? Dilemmas of Justice in a "Postsocialist" Age. *New Left Review*, 212, 68-93.

Fraser, N. 2003. Contributions to Nancy Fraser and Axel Honneth, *Redistribution or Recognition? A Political-Philosophical Exchange*. London: Verso.

Fraser, N. 2005. Reframing Justice in a Globalizing World. *New Left Review*, 36, 69-88.

Fraser, N. and Honneth, A. 2003. *Redistribution or Recognition? A Political-Philosophical Exchange*. London: Verso.

Habermas, J. 1994. Struggles for Recognition in the Democratic Constitutional State, in *Multiculturalism: Examining the Politics of Recognition*, edited by A. Gutmann. Princeton, NJ: Princeton University Press.

Hegel, G.W.F. (1979). *The Phenomenology of Spirit*. Oxford: Oxford University Press (originally published in 1807).

Hobson, B. (ed.). 2003. *Recognition Struggles and Social Movements: Contested Identities, Agency and Power*. Cambridge: Cambridge University Press.

Honneth, A. 1995. *The Struggle for Recognition: The Moral Grammar of Social Struggles*. Cambridge: Polity.

Honneth, A. 2001. Invisibility: On the Epistemology of 'Recognition', *Aristotelian Society Supplementary Volume*, 75(1), 111-26.

Honneth, A. 2003. Contributions to Nancy Fraser and Axel Honneth, *Redistribution or Recognition: A Political-Philosophical Exchange*. London: Verso.

Honneth, A. 2010. Recognition between States. On the Moral Substrate of International Relations, represented at 'The Politics of Misrecognition' conference, University of Bristol, January 2010.

Jenlink, P. 2009. *The Struggle for Identity in Today's Schools: Cultural Recognition in a Time of Increasing Diversity*. Lanham, MD: Rowman & Littlefield.

Konings, P. and Nyamnjoh, F. 2003. *Negotiating an Anglophone Identity: A Study of the Politics of Recognition and Representation in Cameroon*. Leiden: Brill.

Markell, P. 2003. *Bound by Recognition*. Princeton, NJ: Princeton University Press.

Ogbar, J. 2004. *Black Power: Radical Politics and African American Identity*. Baltimore, MD: Johns Hopkins University Press.

Povinelli, E. 2002. *The Cunning of Recognition: Indigenous Alterities and the Making of Australian Multiculturalism*. Durham, NC: Duke University Press.

Ricoeur, P. 2005. *The Course of Recognition*. Cambridge, MA: Harvard University Press.

Sartre, J-P. (1995). *Anti-Semite and Jew*, New York: Schocken Books (French original 1947).

Sayer, A. 2005. *The Moral Significance of Class*. Cambridge: Cambridge University Press.

Seglow, J. 2009. Rights, Contribution, Achievement and the World: Some Thoughts on Honneth's Recognitive Ideal, *European Journal of Political Theory*, 8(1), 61-75

Smith, N. 2009. Work and the Struggle for Recognition, *European Journal of Political Theory*, 8(1), 46-60.

Taylor, C. 1995. The Politics of Recognition, in C. Taylor, *Philosophical Arguments*. Cambridge, MA: Harvard University Press.

Tully, J. 2005. *Strange Multiplicity*. Cambridge: Cambridge University Press.

Tully, J. 2009. *Public Philosophy in a New Key*. Cambridge: Cambridge University Press.

Voswinkel, S. 2005. *Welche Kundenorientierung? Anerkennung in der Dienstleistungsarbeit*. Berlin: Edition Sigma.

Williams, J. 1987. *Eyes on the Prize: America's Civil Rights Years, 1954-1965*. New York: Penguin Books.

Chapter 1
Misrecognition and Ambivalence

Simon Thompson and Paul Hoggett

Introduction

There are circumstances in which good reasons to recognize do not lead to practical acts of recognition. At an individual level, although I may know that I should recognize you, I nevertheless fail to do so. For instance, in spite of my awareness that you have a strong claim on me to care for you, I do not provide you with that care. When you are ill in hospital, I may find excuses not to visit you. Or, at a collective level, one group accepts that another should enjoy a particular right which they do not currently possess, and yet it does not take the action necessary to secure the other that right. In an interesting and important range of cases, good reasons for recognition may be outweighed by other factors, so that one party does not give the other party the acknowledgment it deserves. These failures of recognition, we would suggest, can be understand as instances of misrecognition. Our aim in this chapter is to examine certain reasons for such misrecognition. We are guided by the hope that, if the reasons for such failures of recognition are better understood, then it will be possible more effectively to identify the conditions necessary for success. In other words, such an understanding will make it easier to specify the circumstances in which having good reasons for recognition leads to recognition in practice.[1]

There are, of course, various types of reasons for such failures of recognition. One type of reason is simple ignorance. I may not offer to care for you since I do not know that you are in need of such care. Perhaps because you are ashamed to admit your dependency, you may not be able clearly to articulate your needs to me. But, if you did so, then I would offer you the appropriate care. Another type of reason for misrecognition is self-interest. One group may know that another deserves its recognition, but, since granting such recognition would disadvantage that group, it fails to do so. If the first group did not stand to lose something by recognizing the deserving other, then it would readily provide it with the appropriate

1 With this phrase, we put aside all-too-familiar cases in which two parties disagree about what constitutes good reasons for recognition. In these cases, one party thinks it has good reason to be recognized, but the other party disagrees. Such disagreement is, of course, a central aspect of political struggles for recognition. But we think that the cases in which we are interested, where agreement on reasons for recognition still fails to lead to practical acts of recognition, are both important and generally overlooked.

acknowledgement. In this chapter, we put aside these first two sorts of reasons for misrecognition in order to focus on a third. This sort of reason is to be explained by reference to what may loosely be called 'psychological' factors. Here it is the psychic capacities of individuals and groups which inhibit their ability to give others the recognition that is their due. In order to understand this sort of reason for misrecognition, we shall refer to the work of a number of psychoanalytical thinkers, including Freud, Klein, Winnicott and Bion. Drawing on their work, we place the notion of ambivalence at the heart of our account of the psychological reasons for misrecognition. Ambivalence, according to our interpretation, is to be understood as the constant conjunction of conflicting affects which a subject has toward its object. To take the prototypical case, against a sentimentalized idea of love, an appreciation of ambivalence would enable us to accept that the mother simultaneously loves and hates her child. Put in these terms, then, our central thesis is that the idea of affective ambivalence can provide the basis for an explanation of an important type of reason for misrecognition. If this is right, then it follows that an appreciation of the significance of such ambivalence will make it possible to spell out the circumstances in which psychological factors do not present obstacles to recognition.

It was noted in the introduction to this book that different accounts of recognition give different reasons for recognition. For Nancy Fraser, there is good reason to recognize people who are unable to participate on a par with their peers since they lack the necessary social standing. The practical task in this case is to overcome the inequalities of status, such as those which result from sexism and racism, in order to secure parity of participation (Fraser 2003). On Charles Taylor's account, people have good reason to be recognized if their capacity for rational autonomy or their capacity to create a distinctive identity cannot be exercised. Here what is needed is to guarantee all individuals' basic rights and to give each group a fair opportunity to defend its cultural identity (Taylor 1995). According to Axel Honneth, people ought to be recognized if they need to be cared for by their significant others, or if their fundamental rights are denied, or if the value of their way of life is overlooked. Recognition, in this case, requires the sustenance of a web of relations of care, the maintenance of a system of individual rights, and the preservation of a horizon of value in which contributions to societal goals can be appropriately valued (Honneth 1995).

In this chapter, without denying that Fraser and Taylor – and many others – have valuable insights to offer, we shall take Honneth's account of recognition as the springboard from which our argument will be launched. As we have just mentioned, Honneth identifies three forms of recognition: we love our significant others by responding appropriately to their concrete needs; we respect all others by obeying the laws which treat them as rationally autonomous agents; and we esteem particular others by endorsing a set of values which enable the contributions that they make to shared goals to be duly acknowledged. The first mode of recognition, which has a special place in Honneth's account, is of greatest importance for our argument here. He contends that love is the first mode of recognition in the sense that it is 'conceptually and genetically prior' to respect and esteem (ibid.: 107). It is conceptually prior since it provides the basis for our understanding of the other two modes of recognition, and it is genetically prior since individuals must first be able to love if they are then to be able to respect and esteem others. As Honneth says, love is the 'basic requisite' for the other modes of recognition (ibid.: 176).[2] Since Honneth's account of love as recognition draws on object-relations psychoanalysis, it provides a very suitable basis for our own argument. Also drawing on psychoanalytical sources, we aim to show that his account needs to be supplemented by our idea of affective ambivalence. Although Honneth is aware that there is a struggle for recognition even in the intimate relations between significant others, we believe that he underestimates the role which affective ambivalence plays in all types of relations of recognition.

Given that our declared aim is to bring a psychoanalytical perspective to bear on the issue of misrecognition, it may seem odd for us to begin our argument with a discussion of Aristotle. We do so in the following section since his account of *akrasia*, which can be translated as incontinence, weakness of the will or lack of self-mastery, provides an interesting and important way of explaining why someone who knows what it is right to do may nevertheless fail to do it. Then, by pointing out the limitations of Aristotle's explanation of *akrasia*, we begin to make the case for a psychoanalytically inspired explanation, one which centres on the idea that the self is permanently divided against itself. With this account in mind, we go on to discuss each of Honneth's three modes of recognition in turn. In each case, we suggest how certain affective forces may derail recognition, and we also suggest how it may be possible for them not to do so. To put it in the briefest possible terms, we contend that for love to succeed hatred must be thwarted, for respect to be shown narcissism must be conquered, and for esteem to be expressed envy must be overcome. Our conclusion is that for recognition to succeed, the ambivalence of affect must be taken into account. Our argument will be that by doing so, it will be possible to transform and utilize the energy of negative affects so that misrecognition can be overcome.

The Problem of *Akrasia*

Aristotle, in Book 7 of the *Nicomachean Ethics*, is the first philosopher to conduct a systematic investigation into the problem of *akrasia*. On his account, although the akratic individual knows what it is right to do, he nevertheless fails to do it. In his analysis of this phenomenon, Aristotle is in part responding to Socrates who famously denied the possibility of *akrasia*. In Plato's *Protagoras*, he states that no-one 'who either knows or believes that there is another possible course of action, better than the one he is following, will ever continue on his present course'

2 For a more detailed account of Honneth's conception of love as recognition, see Thompson (2006a: ch. 2) and Yar (this volume).

(358 b.c.). Aristotle suggests that this view 'plainly contradicts the observed facts' (*Ethics*, VII, 2), and, since he wishes to stick as closely as he can to as many of these facts as possible, he is determined to investigate the phenomenon of *akrasia* more closely.[3]

In his analysis, Aristotle is strongly influenced by Plato's division of the psyche into three parts – namely, reason, emotion (or spirit) and appetite. Using this tripartite division, he suggests that *akrasia* occurs when reason is derailed either by emotion or appetite, and he makes particular reference to the emotion of anger and the desire for pleasure as factors which may cause a man to fail to do what he knows is right. On the emotions, he declares that 'there is a sort of man ... whom passion masters so that he does not act according to the right rule' (*Ethics*, VII, 8). So far as appetite is concerned, he states that 'the incontinent man fails to abide by the rule because he delights too much in [bodily things]' (*Ethics*, VII, 9). In addition, Aristotle makes a further distinction between the weak and the impetuous man. Although the weak man exercises his reason in order to determine what it is right to do, he nevertheless acts wrongly. The impetuous man, by contrast, fails to deliberate at all, and so acts wrongly since he is guided by his impulses rather than by considered reason. This man will probably experience regret if, after his hasty action, he deliberates about what he should have done. As Aristotle says, 'the incontinent man is likely to repent' (*Ethics*, VII, 8).

Given this analysis, Aristotle thinks that the nature of the problem is clear: *akrasia* is the result of a lack of virtue. Such a lack means that reason can be overwhelmed by appetite or emotion. In the virtuous man, by contrast, the three parts of the psyche are in the correct alignment. In particular, since reason is the master of both appetite and emotion, we can say that such a man is master of himself. Aristotle suggests that this man will possess *phronesis* – practical wisdom – and so cannot be akratic: 'Nor can the same man have practical wisdom and be incontinent; for it has been shown that a man is at the same time practically wise, and good in respect of character. Further, a man has practical wisdom not by knowing only but by being able to act' (*Ethics*, VII, 9). In other words, a practically wise man not only knows what it is right to do, but also has the qualities of character needed in order to be able to act on this knowledge.

Does Aristotle's analysis help us in our current inquiry? Can it explain why one party may fail to recognize another, despite knowing that it has good reason to do so? To begin with those instances in which reason is derailed by appetite, we may think of a range of cases in which the failure to give appropriate acknowledgement to another is rooted in self-interest. As we suggested above, one party may fail to recognize another since it is not to their advantage to do so. For instance, to recognize you might require me to accept your right to political representation;

---

3 It may be noted that there is a very extensive literature discussing both Aristotle's account of *akrasia* specifically, and the weakness of the will more generally. For the purposes of our argument here, however, we do not need to delve into the many interesting issues raised in this literature.

but it could follow that if you are granted that right, my own influence over the political process is diminished. Or, in order to recognize you, it may be necessary for me to endorse a set of values which ensure that your contribution to societal goals is appropriately valued; but, as a result, I could feel that my own contribution is less highly valued.[4] Or, finally, to recognize you it may be appropriate for me to be responsive to your expression of your needs; but, if I do so, I may be less able to attend to my own needs. It would appear that these cases fall into Aristotle's category of *akrasia* as a result of appetite. That is to say, I fail to recognize you although reason dictates that I should, since to do so would require me to deny myself something that I want. As we have said, however, for the purposes of our current argument we are going to put aside failures of recognition which are rooted in reasons of self-interest.

If we turn now to those instances in which reason is blown off course by emotion, we can think of a range of cases in which one party's failure to give the other appropriate acknowledgement is caused by the action of certain affects. Indeed, it is precisely this range of cases which is of interest to us in this chapter. To take one of Aristotle's own examples, we think he is right to suggest that anger may prevent one party from acting justly to another. For instance, if I make the over-hasty judgement that you have insulted me, I may seek revenge. On reflection, however, I may come to realize that what appeared to be an unwarranted insult was in fact a painful but important truth about me which you sincerely thought I needed to hear. To take a more overtly political example, an angry mob might spray-paint 'paedo' on the front door of a house of a person it believes to be a paedophile, only to realize later on that she is in fact a paediatrician.[5] It is important to note, however, that Aristotle does not endorse a simple account of the relationship between reason and emotion in which reason, which can be entirely without affect, can and should master affect, which is utterly without reason. In particular, he emphasizes that affective states can have cognitive content. For example, he defines anger as the 'desire, accompanied by pain, for revenge for an obvious belittlement of oneself or one of one's dependants, the belittlement being uncalled for' (*Rhetoric*, II, 2: 1378a 31-3). It follows anger can be the appropriate response to our having being unfairly insulted by another.[6] Our argument in this chapter, then, can be seen as an extension of this aspect of Aristotle's thesis.[7]

Having said this, however, we disagree with Aristotle's proviso that our experience of an emotion such as anger should never be so strong as to overwhelm our reason. He makes this proviso since he believes that only if reason ultimately

4 See Cillian McBride (2009) for an account of esteem as a positional good.

5 For further details of this case, see http://news.bbc.co.uk/1/hi/magazine/4719364.stm; last accessed 20/05/2010.

6 For a further elaboration of Aristotle's account of anger, see Thompson (2006b: 129-33).

7 In our previous work, we have sought to defend what we have called 'a passionate rationality' (Thompson and Hoggett 2002).

remains the ruler of the emotions, can the self remain its own master. For us, in sharp contrast, such self-mastery is an impossibility since the self is never completely at home; it is always to some extent divided against itself. It is as this point, then, that we turn from Aristotle's account of a unified self, to Freud's account in which the self is always in conflict with itself. While Aristotle believes that a man can be his own master, Freud denies that the ego can ever be master in its own house (Freud 1923). Against Aristotle's suggestion that the three elements of the soul can be brought into harmony, Freud is adamant that the absence of inner harmony is central to the human condition. Thus, in Freud's scheme, the ego is constantly having to mediate between the demands of the id (which bears some comparison to Aristotle's 'appetite for pleasure' and raging anger) and the super-ego (which is absent from Aristotle's system, since, for him, it makes no sense to think that what is right and what is conventionally correct could come apart). This is illustrated in many of Freud's early cases. In Dora's case, for example, she finds herself caught between an awakening sexuality, aroused in part by an older seducer, and a conscience for which such thoughts and feelings were impermissible (Freud 1905). As it has evolved, psychoanalysis has taken Freud's view of the decentred nature of subjectivity still further. Nowadays psychoanalysts speak in terms of 'different parts of the self' engaged in complex relations with each other (Bollas 1987: 1-2). Indeed, these parts of the self can also be projected into others via projective identification, so that a part of the self becomes located in another person, group or ideal as, for example, when we attribute competitiveness to our colleagues rather than acknowledge it in ourselves.

Building on this account of the divided self, it is important for our current thesis to emphasize that, for Freud, the psyche is founded on contradictory affects. As we put it earlier on, the self experiences a constant conjunction of conflicting affects toward its object. For the early Freud, the battle was between love and hate. For the later Freud, the conflict was between Eros, a unifying life force, and Thanatos, its opposite. After Freud, Klein argued that the principal line of conflict was between envy and gratitude. Psychoanalysis has itself struggled to overcome a dualistic theory of the psyche in which ambivalence is construed in terms of a 'non-dialectical opposition' (Laplanche and Pontalis 1973: 28). Contemporary theory prefers to see this psychic tension less in terms of a binary opposition and more in terms of a tension which can be held or contained. In Kleinian theory this is what differentiates two fundamentally different 'states of mind'. In the pre-ambivalent state the tension is dealt with by splitting objects of love from objects of hate, whereas in the depressive position the connections between love and hate, the loved and the hated, negative and positive, can be more easily tolerated. In the rest of this chapter, then, our aim is to show how the inability to contain ambivalence can help to explain why certain failures of recognition may occur. To be specific, we shall demonstrate that the profound ambivalence that we have to others can prevent us giving them the love, respect and esteem that is their due. At the same time, however, we also want to show how, by facing up to such ambivalence, the power of negative affect can be harnessed in the service of recognition.

Love and Hate

As we said in the introduction to this chapter, love has a special place in Honneth's account of recognition. Indeed it is in a sense the primary mode of recognition since, without it, respect and esteem are impossible. If individuals are loved and cared for by their significant others, then they are able to develop the basic self-confidence which forms the basis of their ability to respect and esteem other people. However, we believe that there is a over-simple developmental story in Honneth's account of love, according to which, under all usual circumstances, parents love their children, those children acquire self-confidence, and then when those children become adults they are able to respect and esteem their fellow citizens. Under normal conditions, it appears, being loved in childhood provides an emotional inoculation which ensures that adults will have the self-confidence they need to take appropriate recognitive attitudes to others.[8] It is revealing, we would suggest, that when Honneth considers the conditions that may undermine self-confidence, he focuses on threats to the physical integrity of the self, singling out torture and rape in particular (1992: 190; 1995: 132). What is missing from this account is a whole range of less serious but all too common circumstances, ranging from poor parenting to abusive adult relationships, which may undermine an individual's self-confidence. Building on this last point, we want to argue in this section that Honneth does not take sufficient account of the continuing presence of love's opposite – that is to say, hatred – in the affective attitudes that individuals take to their significant others.

To make this point, we shall begin by drawing what is admittedly an exaggerated contrast between a romanticized conception of love, and the account we favour which emphasizes the centrality of affective ambivalence to this emotion. According to a romanticized conception of love, it is constant and unwavering emotional force. A good example of such a conception can be found in Carl Rogers' humanistic psychology, in which is located a notion of love as 'unconditional positive regard' (1961: 283-4). In taking this attitude to another, we accept and value another person no matter what they might say or do. In sharp contrast, according to psychoanalytical thinkers such as Klein, Winnicott and Benjamin, the love between mother and child constantly co-exists with a hatred which can never be eradicated. As each party in this relationship will always have good reasons to hate the other, such hatred can only be temporarily vanquished. However, we must emphasize that this is not a shortcoming in relationships of love. It is our contention that love is enriched by hatred that is worked through, by hurt that is forgiven, by ruthlessness that is endured. As we shall suggest in our conclusion, a hate which is temporarily overcome deepens and enriches the quality

8 Compare Anthony Giddens who, in his version of Erik Erikson's notion of 'trust', contends that it is 'the main emotional support or *protective cocoon* which all normal individuals carry around with them as the means whereby they are able to get on with the affairs of day-to-day life' (1991: 40).

of the care that can be provided. To put this in the terms of our current argument, the overcoming of hatred enriches the recognition that is given to the other.

Let us consider the situation in a little more detail. D.W. Winnicott, in his well-known paper 'Hate in the Counter-Transference' (1949), suggests that the mother has many reasons to hate her baby. She endures broken nights' sleep, lacks time for herself, and so on. And yet, despite these reasons, the mother continues to love her baby. Developing this idea, Jessica Benjamin (2004) suggests that the relationship between mother and child goes through phases of breakdown and repair. Breakdown occurs when the mother's patience runs out and she becomes irritated with the child, and repair happens when they manage to re-establish their loving relationship based on their concern for each other. Indeed, ambivalence is part of the experience for both mother and child. From the child's perspective, we could say that he has a devouring affection for his mother. This draws attention to the destructiveness that inheres in appetite, particularly evident in the modern act of consumption. In our terms, this pattern of contrasting phases is the working through of ambivalence. Such a process enables a shift from ruthlessness and ambivalence to ambivalence and concern. According to Winnicott, such a shift may be accomplished if (1) the mother is able to survive the infant's attacks without retaliation or withdrawal, and (2) the infant has a growing confidence in the existence of opportunities for 'contributing-in', that is, for giving, for making reparation. Generosity depends not just on the capacity to give but also on the capacity to receive.

In this case, we need to try to identify the necessary conditions for a mature love, one which does not depend upon the suppression of aggression. When does it triumph? When does it overcome hatred? And also when does such a love fail? Why does it do so? Following her mentor, Carl Abraham, Melanie Klein argued that the capacity to be aware of and tolerant of ambivalence is an achievement, one which alters the quality of both the love and the hate that we feel (Klein 1952). In the 'pre-ambivalent' state of mind, when hatred is aroused so also is persecutory anxiety. The mother, driven to distraction by her child, begins to feel as if the child is persecuting her. She takes it personally, as a calculated, spiteful attack: 'Why is my child doing this to me? What have I done to deserve this? It's not fair'. If such anxiety is too strong, she may withdraw or be driven to retaliate, seeing her own violence as a defensive reaction to the offensive unleashed by her infant persecutor. However, a young baby cannot in reality 'have it in' for his mother; indeed at this age he barely has the ability to conceive of an 'other' at all. In such situations, then, the mother feels persecuted by her own hateful self that she has projected into her infant. Here Klein would say that the less the capacity of the mother to accept and tolerate the loving and hateful parts of herself, the more she will be driven to project the latter into the other when the grounds for hatefulness are accumulating (when, for example, the child is expressing its needs at 3 o'clock in the morning).

Following Klein, our thesis is that such an imagined persecution – provoked by the other in their state of neediness – is immanent in all relations of interdependency.

For Honneth, as we have seen, love is responsiveness to the needs of the other. To be interdependent implies that the other's needs must at times take precedence over one's own. Winnicott's vignette is therefore the primary empirical prototype for all interdependent relationships, between individuals and groups, and therefore between imagined communities, including nations. For interdependency to be successfully sustained, the needs, demands and complaints of each party must be respected and responded to – that is, they must be given recognition – by the other, rather than be seen as an intrusion, an expression of malign intent, or an attack on one's self, one's freedom, one's own rights, etc. We believe, although we do not have space to argue it here, that such interdependency underlies a range of political phenomena, ranging from the solidarity manifest in systems of collective welfare to acts of collective recognition in international relations (Wendt 2003). In all of these cases, in order to enter relations of interdependency, each party requires the capacity to contain its own destructiveness without exporting it into the other individual or group.

Respect and Narcissism

Having argued – and hopefully demonstrated – that it is necessary to take account of the ambivalent character of love, we now turn to consider Honneth's second mode of recognition. For him, respect is an attitude in which one acknowledges the rational autonomy of other persons. If I respect you, I treat you as a person capable of exercising your reason in order to determine how to live your life. As Honneth puts it, I regard you as 'capable of acting autonomously on the basis of rational insight' (1995: 114). In modern political systems, respect for others is typically demonstrated by compliance with the law: 'In obeying the law, legal subjects recognize each other as persons capable of autonomously making reasonable decisions about moral norms' (1995: 109). In this section, our argument will be that the idea of affective ambivalence may also be applied to respect. In this case, we shall contend, narcissism is the affective state that is the constant companion of respect, and it follows that respect is achieved when narcissism is contained.

Now, the state may regard certain groups – such as the criminally insane – as lacking such autonomy, and it may thereby withhold basic rights, such as the right to vote, from them. Hence, as Honneth observes, one part of the recent history of social conflict involves the struggle of groups, such as women or indigenous peoples, to be recognized as rationally autonomous subjects, rather than be treated as immature inferiors who need to be looked after by their mature superiors. However, such struggles for recognition are only partly a matter of obtaining formal rights. In practice, there is often a gap between the formal and the substantive rights of particular groups. The reality is that in many liberal democracies the concept of the rationally autonomous subject has been used in a normative way to construct a 'deficit' model in which the welfare subject is 'constituted in a child like way as someone lacking the capacity to make reasonable judgements about themselves and the others that they have responsibility for' (Hoggett 2008: 66). In education, health and social care, the professional or public official is constructed as the 'one who knows', in contrast to the welfare subject who becomes 'the one who is known'. Anna Yeatman (2007) sees this as a form of patrimonial authority which is concerned with the exercise of patrimonial will over 'dependents'.

When such patrimonial authority is challenged, it can often assume quite prejudicial and vindictive forms. Consider the example of a social worker dealing with a difficult client. The social worker may feel strong ambivalence about her. On the one hand, he wants to treat her with respect. On the other hand, if the client has a history of drug abuse, anti-social behaviour or problematic ways of caring for her own children, the social worker may find it hard to resist feeling that, as a member of the undeserving poor, this client does not merit such respect. Indeed, the client may be difficult to work with and abusive towards anyone – whether family or officials – who seek to offer help. Thus the public official may have many reasons to feel irritated, frightened, or contemptuous towards the client and, like the mother in Winnicott's analysis, may often take the client's abuse of him personally. In such circumstances, the public official may withhold recognition and adopt a patronizing attitude towards the client which assumes she is incapable of rational autonomy. This is an unforgiving stance.

In contrast, if the official can contain his own negative feelings, then he is more likely to be able to take a more generous stance and to sustain respect for his client.[9] In Hannah Arendt's terms, this attitude is more forgiving: the official is able to see that the badness of the other may not be inherent to her, and that she may be 'more than whatever she has done or achieved' (Arendt 1968: 248). Such a stance recognizes the alterity of the other and seeks to establish forms of relatedness which respect this difference. In this case, we approach the other as if they were capable of rational autonomy even if at that moment their behaviour does not seem to warrant this assumption. In other words, we recognize that the other may often act in a self destructive way, in a way which is against their self interest and the interest of others, because of their frailty, powerlessness, or vulnerability, and yet we insist that they are capable of acting differently and hence we avoid treating them in a patronizing or humiliating way. However, to return to the example of the social worker, this does not rule out the possibility that the official may have to act against his client's interests (by, for example, taking her children into care). To return to Winnicott once more, the resort to firmness, the insistence on respect for boundaries, and so on, are not incompatible with respect. While this example of the relationship between the social worker and his difficult client may seem

9 It should be noted that in contemporary psychoanalysis, 'containment' is a technical term. Originating with Wilfred Bion (1972), it describes the capacity to hold on to powerful feelings without suppressing them or getting rid of them by projection or enactment. To contain conflictual feelings, one must be able to hold the tension and use this psychic energy for thought, for 'thinking under fire' as it is often described. We shall say more about this idea in our conclusion.

extreme, our suggestion is that the tendency to regard poorer people, the frail and vulnerable, and children and young people as somehow 'autonomy deficient' continues to characterize the way in which welfare policies are designed and delivered in liberal democracies.

If Honneth's first mode of recognition finds its prototype in maternal love, then perhaps the second mode, embodied in the relation between the state and the citizen as the subject of law, finds its prototype in paternal love. Psychoanalysis considers paternal love in the context of the Oedipal drama and the struggle between the generations. It focuses specifically on the ability of the father to offer a model of good enough authority, one based neither upon paternal absolutism nor abnegation and impotence. Paternal absolutism, captured brilliantly by Michael Haneke in his film, *The White Ribbon* (2009), either crushes the next generation or offers the consolation of identification with the aggressor. In this case, then, adulthood can be entered only so long as the child takes the authority into himself, becoming a narcissistic extension of the father and thereby adopting his stance towards the next generation in turn. In contrast, the 'good enough authority' recognizes the other as a person capable of exercising agency.[10] This is equivalent to the recognition that when the other acts differently to me, they may not be acting irrationally, but simply acting in a way which is different to how I imagine I would act in such circumstances. There is good reason to believe that in asymmetrical group relations, such as in the relation between the liberal state and its citizens, authority must constantly challenge its own assumptions regarding the other if it is not to treat the other narcissistically as a screen for its own projections, so that it is seen as undeserving, 'feral', feckless, etc. Our conclusion, in a phrase, is that respect can only be expressed when narcissism is contained. That is to say, Honneth's second mode of recognition – the acknowledgement of the rational autonomy of the other – can only be achieved and sustained if the other's alterity and capacity for agency is the foundation upon which the state's relations with its citizens is built.

Esteem and Envy

What finally of Honneth's third mode of recognition? Here his suggestion is that every society has a set of 'ethical goals and values' that constitute its 'cultural self-understanding' (1995: 122), and that esteem is a function of one's contribution to those goals and values. As he puts it, 'one is given the chance to experience oneself to be recognized, in light of one's own accomplishments and abilities, as valuable to society' (1995: 130). In other words, individuals who identify themselves with a particular group may enjoy esteem if the contribution which that group makes to shared societal goals is appropriately acknowledged. In this section, we want

10 For an exploration of this idea of 'good authority', see Hoggett, Mayo and Miller (2008: ch. 7).

to argue that the idea of affective ambivalence may also be used the better to understand the necessary conditions of esteem. To be specific, we shall claim that Honneth overlooks the significance of envy as the affect in tension with esteem. Our thesis, therefore, will be that esteem can only be achieved if and when the opposing affect of envy is contained.

Let us begin with a small vignette. In a study of racism and populism in East London which Hoggett conducted in the early 1990s, he examined the relations between the traditional white working class of Tower Hamlets and the emergent Bangladeshi community in the area (Hoggett 1992). Racial attacks on the Bangladeshi minority had increased in intensity, and the National Front had just won a local ward election – marking the first time that an openly fascist organization had claimed such a victory in the UK since the 1930s. As Hoggett noted, '[t]he resentment the whites felt toward the Bangladeshi community was made poignant by the fact that the latter community had many characteristics – extended and intensive kinship networks, respect for tradition and male superiority, a capacity for entrepreneurialism and social advancement – that the white working class in the area had lost' (Hoggett 1992: 354). Our suggestion is that, in this case, the local whites' harassment of the members of Bengali community should be understood as envious attacks on those who represented their lost powers – or, in Slavoj Žižek's words (1993) – those who had stolen their enjoyment. While those Whites who harassed Bengalis may have thought that they did so because they felt that their way of life was threatened by 'incomers', it was clear that they were also motivated by a desire to attack what they had lost, but still valued.

In order to understand the group dynamics at work here, it will be useful to return once more to psychoanalytical theory. In this field, the most important account of the role of envy in psychic life is that of Klein. She takes her definition from Crabb's *English Synonyms*: 'envy is pained at seeing another have that which it wants for itself … The envious man sickens at the sight of enjoyment. He is easy only in the misery of others' (Klein 1957: 182). For Klein, envy lies at the root of human destructiveness. It is an attack on all that is good and life giving. Citing Othello, she describes it as 'the green-eyed monster which doth mock the meat it feeds on' (1957: 182). In an analysis strikingly similar to Klein's, Max Scheler argues that the powerless person feels envy toward the good that the other possesses but he or she has been denied. According to Scheler, to relieve such tension, the envious person engages in 'an illusory devaluation of the other man's qualities or … a specific blindness to these qualities' (1992: 126). As Simon Clarke (2006) notes, the envious person seeks to damage or spoil the very thing that she desires. In this way, Scheler argues, values become inverted, and the objects of desire become devalued. Thus, in London's East End, it is the very values of family, community and enterprise now embodied by the Bangladeshi which become denigrated.

With this psychoanalytical account of envy in mind, let us return to Honneth's conception of esteem. For him, for one party to esteem another involves positively appreciating their contributions to shared social goals. We would suggest that there are circumstances when esteem would be the appropriate response to another's call for recognition, but instead envy leads to a desire to devalue and perhaps even to destroy the other. How can such envy be overcome so that esteem can be secured? Again psychoanalysis can provide us with insights here. Following Freud, we want to argue that the overcoming of envy may provide one of the foundations for group solidarity. We can consider the familial prototype of relations between groups in society in terms of sibling dynamics (with the state unconsciously performing the role of the maternal and paternal authorities). As Freud puts it, 'if one cannot be the favourite oneself, at all events nobody else shall be favourite' (Freud 1921: 117). The siblings resolve the problem of their rivalry by the formation of a contract, a contract in which each of them is guaranteed equal valuation and worth. According to Freud, 'what appears later on in society in the shape of *Gemeingeist*, *esprit de corps*, "group spirit", etc. does not belie its derivation from what was originally envy' (Freud 1921: 117). In multicultural societies, the feeling of one group that another group is being favoured by, for example, being granted special privileges by the state, is a recurring manifestation of such sibling-type dynamics. Hence solidarity between erstwhile rivals requires envy to be contained and overcome. What Freud calls the 'social feeling' is therefore based on the reversal of hostile feelings and their replacement by an identification. As he puts it, 'social justice means that we deny ourselves many things so that others may have to do without them as well' (Freud 1921: 118). In other words, the social contract is based upon the containment of envy and its transformation into an identification with one's fellow sibling citizens.

Conclusion

In this chapter, we have argued that demands for recognition – whether in the form of love, respect or esteem – may be undermined by ambivalent affects. Love may be undermined by hatred, respect by narcissism, and esteem by envy. In this case, it is important to understand that just as love needs hatred to be overcome, so respect needs narcissism to be overcome, and esteem needs envy to be overcome. However, it must be appreciated that overcoming a negative affect is not the same as suppressing or mastering it. It is not possible permanently to defeat such an affect. Indeed, in ending our chapter, we want to emphasize that there are important reasons why we should not try to do so. To explain this point, we need to say a little more about the psychoanalytical the concept of 'containment'. To focus on what we have called the prototypical case, if the mother can contain her hatred, then she can use this negative affect in a creative way. She can get a grip on herself and her own reactions, particularly that part of herself which feels got at and persecuted by her infant. She can use the energy in her aggression to re-find her strength and her capacity to endure, to tough it out, to survive her infant's attacks upon her. She can use the same energy to help find clarity of mind and to act firmly and decisively, but without maliciousness. In short, by containing her negativity, she is able to combine it with her love, creating a psychoanalytic version of 'tough love'. Similarly, to take the case of esteem and envy, we are not arguing that a relationship of esteem can only be established and maintained if feelings of envy are permanently mastered or even eliminated. On the contrary, our thesis is that such a relationship is energized by an envy which is contained and transformed. In the case of all three modes of recognition, then, it is vitally important that the ambivalence of affect is appreciated. Only by doing so, we believe, can the energy of negative affects be transformed and utilized so that misrecognition can be overcome.

Extending this idea a little further, our final thought is this. We have suggested that it is necessary to acknowledge that recognition cannot always be sustained. It is inevitable that breakdowns in relationships of recognition will occur, and that such relationships will then need to be repaired. In this context, Winnicott talks about the necessity of disillusionment: it is important that the infant slowly comes to realize that mum is not perfect, since only by doing so can he change, and so their relationship evolve. Here we can see that repair does not return a recognitive relationship to the *status quo ante*; after repair, the relationship is not was it was before its breakdown. Rather, successive stages of breakdown and repair are necessary if such a relationship is to develop. In this sense, we might say not just that negative affects must be transformed if misrecognition is to be overcome, but more strongly that misrecognition, since it fuels the development of relationships of recognition, has positive potential in its own right.

References

Arendt, H. 1968. *Men in Dark Times.* New York: Harcourt Brace.

Aristotle. 2004. *Nicomachean Ethics*, edited by J. Barnes and J.A.K. Thomson. Harmondsworth: Penguin.

Aristotle. 2005. *The Art of Rhetoric*, edited by H. Lawson-Tancred. Harmondsworth: Penguin.

Benjamin, J. 2004. 'Beyond doer and done-to: an intersubjective view of thirdness', *Psychoanalytic Quarterly*, LXIII, 1, 5-46.

Bion, W. 1972. *Attention and Interpretation.* London: Tavistock.

Bollas, C. 1987. *The Shadow of the Object: Psychoanalysis of the Unthought Known.* London: Free Association Books.

Clarke, S. 2006. *Envy and Ressentiment*, in *Emotion, Politics, and Society*, edited by S. Clarke, P. Hoggett, and S. Thompson. Basingstoke: Palgrave Macmillan, 70-83.

Fraser, N. 2003. 'Contributions to Nancy Fraser and Axel Honneth', *Redistribution or Recognition? A Political-Philosophical Exchange.* London: Verso.

Freud, S. 1905. Fragment of an Analysis of a Case of Hysteria. SE, 7, 3-122.

Freud, S. 1921. Group Psychology and the Analysis of the Ego. SE, 18, 65-143.

Freud, S. 1923. The Ego and the Id. SE, 19, 3-66.

Giddens, A. 1991. *Modernity and Self-Identity: Self and Society in the Late Modern Age*. Cambridge: Polity.

Hoggett, P. 1992. 'A Place for Experience: a Psychoanalytic Perspective on Boundary, Identity and Culture', *Environment and Planning D: Society and Space*, 10, 345-56.

Hoggett, P., Mayo, M., and Miller, C. 2008. *The Dilemmas of Development Work*. Bristol: Policy Press.

Hoggett, P. 2008. 'Relational Thinking and Welfare Practice', in *Object Relations and Social Relations*, edited by S. Clarke, H. Hahn and P. Hoggett. London: Karnac, 65-85.

Honneth, A. 1992. 'Integrity and Disrespect: Principles of a Conception of Morality based on the Theory of Recognition', *Political Theory*, 20(2), 187-201.

Honneth, A. 1995. *The Struggle for Recognition: The Moral Grammar of Social Struggles*. Cambridge: Polity.

Klein, M. 1952. 'The Origins of the Transference', in *The Writings of Melanie Klein*, Vol. 3, London: Hogarth Press, 48-56.

Klein, M. 1957. 'Envy and Gratitude', in *The Writings of Melanie Klein*, Vol. 3, London: Hogarth Press, 176-235.

Laplanche, J. and Pontalis, J-B. 1973. *The Language of Psycho-Analysis*. London: Hogarth Press.

McBride, C. 2009. 'Demanding Recognition: Equality, Respect, and Esteem', *European Journal of Political Theory*, 8(1), 96-108.

Plato. 2005. *Protagoras*, edited A. Beresford. Harmondsworth: Penguin.

Rogers, C. 1961. *On Becoming a Person*, Boston, MA: Houghton Mifflin.

Scheler, M. 1992. *On Feeling, Knowing, and Valuing*, ed. H. Bershady. Chicago: Chicago University Press.

Taylor, C. 1995. 'The Politics of Recognition', in C. Taylor, *Philosophical Arguments*. Cambridge, MA: Harvard University Press.

Thompson, S. 2006a. *The Political Theory of Recognition: A Critical Introduction*, Cambridge: Polity.

Thompson, S. 2006b. 'Anger and the Struggle for Justice', in Simon Clarke, Paul Hoggett and Simon Thompson (eds) *Emotions, Politics and Society*, London: Palgrave Macmillan, 123-44.

Thompson, S. and Hoggett, P. 2002. 'Toward a Democracy of the Emotions', co-authored with Paul Hoggett, *Constellations*, 9(1), 106-26.

Wendt, A. 2003. 'Why a World State is Inevitable', *European Journal of International Relations*, 9(4), 491-542.

Winnicott, D.W. 1949. 'Hate in the Counter-Transference', *International Journal of Psychoanalysis*, 30, 69-74.

Yeatman, A. 2007. 'Varieties of individualism', in C. Howard (ed.) *Contested Individualization*. Basingstoke: Palgrave Macmillan, 45-59.

Žižek, S. 1993. *Tarrying with the Negative*. Durham, NC: Duke University Press.

Chapter 2
Axel Honneth's Antagonism: What Changes When the Mode of Acquiring Recognition Changes

Estelle Ferrarese

Axel Honneth defines his objective as the theorization of a "permanent struggle for recognition" (Honneth 2002: 502), where this permanence is conceived in the form of historical stages, driven by successive struggles, progressing through the expansion of the normative content of recognition. As has been frequently pointed out (see, for instance, Markell 2003), such a permanent struggle is accompanied by permanent reconciliation. In this chapter, I would like to focus on an additional assumption that this argument relies upon, one which has been less frequently highlighted and even less elucidated: the assumption that there is a struggle in the first place.

While Honneth clearly demonstrates that a denial of recognition does not necessarily lead to a struggle, the recognition that is given is generally considered in a context of struggle. From his project to reveal the "moral grammar" of social conflicts in *The Struggle for Recognition* (1995), to his reflections on the recourse to violence in his essay on "Invisibility" (2001), through to his debate with Nancy Fraser, in which he argues that "each principle of recognition has a specific surplus of validity whose normative significance is expressed by the constant struggle over its appropriate application and interpretation" (Honneth, in Fraser and Honneth 2003: 186), his position on this subject has varied little. Even the central thesis of *Reification* (2008) does not question this idea. Admittedly, Honneth now defines "recognition" as a primary form of the relationship to the world in a way that seems to reduce the significance of the motif of conflict: "our actions do not primarily have the character of an affectively neutral, cognitive stance toward the world, but rather that of an affirmative, existentially coloured style of caring comportment. In living, we constantly concede to the situational circumstances of our world a value of their own, which brings us to be concerned with our relationship to them" (Honneth 2008: 38). However, this is a more fundamental level of recognition than that addressed in previous studies, and Honneth's account of it in no way calls into question other modes, including their relations with conflict. As Honneth emphasizes in his response to his commentators, including Judith Butler and Martin Jay, this original form of recognition "is not intended to contain any norms of positive concern or respect. Nor does it claim that certain positive, benevolent feelings are at work" (ibid.: 151). Love and hate, ambivalence and coldness, can all be expressions of this elementary recognition. But at the higher level, where three modes of recognition are distinguished, hate, ambivalence and coldness may be seen as denials of recognition which give rise to struggle.

It is very clear that Honneth reflects on the nature of the moral attitude that causes a person to respond to the other's normative expectations (see, for instance, Honneth 2007a). However, the motif of recognition rarely appears without being accompanied by that of struggle, implying that the potential instance of recognition *resists* my expectations or even my demands.

The self-evident character attributed to the motif of struggle can of course be linked to the thesis – a weak one at that – of a historical realism. According to this thesis, the permanence of struggles is merely what is revealed by the history of modern societies; struggle enjoys prominence simply because it provides a means of obtaining by force that which could not be obtained by any other method.

But if we scrutinize the phenomenology of struggles, they are less self-evident since that they imply that the party to whom the requests for recognition are addressed acknowledges that it is indeed an addressee of requests, but at the same time it *resists* these requests. However, this admission assumes accepting the burden of the justification of the denial. Hence the solution consists in either denying any antagonism, or in redefining the nature or the reason for the interaction. As pointed out by Frantz Fanon, in a well-known footnote of *Black Skin, White Masks*, the White man does not interpret his relationship with the Black man in terms of a struggle where recognition is at stake; what he expects from the Black man is his work (Fanon 1986: 194). At the other end of the spectrum of neglected possibilities, there is the case of recognition granted without struggle. This is particularly true in the framework of reflexive democracies: many colonized societies or dominated groups often no longer have to struggle for their freedom. Rather it is negotiated, obtained through constitutional amendments, or simply given by the colonizer or the dominant groups, and granted in the form of political rights (see Coulthard 2007).

A more demanding explanation would be that the presence of struggle arises from a genuine theoretical necessity, from a constraint internal to Honneth's philosophy. In this case, his social theory should account for the existence of social groups that have an *interest* in the permanence of particular social situations. However, it is difficult to find such an account, for recognition is not posited by Honneth as a scarce good, which would mean as a matter of course that some people's access to this good would deprive others of benefiting from it too. In this case, what people have to gain from resistance is obvious, as it is in the theory of class struggle, where some people's dependency on the position occupied by others in relation to the mode of production makes the struggle to end the existing order inevitable. But there is no room for such an interpretation in Honneth's moral grammar of social conflicts.

Why then, in spite of the fact that struggle does not in any way proceed from a logical constraint, is it put forward? What is lost, on a theoretical level, if we speak of recognition without speaking of struggle? The idea of toleration, brought into play in similar contexts of cultural or religious heterogeneity, does not seem to focus on antagonism. Similarly, the idea of the decent society (Margalit 1998), which is presented as the political and moral antonym of humiliation, is not mediated through the idea of conflict. It therefore seems that it is not its finality (which is shared with theories that do not resort to conflict) that gives struggle the pre-eminence it enjoys in Honneth's theory of recognition. Instead we may put forward the hypothesis that the centrality of struggle derives from something specific to its movement, to its economy, which gives it a character that is as inevitable as it is normatively desirable.

In light of these reflections, I believe it to be necessary to identify the properties attributed to struggle that could explain the central place it occupies in Honneth's system. First, I will consider some hypotheses concerning the history of the concept in order to try to explain the prominence of struggle (1). Then I will examine the effects that the two struggling parties have on each other (2), before considering the effects attributed to struggle in the world in which it emerges (3).

1. Struggle and the History of Philosophy

Hegel would seem to be the inevitable starting point for investigating the association between recognition and struggle. However, approaching the question from this angle turns out to be quite unproductive:

1) When Honneth draws on Hegel, he does not follow the line of thought opened up by Kojève's reading of the dialectic of master and slave, which in the *Phenomenology of Spirit* makes struggle an inescapable fact. In this tradition, "action", defined as the transformation of the world that is hostile, "will begin with the act of imposing oneself on the "first" other man one meets. And since this other, if he is (or more exactly, if he wants to be, and believes to be) a human being, must himself do the same thing, the first anthropogenetic action necessarily takes the form of a fight" (Kojève 1980: 11). But such an anthropology is nowhere to be found in Honneth's writings. He does not interact with this tradition at all.

2) Honneth devotes the first two chapters of *The Struggle for Recognition* to proving the need to reformulate the theory of struggle found in Hegel's Jena writings, because it is impossible to grasp precisely the reasons for the initiation of struggle. But when he describes how he himself fits into the Hegelian heritage, he has the same difficulty. In fact, even though *The Struggle for Recognition* is based exclusively on the Jena writings, it is Hegel's *Philosophy of Law*, from which struggle is conspicuously absent, that Honneth must turn to in order to defend his conviction – shared by all the members of the Frankfurt School – that the cause of society's negative state, the source of social pathologies, is to be ascribed to a deficit of social rationality. According to Honneth, the idea of

Objective Spirit contains "the thesis that all social reality possesses a rational structure, which one can offend against by the practical application of false or inadequate concepts only on pain of prompt repercussions throughout social life itself" (Honneth 2000: 19). And he argues that, in one way or another, all of his predecessors in fact adopted for their own purposes Hegel's idea that social pathologies should be understood as the result of societies' inability to adequately express the rational potential already inherent in their institutions, their practices and their routines (Honneth 2004). But we are left with no explanation – other than the Frankfurt School's passage through Marxism – as to why he then adds that for Critical Theory the Hegelian realization of reason must be understood as a multifaceted *conflictual learning process* in which universally applicable knowledge is produced when the resolution of problems provides improvements, where this occurs against the resistance of dominant groups (ibid). In other words, the deployment of reason derives from a common praxis that creates solutions inextricably linked to conflicts that enable learning. However, this proposition cannot be justified by the framework borrowed from the *Philosophy of Law*, and so we still do not know why the resistance of some to others is the necessary condition for this learning to happen.

3) As already mentioned, for Honneth, the legal and institutional order is changed by a series of struggles for recognition. Indeed, it is merely the product of successive struggles, which, in modernity, have progressively broadened the normative content of the concept of recognition. Here again, he simply assumes that there is resistance, in the sense that the existing institutions actively resist the demands for recognition.

Nevertheless, here we are very far from the metaphor of the siege used by Habermas to characterize relations between the processes of the democratic formation of opinion and the political system: "Communicative power is exercised in the manner of a siege. It influences the premises of judgment and decision making in the political system… It thus aims to assert its imperatives in the only language the besieged fortress understands" (Habermas 1997: 59). In this case, it is easy to imagine (which is not exactly what Habermas does) a fundamental state of conflict between institutions and civil society, the two being strangers to each other in nature, consistency and logic.

Let us consider how Honneth, in *Suffering from Indeterminacy* (2000), reproaches the Hegel of the *Philosophy of Law*. In this work, Honneth interprets *Sittlichkeit* as a concept that refers to all spheres of communication, which, because of their moral assumptions, are capable of producing a reciprocal demonstration of recognition. Thus, he describes a constitutive series of need, self-interest and honour, which form so many degrees of individuation, and which correspond to three institutions, the family, civil society and the state. However, observing that in the case of the intersubjective confirmation constituted by love, it is the family, and not friendship that Hegel uses to develop his thesis, Honneth concludes, with regret, that Hegel favours the *legally institutionalized* forms of *Sittlichkeit*. He sees two reasons for this stance: the stability specific to legally institutionalized forms, which is conferred upon them by the possibility of legal sanctions, and the fact that they can be created by mechanisms that are controllable by state legislation.

While, according to Jean-François Kervégan (2008), the *Philosophy of Law* posits the state at the same time as an (inter)subjective reality, a lived bond, a shared aspiration to living-together, and an objective system of institutions, Honneth sees it as exactly the opposite. According to him, when Hegel comes to question the form of recognition specific to this sphere in the chapter on the state, he shifts from forms of intersubjective recognition, as in the case of the family and civil society, towards vertical forms of recognition between citizen and the state (§260), with the result that the intersubjective dimension of the state is lost.

Honneth opposes a conception of the institution, derived from the work of Arnold Gehlen, as a "practical set of actions … that have taken the form of intersubjectively shared routines and habits" (Honneth 2001a: 115). According to Gehlen, to whom Honneth devotes an extensive discussion in *Soziales Handeln und Menschliche Natur* (1980) – an early work written with Hans Joas – institutions unburden man (who is described as a being abandoned by his instincts) of the complexity of the world. Institutions are seen as coagulations into forms, and include morality, legal relations and stereotyped models of behaviour.

The question that then arises is why such institutions should resist demands for recognition, and thus always make struggle necessary. Here we are dealing with institutions in the way Vincent Descombes (1997) defines them, in terms of the grammatical rule and the shared meanings which individuals find themselves faced. In other words, the strength and form of the institutions can be illustrated by language, the use of which is possible only as long as it conforms to pre-existing constraints. Understood in this way, at best institutions are unavailable to constant change. However, to speak of resistance and confrontation in this context makes little sense. Can one struggle against language?

The intention here is not to deny the autonomy of the system of norms that constructs institutions from every individual's opinions. But the most obvious thesis regarding the ineluctability of struggles against institutions, that of the solidification of norms and representations in positive law and in state apparatuses, which become intangible and self-centred, is swept aside by the very type of reproach that Honneth directs at Hegel.

If the theoretical background from which the idea of recognition is extracted does not suffice to explain the centrality attributed to struggle for recognition, we must turn our attention to the attributes which struggle assumes in its material expression, according to Honneth. From a logical point of view, we can consider three possible effects specific to struggle: it transforms A who demands; it transforms B who resists; or else it modifies their interaction and the world that gives shape to it (in a way that the absence of combat would not allow). Let us begin by considering the effects that the two struggling parties have upon one another.

2. Struggle and the Struggling Parties

First, let us examine the ability of struggle to affect the party to whom the requests for recognition are addressed: the most radical possibility here would be to put an end to the denial of recognition by doing away with this party, rather than forcing it to take my existence into consideration. This is the model of the struggle to the death. Unsurprisingly, it has no place in Honneth's work, and more fundamentally, the motif of confrontation must remain compatible with the following: "A decentering takes place in the recognizing subject because she concedes to another subject a 'worth' that is the source of legitimate claims infringing upon her own self-love. 'Confirmation' or 'affirmation' thus means that the addressee is equipped with as much moral authority over one's person as one knows oneself to have in being obligated to carry out or abstain from certain classes of actions" (Honneth 2001b: 122). In other words, we are not in an agonistic perspective in the full sense of the term, where the temporary end of the conflict does not result from renewed understanding, but purely and simply from the *victory* of one of the two parties.

The project of the proponents of "agonism", such as Chantal Mouffe and Ernesto Laclau, just the same as Honneth, is to demonstrate that antagonism is constitutive of the social. Mouffe thus defines 'the political' as opposed to 'politics', as "the dimension of antagonism inherent in human relations" (2000: 101). However, this perspective is founded on a denial of the moral dimension of the human relations. According to these authors, the refusal of morality is the condition of a democratic politics whose purpose is to "construct the "them" in such a way that it is no longer perceived as an enemy to be destroyed, but as an "adversary", that is, somebody whose ideas we combat but whose right to defend those ideas we do not put into question" (ibid.: 102).

For Honneth, by contrast, social conflicts that concern the adequate interpretation of dominant standards of recognition necessarily have a *moral* point. "What makes such claims moral is, first, that they concern the social conditions of undistorted subjectivity and agency, and second, that they require of social agents an attitude that goes beyond an immediate concern with their self-interest in being responsive to the needs of others" (van den Brink and Owen 2007: 6). If we have to abandon the proposition that struggle is simply what makes the other submit, we must dismiss the idea of a struggle whose result would be to force others to accept as true what is already true for oneself, that is, to win a cognitive victory. Contrary to this model, which posits that awareness of the other bestows truth to the certainty that the winner has of his being, for Honneth, the instance of recognition is not merely required to passively ratify an existence or an identity, since it must be involved in co-producing it.

Let us now consider how struggle changes individuals who enter into it. One might claim that it is important that the person who has experienced a denial of recognition frees himself of it himself, because struggle is a process in which a subjectivity is revealed to itself and at the same verifies itself. Here, subjectivation is to be understood as the emergence of a political subjectivity. I will leave aside the question of ontogeny, which would mean engaging in psychological considerations that have no place here.

The intertwining of subjectivation and antagonism is put forward by Jacques Rancière in *Disagreement*. He considers the process of subjectivation, not as the acquisition of awareness and voice in an entity existing prior to this confrontation, but as taking form through a series of operations involving the production of a new field of experience, operations with which it remains co-extensive. "By subjectification I mean the production through a series of actions of a body and a capacity for enunciation not previously identifiable within a given field of experience, whose identification is thus part of the reconfiguration of the field of experience" (Rancière 1995: 56).

Honneth hints at a move in this direction in *The Struggle for Recognition*, when he writes that social shame is "a moral emotion that expresses the diminished self-respect typically accompanying the passive endurance of humiliation" from which one can be liberated only through active protest and resistance (Honneth 1995: 121).

However, the idea that struggle creates the subject engaged in it remains in the background for Honneth, who restricts himself to considering the effect of struggle on the relationship to self and qualifies it as a "secondary motivation" (Honneth 1995: 163) of the conflict. This idea was a lot more in the foreground for Fanon, for whom the irreducibility of the motif of confrontation in the logic of recognition proceeds quite plainly from the self-affirmative function attributed to struggle. To the extent that he did not *make* the other recognize him, the French Negro was "acted upon"; only confrontation enables him to free himself from "the inessentiality of servitude" (Fanon 1986: 194).

It is worth also noting that in Honneth's theory absolutely no room is given to the establishment and assertion of a collective subject, or even just a collective consciousness. The process of transition to struggle is described in its collective dimension, but we know nothing about the nature of this collective or its reason for being. We are told that only if the individual is able to express his feelings in a context of intersubjective interpretation that identifies him as typical of a whole group, then the transition to struggle is possible. In other words, the effectiveness of the struggle depends on the existence of a collective semantics (Honneth 1995: 163). Honneth therefore only clarifies the formation of a collective entity in terms of the availability of grammatical, almost cognitive resources that make certain formulations and the articulation of certain demands possible. However, nothing is said of the process of producing the common inherent to the struggle itself. He does not consider struggle as a modifier, and even less as a generator of this collective, although this is the approach taken by Georges

Sorel, whom he quotes. Considering that Marx is mistaken in his belief that society is divided into two fundamentally antagonistic groups, Sorel attributed violent struggle with the function of dividing the society "into two camps, and only into two" (Sorel 2007: 164). In this way, he accounts for the unifying and auto-transformative logic of struggle and for the shaping of the collective entity that carries it. By failing to do the same, Honneth seems to postulate a given consciousness and an identity that precede the conflict.

Generally speaking, for Honneth, struggle has no ability to act as a force of revelation of self to self – except in the margins: "the idea of a struggle for recognition does not necessarily imply that subjects struggle merely on the basis of a diffuse feeling of being disrespected totally, thus only gaining a clear conception of their actual goal in the course of their social struggle. Rather, what generally motivates these struggles is the still unclear and merely negatively formulated realization that one possesses the same qualities and abilities as those who have been recognized (institutionally), but without enjoying corresponding public recognition" (Honneth 2007: 364).

I have thus made clear that struggle is not prominent in Honneth's theory because of its possible effects on the struggling parties. Let us therefore examine the last theoretical option: the effects one can attribute to struggle in the world in which it emerges.

3. Struggle and the World

At first glance, this explanation seems to be the easiest to defend, since for Honneth struggles for recognition move nothing less than history itself. As the instrument by which societies experiencing moral progress gain in rationality, such struggles are seen as the condition of possibility for the learning process described above. Here we are dealing with a clearly Hegelian postulate. As Honneth himself points out in *Disrespect*, Hegel's model includes the "venturesome but challenging idea that ethical progress unfolds in a series of three levels of increasingly demanding patterns of recognition, and that an intersubjective struggle mediates between each of these levels, a struggle that individuals conducts for the purpose of having their identity claims confirmed" (Honneth 2007a: 132).

Nonetheless, Honneth distances himself partly from the Hegelian position because for him conflict does not have the function of motivating the transition to the next ethically-constituted institutional step. Each sphere must be marked by an internally-caused conflict over the legitimate application of the principle of recognition in question (Honneth, in Fraser and Honneth 2003: 144). It remains the case that struggle is normatively justified as the engine of evolution, both at the level of the species and at that of individuals. This is most certainly related to an idea that has no explicit foundation, apart from at the individual level: there is no access to the principles of justice except negatively. This is the reasoning that Honneth develops from the role played by the emotions in the transition to struggle, emotions that he endows with a cognitive dimension. The expectation of recognition is integrated into the structure of interactions, to the extent that the individual implicitly expects to be taken into account in the projects of others in a positive way (Honneth 1995: 45). It is on the occasion of failures of recognition, and through the emotions they arouse, that the subject discovers himself to bear normative expectations which relate to his vulnerability. The attention of the disappointed subject shifts to his own expectations, making him simultaneously aware of the cognitive elements – in this case the moral knowledge – that governed his action (Honneth 2001c: 110).

We are given less explanation about the evolutionary effect of what is (sometimes) the later stage – that is, collective struggle. We are simply informed that it unfolds the surplus validity of the norms of recognition in force, against the dominant interpretative praxis. This characteristic calls for two remarks.

1) One might think, since struggle creates a normativity that would otherwise remain out of reach, that confrontation is the necessary condition for an act of recognition to be normatively valid, in the sense that struggle would qualify the justice or the fairness of the result. But here we encounter a problem: for, when Axel Honneth examines the ideological – that is to say, normatively false – forms of recognition, it is not struggle that constitutes the evidence of a non-ideological recognition. Rather, such recognition stands out because "something in the physical world – be it modes of conduct or institutional circumstances – must change if the addressee or addressees are to be convinced that they have been recognized in a new manner" (Honneth 2007c: 342).

I will therefore propose the following thesis: struggle has a mediate role in Honneth's schema. The fact that it occurs does not directly imply that the act of recognition to which it leads is normatively valid, but it is proof that the world has changed.

In modern societies characterized by reflexivity, there are two possibilities. Either the denial of recognition perceived by a group is "justified", in the sense that another group in a position of domination has integrated the practice of denial, by means of a coherent legitimating discourse, in a social order apparently neutral from the moral and epistemic point of view. Or else the denial quite simply does not appear, as the available grammar precludes the characterization of what certain subjects undergo. Bringing to light the denial thus implies overcoming the epistemic deficit which hinders a person from making a lived experience intelligible to himself and to others. But the impossibility for the victim of making heard the wrong it has undergone results from unequal participation in the creation of collective models of interpretation. This is also what Nancy Fraser highlights, when she states: "it is unjust that some individuals and groups are denied the status of full partners in social interaction simply *as a consequence of institutionalized patterns of cultural value in whose construction they have not equally participated* and which disparage their distinctive characteristics or the distinctive characteristics assigned to them" (Fraser, in Fraser and Honneth 2003: 29). Because as much as the justifications made for some denials of recognition – and the existence of an epistemic deficit which masks others – result from power relations, their contestation always implies the claim to, or the appropriation of a power to construct meaning and hence the world.

2) Furthermore, it should be noted that the idea of surplus validity – as unfolded by struggle – refers to something that already exists as potential: it is not about creating something new, but about making a potential actual. Indeed, Honneth considers it as part of the legacy of leftist Hegelianism, which he claims as his own, that there must be an identifiable element of practice or experience that is a piece of socially incorporated reason insofar as it contains a surplus of rational norms or organizational principles *pressing for their own materialization* (Honneth, in Fraser and Honneth 2003: 238).

However, if it is then a question of actualization, we must clearly understand what is meant by this concept. It was defined by Axel Honneth in a debate initiated by Arto Laitinen, who, in discussing the nature of the act of recognition, attempted to overcome the choice between the constructivist model of attribution, and the response model (which treats acts of recognition as responses to pre-existing reasons that reside in what the subjects claiming recognition *really* are – that is to say, what they are *already*). In this context, an act of recognition merely actualizes an identity, a quality or a capacity existing as potential. However, Honneth adopts this proposal in order to give it a particular meaning (Honneth 2002: 510). His inquiry proceeds from the difference between the qualities that we know intellectually and those that we embrace emotionally, precisely the movement that is covered by the concept of actualization: "I intended this notion to indicate the act by which subjects become capable of identifying wholly with the evaluative qualities of which they are already culturally aware. … The distinction between potentiality and actuality indicates neither an epistemic gap nor a space to be bridged over, but a rift between ethical knowledge and social expression" (Honneth 2007b: 356). It seems to me that *this* is the function performed by struggle; it confers the quality of world-changer to the party demanding recognition.

In bringing together these last two points, we can understand the importance of struggle in the motif of recognition. To be sure, Honneth's reasons for his preference for antagonism remain unclear. But this inquiry into his theory allows us to reconstruct the following justification. Extracting the *ability* to modify the state of the world seems always to be the object of the struggle for recognition, whether explicitly or implicitly, accompanying a claim to be recognized as a member of a polity or as the bearer of particular identity. In the same way that requests for visibility are doubled in reality – as demonstrated by Axel Honneth – by more fundamental expectations relating to the status of being worthy of moral consideration, an attentive reading of the confrontational movement, so obvious and yet so rarely questioned directly in the constellation of contemporary theories of recognition, teaches us that any struggle for recognition comes with a double meaning: on the one hand, it is about the designated object (identity, lifestyle, contribution to the common project, status, etc.), and it is also about a power of construction, or, to put it in other terms, the world-changer status. And this double meaning then provides us with an explication for the unspoken necessary motif of resistance. The status of world-changer can only result from a struggle against an enemy that resists; for if the latter anticipates the request, or even the expectation, for recognition, it maintains its monopoly over this status.

Thus, at the conclusion of my examination of the idea of struggle in analyses of recognition, it turns out that the initial reticence of the instance, which nonetheless ends up yielding to good reasons, is the sign – because it is defeated during the struggle – of my ability to alter the world. In other words, the logic that explains the prominence of struggle in Honneth's theory of recognition, far from revealing simple fidelity to the Hegelian reference, covers the three points of analysis that I set myself: struggle is necessary and desirable because it triggers the transformation of A who demands, B who resists, and the world; and each is changed because all the others are changed. In this sense, there is never a return to a commonness preceding the struggle, even though the recognition of the subjects having engaged in struggle would not seem to have modified the social and political order.

References

Coulthard, G.S. 2007. Subjects of Empire: Indigenous Peoples and the Politics of Recognition in Colonial Contexts. *Contemporary Political Theory*, 6, 437-60.

Descombes, V. 1997. *Les Institutions du sens*. Paris: Minuit.

Fanon, F. 1986. *Black Skin, White Masks*. London: Pluto Press.

Fraser, N. and Honneth, A. 2003. *Redistribution or Recognition: A Political-Philosophical Exchange*. London and New York: Verso.

Habermas, J. 1997. Popular Sovereignty as Procedure, in *Deliberative Democracy*, edited by J. Bohman and W. Rehg. Cambridge, MA: MIT Press.

Honneth, A. 1995. *The Struggle for Recognition*. Cambridge: Polity.

Honneth, A. 2000. *Suffering from Indeterminacy*. Amsterdam: Van Gorcum.

Honneth, A. 2001a. *Leiden an Unbestimmtheit: Eine Reaktualisierung der Hegelschen Rechtsphilosophie*, Stuttgart: Reclam Verlag.

Honneth, A. 2001b. *Das Andere der Gerechtigkeit*. Frankfurt/M: Suhrkamp.

Honneth, A. 2002. Grounding Recognition: A Rejoinder to Critical Questions. *Inquiry*, 45(4), 499-519.

Honneth, A. 2004. Eine soziale Pathologie der Vernunft. Zur intellektuellen Erbschaft der kritischen Theorie, in *Axel Honneth: Sozialphilosophie zwischen Kritik und Anerkennung*, edited by C. Halbig and M. Quante. Münster: LIT Verlag.

Honneth, A. 2007a. *Disrespect*. Cambridge: Polity.

Honneth, A. 2007b. Rejoinder, in *Recognition and Power*, edited by B. van den Brink and D. Owen. Cambridge: Cambridge University Press.

Honneth, A. 2007c. Recognition as Ideology, in *Recognition and Power*, edited by B. van den Brink and D. Owen. Cambridge: Cambridge University Press.

Honneth, A. 2008. *Reification: A New Look at an Old Idea*. Oxford: Oxford University Press.

Honneth, A. and Joas, H. 1980. *Soziales Handeln und menschliche Natur: anthropologische Grundlagen der Sozialwissenschaften*, Frankfurt/M, Campus.

Honneth, A. and Margalit, A. 2001. Invisibility. On the Epistemology of 'Recognition'. *Proceedings of the Aristotelian Society*, 75, 111-39.

Kervégan, J-F. 2008. *L'Effectif et le rationnel. Hegel et l'esprit objectif.* Paris: Vrin.

Kojève, A. 1980. *Introduction to the Reading of Hegel: Lectures on the Phenomenology of Spirit*. Ithaca: Cornell University Press.

Margalit, A. 1998. *The Decent Society*. Cambridge, MA: Harvard University Press.

Markell, P. 2003. *Bound by Recognition*. Princeton University Press.

Mouffe, C. 2000. *The Democratic Paradox*. London: Verso.

Rancière, J. 1995. *La Mésentente. Politique et philosophie*. Paris: Galilée.

Sorel, G. 2007. *Réflexions sur la violence*. Paris: Editions Labor.

van den Brink, B. and Owen, D. 2007. Introduction, in *Recognition and Power*, edited by B. van den Brink and D. Owen. Cambridge: Cambridge University Press.

Williams, R.R. 1997. *Hegel's Ethics of Recognition*. Berkeley and Los Angeles: California University Press.

Chapter 3
Overcoming the Injuries of ‘Double Consciousness’

Nasar Meer

Introduction

In the forethought to his *Souls of Black Folk*, William Edward Burghardt Du Bois (b. 1868-1965) contemplates ‘the strange meaning of being black here in America’ (Du Bois 1903: 5), a question of significance to both White and African-American readers since ‘the problem of the twentieth century is the problem of the colour line’ (ibid.). These words feature as some of the most frequently quoted in scholarly accounts of ‘race’ and colour racism. The core argument of this chapter is that while these few words bear a historical resonance they also constitute part of a body of thought that has a profound but overlooked contemporary relevance.[1] That is to say that while Du Bois focused mainly upon the racialized and very particular existence of late nineteenth and early to mid-twentieth century African-Americans, his account offers a broader illustration of how minorities will posses an impaired civic status if the terms of incorporation misrecognize their sensibilities. This is because they will be prevented from participating in the social and political life of their society in a manner that affords them equal opportunity, dignity and confidence; diminishing their citizenship and giving rise to the ‘peculiar sensation’ that they are ‘a problem’.

This should not be taken to suggest that Du Bois has been ignored by the academy. On the contrary, there has of late been an increasing recognition of Du Bois a ‘founding figure’ of sociology (Young, Jr. et al. 2007). Examples include how in 2006 a group of sociologists led a successful campaign to rename the American Sociological Association’s (ASA) highest award, the Career of Distinguished Scholarship Award, after Du Bois. Elsewhere Burawoy’s (2005: 417) seminal intervention on the role of contemporary social science names Du Bois ‘as perhaps the greatest public sociologist of the twentieth century’. While not exhaustive, each of these accolades follow Zuckerman’s (2004: 3) proclamation that Du

1 This chapter limits itself to re-reading the cited work instead of reconciling the trajectories of Du Bois’ contribution. These are varied and include intellectual and political excursions during later life that led Du Bois to embrace Communism and Pan-Africanism (indeed, Du Bois died in Ghana in 1963 and was given a state funeral by President Kwame Nkrumah).

Bois was 'one of the most imaginative, perceptive, and prolific founders of the sociological discipline'.

This chapter seeks to extend this renewed interest in the work of Du Bois by taking the opportunity provided by the present collection to invite an emerging scholarship on the politics of misrecognition to re-examine Du Bois' contribution. More precisely the chapter argues that with the concept of 'double consciousness' Du Bois bequeaths to us a rich account of reciprocal moral obligations within a national community that helps us to understand how forms of minority 'consciousness' can underpin minority social formations that emerge both *in* and *for* themselves. This describes the movement from a minority consciousness that is derived from the treatment of a dominant party, existing *in* itself and bearing a historically ascribed identity, to a minority consciousness that is capable of mobilizing on its own terms for its own interests, and which emerges *for* itself in adopting a politically self-defined identity. As such, and through an original reading of his concept, Du Bois is cast as a pre-cursor to later exponents of the politics of 'difference' (Young 1990), 'cultural diversity' (Parekh 2000), and 'recognition' (Taylor 1994), respectively. Prior to this, however, and due mainly to their similar conceptions of consciousness and ideas of reciprocity, it is argued that a rewarding method of decoding novel implications from Du Bois' concept is to dialogue it with Hegel's Master-Slave dialectic (hereafter MSD) outlined in the *Phenomenology of Spirit*.[2]

The next section will show how an understanding of Hegel's MSD is helpful in grasping how Du Bois conceives of the power held by a dominant group to afford status, invoke complicity or use coercion in denying recognition or affording misrecognition to a minority, and that the constituent parts of double consciousness emerge as an outcome and a resource in relation to the need to maintain a sense of *self* in response to this misrecognition. The subsequent section will explicate each of the four aspects it is argued constitute Du Bois' idea of double consciousness, as well as how Du Bois appropriated these insights in his political assessment of the future of African-American life. The final section will relate the preceding discussion to some core authors that have profoundly shaped the study of the politics of identity broadly conceived. The chapter will conclude that the rationale behind revisiting Du Bois' concept is to probe the dilemmas facing minorities who aspire to be full participants in society. This can be characterized as a schema which becomes progressively 'thicker' in capturing (a) the political dimension in which minority subjectivity is formed, (b) the nature and form of this subjectivity *in* and *for* itself, alongside (c) the transformative potential it heralds for society as a whole. This includes an examination of both the conflicting accounts evident in

---

2 It is worth noting, as Zamir (1995) does, that Du Bois does not always make explicit reference to Hegel in his work, which informs Reed Jr.'s (1997) rebuttal of the view that Hegel's influence on Du Bois is obvious. The complementarity of the two thinkers that is of greatest interest here and it is equally accepted that reading Du Bois into Hegel could be just as fruitful as looking for the Hegel in Du Bois.

the construction of the *self*, and the grounds on which racial and ethnic minorities who are subject to exclusionary discourses can strive for political recognition and incorporation.

Hegelian Consciousness

In his allegory of the master and the slave, Hegel outlines a series of conflicts and their dialectical relationship to different forms of consciousness. In examining reciprocal relations of power, he attempts to 'lift the veil' and reveal the processes mediating the transformation of a consciousness from dependence to one of self-consciousness and independence. It is worth clarifying at the outset that rather than providing an empirical account of power-relations in actual slave societies, Hegel's master-slave dialectic should instead be understood as an abstracted 'state of nature' argument conceived as a corrective to Hobbes' (Davis 1975). By this it is meant that through the MSD, Hegel is trying to draw our attention to the manner in which a Hobbesian war of 'all against all' is unable to maintain the very individuality or independence upon which it is premised. This is perhaps best captured in Binder's (1989: 1435) interpretation of the MSD as an attempt to show that 'freedom [has] to be conceived as some form of association rather than independence; and that it [has] to be mediated by politics rather than defended from politics'. Besides stressing the primacy of the political, Binder positions the MSD as 'an intellectual foundation for modern communitarian conceptions of freedom in its devastating critique of the ideal of independence' (ibid.: 1437).

The reason why Binder makes such a bold claim stems from a question that Hegel posed himself, namely: how does a person come to conceive herself as an independent being and/or when do they become conscious of themselves as such? Hegel's answer rests on a process of objectification which reasons that we must first identify – outside of ourselves – some 'purposive intelligence' (Binder, ibid.) from which it proceeds that others are required to establish our own independent selfhood or identity, described in the following terms:

> A self-consciousness has before it another self-consciousness; it has come outside itself. This has a double significance. First it has lost its own self, since it finds itself as an *other* being; secondly, it has thereby sublated that other, for it does not regard the other as essentially real, but sees its own self in the other. (Hegel 2003 [1910]: 105)

What prevents our collapse into our own perceptions, insists Hegel, is our ability to see 'our own self in the other'. The ethical basis this provides in terms of its potential normative, political implications for Du Boisian conceptions of consciousness is what this first section on Hegel seeks to establish. To this end, it will be argued that we cannot receive recognition outside of a political community characterized by reciprocal or mutual recognition. That is, the obligations rendered under conditions of *Sittlichkeit*[3] or ethical life, 'by virtue of being members of one of the ongoing bonded communities of common life and common freedom' (Taylor 1989a: 864). To satisfactorily understand the meaning of this, we must unpack the complexities and rewards of the MSD.

Hegel's dialectic, presented as an allegory or vignette, begins with two independent beings that – at an underdeveloped stage of history – try to 'wrest recognition from one another without reciprocating' (Taylor 1975: 153). The reason 'each aims at the destruction and death of the other' (Hegel 2003 [1910]: 12), or is driven to demand recognition while conferring none, fighting for it instead of cooperatively conferring it, is because each carries a distorted conception of individual identity, struggling for Hobbesian survival. Unlike the Hobbesian predicament (see footnote 7), however, Hegel's framing of this 'state of nature' scenario posits that when this struggle takes place and one of the protagonists is defeated, rather than being slain they are instead enslaved by the victor. According to Hegel, this is because the victor cannot receive the desired recognition from the defeated if they do not exist, and so the whole process would have been futile. The completion of this first conflict is best described in Hegel's own terms:

> The dissolution of that simple unity is the result of the first experience; through this there is posited a pure self-consciousness and a consciousness which is not purely for itself [...] The one is independent, and its essential nature is to be for itself, the other is dependent, and its essence is life or existence for another. The former is the Master, or Lord, the latter the Bondsman. (Hegel 2003: 108)

The master is thus positioned as an independent being and is recognized as such by the enslaved. At this point there emerges, however, a discrepancy between the master's consciousness and the reality of the situation; between the master's idea of himself as a true independent being, and his concept of the outside world. This is because the master's conception of himself – as truly independent and recognized as such by the slave – is necessarily mediated through this two party relationship. Having argued that the master achieves a dependent rather than an absolute status, Hegel insists that it is in fact the very freedom of the master that is determined through his relation to the slave, specifically because the consciousness of the one party is necessarily mediated through its relation to the other:

> In all this, the unessential consciousness is, for the master, the object which embodies the truth of his certainty for himself. But it is evident that this object does not correspond to its notion; for just where the master has effectively achieved Lordship, he really finds that something has come about quite different from an independent consciousness. It is not independent, but rather a dependent consciousness that he has achieved. (ibid.: 109-10)

3 Defined by Taylor (1975: 376) as referring to 'the moral obligations I have to an ongoing community of which I am a part'.

Before we critically assess this understanding, by writing in the next section of *dialectics* in the plural rather than the singular, we should recognize that Hegel's position brings the master to a point which Kojève (1969: 22) describes as an 'existential impasse', where the recognition sought by the master during the initial conflict is not what is achieved. For in enslaving the other and relegating them to a position of subordination, the master cannot receive the recognition of them self as an independent being because (a) their own notion of mastery is dependent upon that of the slave, and (b) recognition is not of sufficient value coming as it does from one relegated in status. As Hegel argues above, at first the master does not realize the disparity between the reality of the situation and their impression of it.

Teleology, Group Psyches and Multiple Dialectics

Following the initial conflict then, Hegel sees the dialectic as a representation of how the fate and consciousness of the two parties is no longer independent but, albeit unequally, *interdependent* in that they have become inextricably linked in a process that necessitates some form of resolution; that they effectively have to sink or swim together. Taylor (1975: 155) shares this interpretation when he stresses that the process of coming to self-consciousness is a 'dualistic' one. For both Taylor and Kojève the slave must recover their self-consciousness not only for their own survival, but also to resolve the existential impasse of the master. Similarly, the master must recognize the fact that their fate is now directly dependent upon the development of the consciousness of the slave. The anticipated independence of the master becomes not only a dependence upon the slave for his present form of self-consciousness, but, more importantly, rests upon the possibility of the future development of that consciousness to a state of true self-consciousness or independence. Specifically: the movement from a self-consciousness *in* itself to the transformative potential of a self-consciousness *for* itself, or from one's historically *ascribed* identity to one's politically *self-constructed* identity.

There is of course a teleological prescription in some of these readings but what is of interest is the way in which something valuable can be stated, as it was by Du Bois, without it necessitating a teleological course, and this is no less true with the leap that Hegel makes from individual to group psyches. In common with a tradition amongst philosophers to begin with the rational self, Hegel also starts with the self but, as we have seen, argues that this cannot exist in a *self substantiating process*, and so therefore communalizes it. Thus in contrast to Hobbes who argued that in leaving a 'state of nature' we lose freedom, Hegel shows that the social and the political *is* the condition of freedom in which self is a social or communal self.

As it is argued below, however, the sorts of multicultural recognition that Du Bois espouses does not follow from this alone. That is that the case for mutual recognition does not on its own establish the legitimacy of multicultural inclusion for Du Bois. As we shall see, Du Bois merges ideas of difference with citizenship, centred around modernist ideas of hyphenated identities, in making a universalistic ethical move in arguing for the equal but differentiated inclusion of different groups on the basis of their common membership of a polity. This is retuned to below, but what is required at this stage is a closer inspection of the internal logic of Hegel's dialectic, where it is revealed that during his initial discussion of the development of consciousness, Hegel fails to distinguish between what appear to be three *separate* constructs in the MSD.

These multiple dialectics roughly divide between (a) the *present-focused* as a logical interaction or binary, which distinguishes between the existence and non-existence of an interaction between two parties and (b) the *empirical possibilities* to emerge from the power retained by the master who, in the final analysis, possesses an autonomy that the slave lacks. These possibilities shape the future of this relationship and the ways in which it might continue (reciprocity being one possibility, coercion another). The nature of the relationship as it exists and changes may then be described by tracing (c) the moral dialectic, which seeks to engage – through the masters' authoritative paternalism – the slaves' reciprocal complicity in the dialectic, serving to externalize and normalize the ethical constraints of this relationship. In what one might cite as an unreasoned inference, Hegel utilizes the two constructs of the dialectic, outlined as (a) and (c), which herald a mutual dependency for attaining *status* (however uneven that may be) between the master and the slave, before – without clear reason – moving to tie the very development of consciousness upon this struggle for status recognition. Hegel circumvents a step in his allegory (b) which pertains to the empirical possibilities that, should the slave refuse to acquiesce with the master's dominance, the master can coerce the slave as a subordinate and thwart the reciprocity required to make the dialectic function on the basis of recognition alone.

Regardless, therefore, of the appropriate recognition granted to the master by the slave, the slave is dependent upon the Master for their coming to self-consciousness, whilst the master retains the agency to minimize their own dependence upon the slave. Thus, Hegel ignores the extent to which coercion can be either a competitor or partner of recognition. In light of this, it might be more helpful to speak of master-slave *dialectics* in the plural, rather than the singular, and to suggest that there are actually three different interactions taking place in this allegory. This appears to be a more promising insight than the initial reading offered by Taylor and Kojève, specifically because it can be employed to probe the intricacies of forms of consciousness developed in the present-focused and moral dialectic outlined by Hegel, in order to distinguish between these and the empirical dialectic of majority-minority relations that so occupied Du Bois.

Leaving the master at the impasse earlier identified by Kojève, Hegel turns his attention to the position of the slave, which is also contrary to what might be expected, since the consciousness of the slave is essentially in a position of 'potentiality':

> Just as lordship showed its essential nature to be the reverse of what it wants to be, so, too, bondage will, when completed, pass into the opposite of what it immediately is: being a consciousness repressed within itself, it will enter into itself, and change round into real and true independence. (Hegel 2003: 110)

In a strong reading, Kojève (1969: 22) places the slave as the instrument and agent of all historical change:

> There is nothing fixed in him. He is ready for change; in his very being, he is change, transcendence, transformation, education; he is historical becoming at his origin, in his essence, in his very existence … the experience of the fight predisposes the slave to transcendence, to progress, to History.

Given the tension we have identified, Kojève's deterministic reading might better be interpreted as offering only a potential avenue rather than a determinate outcome. The transformative possibility provided by this sort of context can be contrasted with Du Bois' reading of the broader sense of consciousness developed among African-Americans, and particularly in their conception of freedom as newer, and possibly richer, because:

> … out of slavery and out of the later striving of black folk … in an oppressive white world came a rising sense of black soul. Thus it was that white thesis bred black antithesis, which took the best of white culture and moved it upward towards a new synthesis. (Williamson 1984: 405)

This end stage of the dialectic, however, does not generally constitute our main concern. Of far greater relevance in contrasting Du Bois with Hegel are the intricacies in the processes of the development of consciousness. As Binder (1989) suggests, rather than being a specific model of dominance and submission, the MSD is a series of wheels within wheels; an attempt to explain historical processes, through an examination of the transformation of consciousness within a social relationship that is, itself, transformed by and through these shifts in consciousness. With the distinction between those three separate constructs in mind, we can infer from Binder some sympathy to the multi-faceted nature of the development of consciousness.

What is Double Consciousness?

Like all forms of dialectic, the MSD is a process in which concepts and categories are never static but are marked by constant transformation and mediation. This becomes evident in Du Bois' account of the political development of America in that – just as it is the case for the master and the slave – in *Of Our Spiritual Strivings* (1903) the fate of American consciousness is dependent upon the unfolding relationships and the dialogue or interaction between minority and majority subjectivities, as two separate but entwined forms of consciousness. It is, moreover, these *dialectics* which will, for Du Bois, determine the course of American history.[4] Du Bois introduces his account of double consciousness in the following passage from *Strivings*, and since this is the main text that I wish to focus upon in the proceeding discussion, it is worth quoting at length:

> … the Negro is … born with a veil, and gifted with a second-sight in this American world, – a world which yields to him no true self consciousness, but only lets him see himself through the revelation of the other world. It is a peculiar sensation, this double-consciousness, this sense of always looking at one's self through the eyes of others, of measuring one's soul by the tape of a world that looks on in amused contempt and pity. One ever feels his twoness, – an American, a Negro; two souls, two thoughts, two unreconciled strivings; two warring ideals in one dark body, whose dogged strength alone keeps it from being torn asunder. The history of the American Negro is the history of this strife,-this longing to attain self-conscious manhood, to merge his double self into a better and truer self. In this merging he wishes neither of the older selves to be lost. He would not Africanize America, for America has too much to teach the world and Africa. He would not bleach his Negro soul in a flood of white Americanism, for he knows that Negro blood has a message for the world. He simply wishes to make it possible to be both a Negro and an American, without being cursed and spat upon by his fellows, without having the doors of Opportunity closed roughly in his face. (Du Bois 1999 [1903]: 10-11)

On the surface, this passage has as its fundamental theme a duality in African-American life. Fuelled largely – but not exclusively – by colour racism, this duality is a kind of paradox which stems from being intimately part of a polity while excluded from its public culture, or, as Du Bois characteristically puts it, 'being an outcast and stranger in mine own house (ibid.)'. Yet further scrutiny reveals four different issues, loosely grouped into two sets, which encompass much more than an outcome predicated upon the effects of colour racism. Moreover, since there are a range of issues signalled in his description of double consciousness, and because this range attempts to mediate between agency and structure, individual and society, and between minority and majority subjectivities, there has on occasion been a tendency to conflate, reduce or confuse the role of one to the other. This concern further instils the need to unpack Du Bois' description before we analyse and adapt it for conceptual use in any normative sense.

4 Gooding-Williams (1987) argues that Du Bois explicitly offers a kind of Hegelian philosophy of African American history, and that the philosophical model for Du Bois' conception of historical process is Hegel's *Phenomenology of Spirit*. See footnote 5 of this chapter.

In the opening half of the passage, Du Bois outlines his reading of the *self*, specifically the significance of (1a) the internalization by African-Americans of the contempt white America has for them, and (1b) the creation of an additional perspective in the form of a 'gifted second sight' to which experiencing this gives rise. In the second half of the passage he identifies how societal incongruencies emerge from (2a) conceiving of African-Americans as having fewer civic rights but no less the duties or responsibilities of an ideal of American citizenship, and (2b) diverging sets of un-reconciled ideals or 'strivings' held by African-Americans which are objected to by white society, specifically emerging from an 'enduring hyphenation' signalled in his notion of 'twoness'. In sum, these four interacting constructs give rise to a condition of double consciousness as Du Bois understood it. The function of descriptive metaphors such as the 'veil' cut across and straddle these interacting issues, and are therefore discussed when they appear relevant.

The Conflicted Construction of the *Self*

The notion of the *self* plays an important role in Du Bois' concept, and – beginning with his reference to looking at one's self through the eyes of others – Du Bois, like Hegel, seeks to illustrate how our sense of *self* is necessarily constructed in a social context that is continually subject to implicit power relations. If we recall, Hegel suggests that our idea of ourselves, what we claim to be, and what we really think we are, can be dependent upon how others come to view us, to the extent that our sense of *self* is developed in a continuing dialogue.[5] Self-consciousness exists here 'only by being acknowledged or recognised'. Thus, like the master and the slave, each of us derives our sense of *self* through an interaction with others, through coming to view our individual selves as others see us, such that the refusal of others to acknowledge our humanity, our existence or our faculty to contribute something meaningful, inevitably underscores a sense of alienation.[6]

In using this Hegelian perspective to understand the Du Boisian position, it can be argued that Du Bois sees something unique about the consciousness of the *self* among African-Americans. As an Other and as 'a problem', 'black folk'

5 Of course all theories of the self in sociology emphasize the importance of the 'generalized other' but the distinction here is between a benign self-other relationship from one predicated on subordination.

6 Taylor (1994) goes further in sharing with Du Bois the view that systematized mis-recognition or negative disapproval compromises our sense of self worth and constitutes a moral injury; Young (1990) characterizes such a tendency as a form of majoritarianist oppression, whilst Parekh (2000) deploys a pluralist argument beginning with a communitarian account of the culturally embedded self and the necessity of recognizing how the self is formed, before making the stronger case that cultural diversity is an intrinsic value.

developed a double consciousness where they have a sense 'of always looking at one's self through the eyes of others'. This is because negative disapproval in the form of presenting African-Americans as possessing a degraded cultural heritage or limited contribution to American life creates an internal echo of white America's racist judgements. It should be clear then that this conception of the *self* is not, for Du Bois, a reflection of the atomistic *self*. It is instead conceived of as culturally embedded and socially mediated; leading Du Bois to argue that self recognition is a form of cultural recognition which, necessarily, sees one's cultural identity in connection with the cultural identities of other members of one's community. Hence the injuries suffered from prejudice are not only due to the overt hostility from the majority, but also come from minority invisibility. This first source of conflict in Du Bois' passage can then be seen as contributing to a sense of double consciousness through the unwillingness of one group, contingent on their historical dominance as 'master', to recognize African-Americans satisfactorily, to the extent that the consciousness of *self* is established distortedly through that of another.

The Creation of an Additional Perspective or 'Gifted Second Sight'

Accompanying Du Bois' understanding of the *self* is the role of subjectivity, for he situates the standpoint developed within minority-majority relations at the centre of his account of double consciousness. This is exemplified in his suggestion that the experience of oppression allows African-Americans to understand the promise of freedom in a way that white Americans cannot.[7] In the passage from *Strivings* Du Bois refers to this as 'a second sight', a way of seeing things that escape the notice of the majority, specifically the distance between democratic ideals and the practice of racial exclusion, so that 'once in a while through all of us there flashes some clairvoyance, some clear idea of what America really is. We who are dark can see America in a way that Americans cannot' (Du Bois 1971: 416). This is realized in everyday scenarios where it is raised to a conscious level, serving as a means to probe deeper meanings and contradictions of a racialized experience and providing the resource for transformative change. For Du Bois, then, racial alienation is arguably similar to forms of class alienation in its potential for initiating change.

This notion of 'second sight' also ties into his metaphor of the *veil* which, in the passage, serves as an expression of how those behind it – African-Americans – see the dominant society, whilst those in front of it – white America – may

7 Lukács (1971) later argued that structurally defined class positions could offer a superior vantage point with which to view social realities. Later still some feminists, particularly Harding (1986), put forward the idea of 'standpoint epistemologies' which stressed that women's experiences and location – their standpoint – could provide a better place from which to view knowledge production.

not see the excluded as full co-members of their polity. In this way, it might be argued that Du Bois presents an inverted version of the early Rawlsian thought experiment of placing a 'choosing subject' behind 'a veil of ignorance' in an effort to ascertain unbiased, and transcending, propositions of human interest. What such an understanding means is that the Du Boisian subject is looking out from behind a socially constructed apartheid, in full knowledge of critical aspects of their identity. Moreover, and unlike the early Rawls (1971), Du Bois does not consider it possible to presuppose that a person can be detached from the contingent aspects provided by society, history and culture. Du Bois' *veil* might then best be described as a one-way mirror, with the minority seeing the majority through the glass, whilst the latter sees only their own reflection (of mastery or dominance) as the former remain hidden behind the mirror. This quite obviously complements Hegel's MSD, specifically in Du Bois' suggestion that *those without power are able to see those with power in a different light*, since the actions of those without power must always take the powerful into account. Reading his account in this manner adds further import to the second of Hegel's dialectics, specifically that the master can coerce the slave with a power that the slave lacks, which may explain why Du Bois argues that 'second sight' is both a gift and a burden.

Bound by the *Requirements* but not the *Rewards* of Citizenship

The overarching structural factors which Du Bois identifies as contributing to a sense of double consciousness are twofold. The first is revealed in his assertion that historically embedded racial dualism in mainstream American society denies African-Americans the civic rights afforded to their white counterparts. Simultaneously, however, this racial dualism continues to conceive of African-Americans as having no less the duties or responsibilities of an ideal of American citizenship. He thus argues that within the rhetoric of democratic citizenship and its attendant ideals, 'the Nation has not yet found peace from its sins; the freedman has not yet found in freedom his promised land' (Du Bois 1999 [1903]: 12). This 'promised land' is of course the stage in which racial and cultural differences are not taken as grounds for the justification of natural inequality or superiority.

For Du Bois however, an important symptom of this dichotomy is the effect it has in stifling internal criticism and dissent, giving rise to what he describes as a 'moral hesitancy that is fatal to self confidence' (1999 [1903]: 127). This is because internal criticism is impeded or sacrificed within the minority group, because the starting point of representation takes the form of a combative defence against societal biases. Du Bois calls these 'peculiar problems of inner life' which occur because 'our worst side has been so shamelessly emphasized that we are denying that we ever had a worst side [so that] in all sorts of ways we are hemmed in' (ibid.).

Diverging Strivings and Two-ness

The second structural factor which Du Bois identifies as contributing to a sense of double consciousness is outlined both in his discussion of different sets of 'strivings' or claims upon the public sphere, and *twoness* as a hyphenated identity. These are both quite distinct from the potentially debilitating effects evident in the first two, since they, like the third, provide a resource for something beneficial to both minority and majority and reflect a new synthesis. This derives from 'strivings' or cultural attributes amongst African-Americans who seek to affirm both their American *and* African identities. The following statement, repeated from the passage taken from *Strivings*, tries to sketch this out:

> The history of the American Negro is the history of this strife … to attain self-conscious manhood, to merge his double self into a better and truer self. In this merging he wishes neither of the older selves to be lost. He would not Africanize America for America has too much to teach the world and Africa. He simply wishes to make it possible for a man to be both a Negro and an American, without being cursed and spit upon by his fellows, without having the doors of opportunity closed in his face. (Du Bois 1999 [1903]: 10-11)

Du Bois here is encouraging a reflexive understanding between origin and destination, between what Gilroy (1993) has called 'roots' and 'routes', and not only arguing that there is space for both, but that both be positively cultivated in an effort to maintain a critical perspective towards a new synthesis or hyphenation. As he put it in another essay, *The Conservation of Races*, from a similar period:

> Here, then, is the dilemma, and it is a puzzling one, I admit. No Negro who has given earnest thought to the situation of his people in America has failed, at some time in life, to find themselves at these crossroads; has failed to ask at some time: What, after all, am I? Am I an American or am I a Negro? Can I be both? … We are Americans, not only by our birth and citizenship, but by our diverging political ideals… . (Du Bois 2003 [1897]: 24)

This is then an unapologetic objection to forms of cultural assimilation or separatism, strongly endorsing a view that cultural and/or moral diversity may be captured within hyphenated identities.

'Enduring Hyphenation'?

Expressions of double consciousness are neither mutually exclusive nor one and the same. By definition they must interact, but are suitably distinctive to be discussed separately. What they all have in common is the sense of an unresolved – but not irresolvable – conflict, anchored in a process of structural and discursive misrecognition. Thus, although formed in a specific context and concerned with the conditions of a particular peoples, it is clear that in many ways Du Boisian conceptions of consciousness are relevant to the contention that socio-cultural self-esteem emerges from forms of group recognition, alongside personal recognition. The relationship between personal and group recognition that is alluded to in Du Bois' account is characterized by the idea that the 'inner strife' affecting African-Americans individually is informed by the mastery or dominance possessed by white Americans in depreciating their African-American counterparts. This is captured well in the following passage:

> ...that nameless prejudice that leaps beyond all this, he stands helpless, dismayed and well-nigh speechless; before that personal disrespect and mockery, the ridicule and systematic humiliation, the distortion of fact and wanton license of fancy, the cynical ignoring of the better and boisterous welcoming of the worse, the all pervading desire to inculcate disdain... . (Du Bois 1999 [1903]: 15)

In this sense, the subject group are more disenfranchised than alienated so that it is not so much cultural *difference* but *cultural disfranchisement* that shapes their struggle. This means that institutions and social practices attribute minority status to some inherent qualities in the minority group, as if those qualities were the *reason* rather than the *rationalization* for not taking their sensibilities into account. This leads Du Bois to raise the following question: how can one achieve a mature self-consciousness and an integrity or wholeness of *self* in an alienating environment? If, in the eyes of another, your humanity is perceived as lacking self-evidential qualities, how do you go about showing its existence?

Self assertion holds many benefits, but for Du Bois – and this is where he differs from some of his contemporaries and later Black Nationalists – overzealous self-assertions appear (a) unnecessarily outwardly threatening, (b) too often draw upon fictitious claims of authenticity, so that (c) they are, in the end, counter-productive. To openly plead for respect on the other hand would effectively forfeit any self-respect in the process. The solution that Du Bois points to is not one of abandoning the double self but is, instead, to merge the 'double self into a better and truer self'– one that does not deny experience and history but seeks to build on it. As Lewis (1993: 281) argues:

> The genius of *The Souls of Black Folks* was that it transcended this dialectic in the most obvious way – by affirming it in a permanent tension. Henceforth, the destiny of the race could be conceived as leading neither to assimilation nor separatism but to proud, enduring hyphenation.

This is a kind of multiculturalism in which minorities can espouse a hyphenated identity, contribute and participate equally but not necessarily uniformly. This would not only produce a better America, but the 'better and truer self' Du Bois thought possible. At the same time, and although Du Bois implies the eventual resolution of this paradox of a divided self in time, much of what he writes simultaneously suggests that African-Americans should accept – and embrace – this contradiction arising from dual consciousness. This is because 'living in two worlds at once' furnishes the minority subjectivity with powers to see what the majority are blind to and so, through 'second sight', add something to the equation of diversity in the way Parekh (2000) would later describe as an expansion of each other's horizons of thought and human fulfillment. Du Bois is, therefore, trying to reconcile the strivings for group recognition with more traditional accounts of the nation-state, in an effort to capture a multiculturalism in which cultural and/or moral diversity would be considered an asset. In this sense, he leaves us with the basis of a normative concept in debates advancing an ethic of multiculturalism that encompasses a pragmatic logic, beginning with a rebuttal of narrow preferences for territorial and cultural congruencies.

The following sections explore this with reference to three prominent thinkers who have made seminal contributions to what May et al. (2004: 1-19) have described as the 'multicultural turn' in recent social and political theory. The selection of only three obviously omits many others of significant standing but, it is argued, that these three in particular share with Du Bois a striking yet overlooked similarity in key aspects of their work. The aim, therefore, is not to offer a descriptive commentary and overview, but to pick out some points of convergence that help further elucidate the operation of minority consciousness and double-consciousness. For example, how do ideas of difference, diversity and recognition, as they are presented in Du Bois' contributions contrast with those of Iris Marion Young (1990), Bhikhu Parekh (2000) and Charles Taylor (1994), respectively?

Young's 'Difference', Parekh's 'Diversity', and Taylor's 'Recognition'

In her landmark *Justice and the Politics of Difference*, Iris Marion Young (1990) presents a series of objections to modes of political incorporation which, as a precondition of being afforded full and unimpaired civic status, require minorities to reject their own particularity in a process of cultural assimilation to the dominant norms, values and customs of that society or polity. In Young's view such a requirement is unjust because 'assimilation always implies coming to the game after it is already begun, after the rules and standards have been set, and having to prove oneself accordingly' (1990: 165). Although Young argues that there are different types of assimilation which can seek to assimilate different things, what they all share in common is the disproportionate burden of change that they place upon the minority. Assimilation is certainly an obstacle to the sorts of strivings imagined by Du Bois, memorably objected to by his belief that the African-Americans would not 'bleach' their 'Negro soul in a flood of white Americanism', for, with their message for the world, they simply wish to make it possible for 'to be both a negro and an American'. This is a good example of *twoness* as an expression of 'enduring hyphenation' which contests the singularity of a civic status that cannot, for example, incorporate the public recognition of identities marked by 'difference'.

Young's work is a response to the view that citizenship achieved through individual rights alone, based upon blindness to difference, can satisfy principles of social justice by, for example, relegating differences to the private realm in favour of equal treatment in the public sphere. By drawing attention to the context of groupings that are founded upon non-voluntary aspects of social identity, she points to the disproportionate impact of past domination or present disadvantage. She thus argues that focusing upon individuals ignores how citizenship already fails to treat people equally, or where 'blindness to group difference disadvantages groups whose experience, culture and socialized capacities differ from those of privileged groups' (ibid.: 165). Not being attentive to group differences can, therefore, lead to a form of oppression in itself and/or can contribute to further oppression:

> …by allowing norms expressing the point of view and experiences of privileged groups to appear neutral and universal. […] Because there is no such unsituated group-neutral point of view, the situation and experience of dominant groups tends to define the norms of any such humanity in general. Against such a supposedly neutral humanist ideal, only the oppressed groups come to be marked with particularity; they, and not the privileged groups, are marked, objectified as the Others. (Young 1990: 165)

It is striking how, in holding this view, she offers a similar objection to the idea of neutrality presented by Du Bois in his account of the operation of the *veil.* Since 'privileged groups implicitly define the standards according to which all will be measured…their privilege involves not recognizing these standards as culturally and experientially specific' (Young 1990: 165). If we recall, the Du Boisian *veil* imagines that those who are 'veiled' become marked by dominant society as deviating from the 'norm', while those in front of it may not see anything other than their own rightful mastery or dominance. It was argued that this presents an inverted version of the Rawlsian 'veil of ignorance', for what such an understanding means for Young, like Du Bois, is that the minority looks out from behind a socially constructed disparity, in full knowledge of critical aspects of their identity. By the very nature of this state of affairs, where past dominance informs contemporary disparities in power, she argues that it is periodically raised to a conscious level:

> When participation is taken to imply assimilation, the oppressed person is caught in an irresolvable dilemma: to participate means to accept or adopt an identity one is not, to try to participate means to be reminded by oneself and others of the identity one is. (Young: ibid.)

This double consciousness, this sense of looking at oneself through the eyes of another, accords with Du Bois' insistence that self recognition is a form of cultural recognition which, necessarily, sees one's own cultural identity in connection with the cultural identities of other members of one's community. Hence, the injuries suffered from prejudice are not merely due to the overt hostility from the majority, but also arise from minority invisibility in not being recognized or represented as a legitimate constituent of society. This links to Young's complaint that it is an unhelpful liberal fetishism to presuppose that a person can be detached from the contingent aspects of their social identity, history and culture. These separate points are nicely drawn together by her advocacy of the institutional incorporation of group identities into a democratic cultural pluralism, one that can reconcile a general system of rights that is the same for all, and a more specific system of group-conscious policies such that:

> …a democratic public should provide mechanisms for the effective recognition and representation of the distinct voices and perspectives of those of its constituent groups that are oppressed or disadvantaged. Such group representation implies institutional mechanisms and public resources supporting (1) self organization of group members so that they achieve collective empowerment and a reflective understanding of their collective experience and interests in the context of society; (2) group analysis and group generation of proposals in institutionalized contexts where decision makers have taken group perspectives into consideration… . (ibid.: 184)

This is a particularly 'thick' advocacy of policies capable of instantiating the recognition and inclusion of minorities in a reorganized public sphere with the aim of preventing minorities from being further frozen out or overwhelmed by majorities. Although it is expressed in a less technical fashion, the maintenance and promotion of such plural constituencies is similarly championed by Bhikhu Parekh and is expressed in his *Rethinking Multiculturalism.* There is a great deal in this offering and what is of most concern to this discussion probably captures the main thrust of Parekh's argument within this text as elsewhere. This is that cultural diversity and social pluralism are of an intrinsic value because they challenge people to evaluate the strengths and weaknesses of their own cultures and ways of life. This distinguishes him from liberals and communitarians thus. Where the latter might recognize that cultures can play an important role in making choices meaningful for their members (Kymlicka 1995), or play host to the development of the *self* for the members of that culture (Tully 1995), or that different cultures increase autonomy by providing further 'options' in ways of living for society as a whole (Raz 1986) – they maintain that culture is important for individual group members but do not succeed in explaining why cultural diversity is necessary in itself. To this Parekh offers the following explanation:

> Since human capacities and values conflict, every culture realizes a limited range of them and neglects, marginalizes and suppresses others. However rich it may be, no culture embodies all that is valuable in human life and develops the full range of human possibilities. Different cultures thus correct and complement

> each other, expand each other's horizon of thought and alert each other to new forms of human fulfillment. The value of other cultures is independent of whether or not they are options for us ... inassimilable otherness challenges us intellectually and morally, stretches our imagination, and compels us to recognize the limits of our categories of thought. (Parekh 2000: 167)

Thus there is an active promotion of cultural difference here, a clear argument in favour of diversity in and of itself which complements an over-arching Du Boisian prescription. This emerges in Du Bois' sense of the need for African-Americans to develop their 'traits and talents' so that 'someday on American soil two-races may give each to each those characteristics both sadly lack' (1999 [1903]: 9-10).

Du Bois was convinced that moral truths are discovered as members of a culture reflect on their particular historical experiences, and this idea sustained his insistence that different groups are capable of discovering different moral truths. Much like Parekh, Du Bois' position is not an orthodox liberal one that argues people have a right to pursue their own conceptions of the good, and that if the state neglects them benignly, rather than intervening coercively, then each state is likely to house many different cultures. Nor is it that Du Bois believes exposure to other ways of life increases the choice of options available to all in a society. His argument is rather that, because each culture has something to teach others, members of minority cultures should be allowed to cultivate moral and aesthetic insights for humanity as a whole. This is supported by his call to African-Americans to fulfil their 'duty' and 'maintain their race identity [because they] have a contribution to make to civilization and humanity which no other race can make'. This is not limited to African-Americans, however; this is an issue of plurality as a consequence of particularity. What is being advocated is both a deepening of cultural particularities and a broadening of these insights from different cultures. This is something that sits comfortably with Parekh's (2000: 167-8) view that cultural diversity is an objective good since it 'fosters ... human freedom as self-knowledge, self-transcendence and self criticism'.

The conception of recognition that emerges from both Parekh and Young, however, is most recognizable in Charles Taylor's (1994) account of the emergence of a modern politics of identity. In this Taylor suggests that the idea of 'recognition' as we understand it today has developed out of a move away from conceiving historically defined or inherited hierarchies as the sole provenance of social status or honour (in the French sense of *préférence*), and towards a notion of dignity more congruent with the ideals of a democratic society or polity, one more likely to confer political equality and a full or unimpaired civic status upon all its citizens.[8] Drawing upon his previous, densely catalogued account of the emergence of the modern self (Taylor 1989b), he maps the political implications of this move

8 Thus making equal recognition an essential part of democratic culture, a point not lost on Habermas (1994: 113) who argues that 'a correctly understood theory of [citizenship]

onto two cases of Equality. The first is the most familiar and is characterized as a rights-based politics of universalism, with the prospect of affording equal dignity to all citizens in a polity. The second denotes a politics of difference where the uniqueness of context, history and identity is salient and potentially ascendant.

For Taylor, this coupling crystallizes the way in which the concept of recognition has given rise to a search for 'authenticity'. This is characterized as a move away from the prescriptive universalisms that have historically underwritten ideas of the Just or the Right, in favour of the fulfilment and realization of one's true self, originality or worth. That is why, according to Taylor, people can no longer be recognized on the basis of identities determined from their positions in social hierarchies alone but, rather, through taking account of the real manner in which people form their identities. The interface between these two issues – dignity and difference – forms the basis of Taylor's account of the politics of recognition, expressed as a dialogical interlocutor. So how does this relate to Du Bois?

In the first instance, Taylor's emphasis on the importance of 'dialogical' relationships rehearses Du Bois' view that it is a mistake to suggest that, in Taylor's terms, people form their identities 'monologically' or without an intrinsic dependence upon dialogue with others. We have seen how Du Bois expresses this process, and Taylor (1994: 33) characterizes it in a similar manner, arguing that we define our identity 'always in dialogue with, sometimes in struggle against, the things our significant others want to see in us'. Here Taylor is openly drawing upon Hegel who, if we recall, suggests that our idea of ourselves, what we claim to be, and what we really think we are, can be dependent upon how others come to view us to the extent that our sense of *self* is developed in a continuing dialogue. Self-consciousness exists 'only by being acknowledged or recognised', and the related implication for Taylor, just like Du Bois, is that a sense of socio-cultural self-esteem emerges not only from personal identity, but also in relation to the group in which this identity is developed. This is expressed at the beginning of Taylor's (1994: 25-6) account that:

> ….our identity is partly shaped by recognition or its absence, often by the misrecognition of others, and so a person or group of people can suffer real damage, real distortion, if the people or society around them mirror back to them a confining or demeaning or contemptible picture of themselves. Non recognition or misrecognition can inflict harm, can be a form of oppression, imprisoning some in a false, distorted, and reduced mode of being.

It is worth noting here how Taylor's concerns rest on the need to prevent the outcome described in the first part of Du Bois' concept, namely an internalization by a minority of the contempt a majority hold for them. Less directly, but equally

---

rights requires a politics of recognition that protects the individual and the life contexts in which his or her identity is formed'.

present, is the thrust of the second part which referred to the creation of an additional perspective to which this experience might lend itself, as is evident in Taylor's characterization of liberalism as a 'fighting creed' and what this means to those being fought:

> Liberalism is not a possible meeting ground for all cultures, and quite incompatible with other ranges. … [A]s many Muslims are well aware, Western liberalism is not so much an expression of the secular, postreligious outlook that happens to be popular amongst liberal *intellectuals* as a more organic outgrowth of Christianity … All this is to say that liberalism is also a fighting creed. (Taylor 1994: 62)

What Taylor is drawing our attention to here is 'a particularism masquerading as the universal' (ibid.: 43). Simultaneously, he identifies the limitations of his own conception of recognition politics, concluding that the boundaries marking the legitimacy of recognition politics must be drawn somewhere, and that nowhere is more appropriate than on issues of Muslim claims-making. This is necessary, Taylor argues, because in Islam 'there is no question of separating politics and religion in the way we have come to expect in Western liberal society' (ibid.: 62). Whether this sort of exclusivity in predetermined notions of incompatibility masks a complex partiality or whether it represents legitimate caution, what nevertheless emerges *here* is Taylor's divergence from a Du Boisian idea of recognition, since the latter is more genuinely dialogical and does not seek *a priori* to exclude some minority claims-making from the process of politics. Is it therefore fair to query the extent to which Muslim-consciousness is disproportionately objectified by liberalism's 'fighting' creed? Like Hegel's master, could Taylor's conception of recognition be guilty of the same sleight of hand that is only ever revealed when recognition is replaced by coercion?

Conclusions

The purpose of this chapter has been to unpack and explore Du Boisian ideas of minority consciousness and double consciousness; to elaborate why they are of value and worth redeeming, and where they sit in relation to some other, more recent, ideas in the areas of multiculturalism and recognition. It is argued that Du Bois' concept is premised upon the idea that a consciousness *for itself* is characterized by an active mobilization, one that is striving to be recognized, but one that turns inward and becomes a double consciousness when it is benignly ignored or malignly coerced. Double consciousness thus captures the dual character of unrecognized minority subjectivities and their transformative potential, alongside the conditions of impaired civic status that are sometimes allocated to minorities by mainstream society. The rationale behind revisiting Du Bois' concept is to probe the dilemmas facing minorities who aspire to be full participants in society. This can be characterized as a schema which becomes progressively 'thicker' in capturing (a) the political dimension in which minority subjectivity is formed, (b) the nature and form of this subjectivity *in* and *for* itself, alongside (c) the transformative potential it heralds for society as a whole. This includes an examination of both the conflicting accounts evident in the construction of the *self*, and the grounds on which racial and ethnic minorities who are subject to exclusionary discourses can strive for political recognition and incorporation.

References

Binder, G. 1989. Mastery, Slavery, and Emancipation. *Cardozo Law Review*, 10(5-6), 1435-80.

Burawoy, M. 2005. For Public Sociology. *The British Journal of Sociology*, 56(2), 260-90.

Davis, B. 1975. *The Problem of Slavery in the Age of Revolution, 1770-1823*. Ithaca: Cornell University Press.

Du Bois, W.E.B. 1971. Does the Negro Need Separate Schools?, in *The Seventh Son: The Thought and Writings of Web Du Bois*, edited by J. Lester. New York: Random House.

Du Bois, W.E.B. 1995 [1897]. *The Conservation of Race*, in *W.E.B. Du Bois: A Reader*, edited by D. Lewis. New York: Henry Holt.

Du Bois, W.E.B. 1999 [1903]. *The Souls of Black Folk* Centenary Edition, edited by H.L. Gates Jr. and T. Oliver. Oxford: Oxford University Press.

Gilroy, P. 1993. *The Black Atlantic: Modernity and Double Consciousness*. London: Verso.

Gooding-Williams, R. 1987. Philosophy of History and Social Critique in the Souls of Black Folk. *Social Science Information*, 26(1), 99-114.

Habermas, J. 1994. Struggles for Recognition in the Democratic Constitutional State, in *Multiculturalism. Examining the Politics of Recognition*, edited by A. Gutmann. Princeton: Princeton University Press.

Harding, S. 1986. *The Science Question in Feminism.* Milton Keynes: Open University Press.

Hegel, G.W.F. 2003 [1910]. *The Phenomenology of Mind*, translated by J.B. Baillie. London: Allen and Unwin.

Kojève, A. 1969. *Introduction to the Reading of Hegel*, assembled by Raymond Queneau, translated by James H. Nichols, Jr. New York: Basic Books.

Kymlicka, W. 1995. *Multicultural Citizenship.* Oxford: Oxford University Press.

Lukács, G. 1971. *History and Class Consciousness.* Merlin: London.

May, S., Modood, T. and Squires, J. (eds) 2005. *Ethnicity, Nationalism, and Minority Rights*. Cambridge: Cambridge University Press.

Parekh, B. 2000. *Rethinking Multiculturalism: Cultural Diversity and Political Theory.* London: Palgrave.

Rawls, J. 1971. *A Theory of Justice.* Cambridge: Harvard University Press.
Raz, J. 1986. *The Morality of Freedom*. Oxford, England: Clarendon Press.
Reed, A.L. Jr. 1997. *W.E.B. Du Bois and American Political Thought*. New York: Oxford University Press.
Taylor, C. 1975. *Hegel.* Cambridge: Cambridge University Press.
Taylor, C. 1989a. Hegel's Ambiguous Legacy for Modern Liberalism. *Cardozo Law Review*, 10(5-6), 857-70.
Taylor, C. 1989b. *Sources of the Self: The Making of the Modern Identity.* Cambridge: Harvard University Press.
Taylor, C. 1992. *The Politics of Recognition* in *Multiculturalism and the Politics of Recognition*, edited by A. Gutmann. Princeton, NJ: Princeton University Press.
Tully, J. 1995. *Strange Multiplicity*. Cambridge: Cambridge University Press.
Williamson, J. 1984. *Crucible of Race.* New York: Oxford University Press.
Young, A.A. Jr., Lemert, C., Watts, J.G., Marable, M. and Higginbotham, E. 2006. *The Souls of W.E.B. Du Bois*. Boulder, CO and London: Paradigm Publishers.
Young, I.M. 1990. *Justice and the Politics of Difference*. Princeton NJ: Princeton University Press.
Zamir, S. 1995. *Dark Voices: W.E.B. Du Bois and American Thought, 1888-1903.* Chicago: Chicago University Press.
Zuckerman, P. 2004. *The Social Theory of Du Bois.* New York: Columbia University.

Chapter 4
'The Imprison'd Absence of Your Liberty'[1]: Slavery, Recognition and Belonging

Laura Brace

Introduction

This chapter explores some of the complex threads we can draw between slavery and recognition. It draws in particular on Axel Honneth's suggestion that the concept of social death helps us to understand how 'victims of slavery collectively cope with the denial of rights and exclusion from society' (Honneth 1995: 135). He argues that the form of disrespect associated with slavery is understood as an injury that endangers the identity of human beings, but also makes the slaves aware of the state they are in, and allows us to see what the integrity of human beings might mean by looking at an example of its loss (1995: 135). He concludes that 'the negative emotional reactions accompanying the experience of disrespect could represent precisely the affective motivational basis in which the struggled-for recognition is anchored' (Honneth 1995: 135). In what amounts to an aside, we can see how, for Honneth, social and political agency emerges from physical injury and moral suffering, and so directly from the experience of struggling for recognition (McNay 2008: 126-7). By drawing on the work of Orlando Patterson to explore the concepts of social death, natal alienation, and permanent exclusion, this chapter provides a critical assessment of the idea of rooting our understandings of slavery and agency in a founding moment of torture, physical injury, disrespect or objectification.

Patterson's approach (and Honneth's suggestion) focus on the excluded status of the slave and on the permanence of that exclusion, making the opposite of slavery not freedom, but belonging. It is an account that places violence and injury at the heart of slavery, making it the defining feature of the experience and the institution. This means that from the outset, slavery is understood as a relationship, and as defined by powerlessness and loss. The trauma of slavery, on this account, is all about being violently torn away from your home, roots and family, and left defenceless to fend for yourself without the ethical bonds and the emotional connections we all require as humans. It is not so much being property that makes

1 Shakespeare, Sonnet 58.

a slave a slave, or being coerced to perform back-breaking labour, but being an outsider, forced to live outside the ethical bonds of society. This can in turn reinforce a powerful discourse of suffering that is all about disrespect and damage to identity. It is a variation on the 'rhetoric of personal pain' (McNay 2008: 10), where the pain involved is the pain of others, and our response is sentimentalized to teach us the meaning of integrity. My argument is that this rhetoric can itself be a form of misrecognition.

To make this argument, we need to start by thinking about how slavery fits into the classical liberal framework, where it is part of an abstract account of personhood where actions are motivated by rational interest (McNay 2008: 6). In the classic liberal framework what is damaged and broken by slavery is our own rational capacity to own the self and to exercise independent control over the self and its objects. Self-ownership takes the individual as the ultimate principle of justice, and has a vision of autonomy structured by self-control, rationality and individual choice (Willett 2001: 104). It is these that are at stake in slavery, and fundamentally undermined by the possibility of being owned by somebody else. Cynthia Willett points to the binary between autonomy and dependence, used as a scale to measure moral maturity and rational choice, and argues that inequalities 'grow out of the fact that liberal theory categorizes individuals into those who are viewed as responsible for their own lives and those who are entangled in relations of dependency' (2001: 3).

There are several implications for an account of slavery that takes this dichotomy as its starting point. Self-ownership is, as Janet Coleman points out, an intensely individualized concept (Coleman 2005: 128). A world governed by self-ownership is a world of self-interested, unsocial agents, radically abstracted from one another. This entails a particular set of assumptions about slavery. Slaves are the most hopelessly entangled of all of us in relations of dependency and force, and slavery is the ultimate injustice in liberal theory because it robs individuals of their rational decision making, their individuality and their rights and so of the basis of their personhood. In thinking about slavery in terms of the ownership of the self, this approach assumes that if it is possible for us to own ourselves, then it is a logical possibility for us to be owned by others. The focus on ownership, and on consent and contract, tend to produce a non-historical and non-social approach to slavery within which the slavery contract is not a right violation, since each of us can waive our right not to be enslaved (Kershnar 2003: 531). Given the general presumption in favour of liberty of contract, the transaction ought to be permitted. An individual 'may waive her moral claim not to be a slave in return for payment or something of value, since she has the relevant moral powers over the claims and liberties that in part constitute the right not to be a slave' (Kershnar 2003: 519).

An approach to slavery that takes recognition as its starting point might be expected to overcome some of the weaknesses of the 'intensely individualized' self-ownership account. Taking slavery and belonging as opposites means beginning from a model of psychic and economic interdependence, expressed through friendship, intimacy and co-operation, and based in what Cynthia Willett terms 'the rights of the social person' (Willett 2001: 16). This is close to Honneth's argument that every philosophical theory of society must proceed 'not from the acts of isolated subjects but rather from the framework of ethical bonds, within which subjects always already move' (Honneth 1995: 14). Thinking about slavery as the ultimate denial of recognition involves exploring some of the ways in which the connections that we make with another can be fractured and broken, illuminating part of the wrong of slavery which is not to do with self-control and rationality, or with ownership of the self. There are great strengths to this approach, but taking violence as the fundamental structure of slavery raises its own tensions and contradictions, making the experience of slavery all about the binary between exclusion and belonging, and then about the permanence of that exclusion, and so about how victims of slavery 'cope' with social death and the damage it does to their identity. This risks relying on a 'reductive understanding of power' that rests on identity claims to understand the complex social and power relations at work in slavery and in prostitution (McNay 2008: 2).

Slavery and Recognition

Taking violence as the starting point means that slavery is understood as a status violation, an assault on social relationships and the rights of social persons. This gets us beyond a narrowly economic analysis of the slave as a worker, and builds on Rousseau and Hegel's crucial insights to explain the intersubjectivity of slavery and its effects on masters as well as slaves. The focus is on the 'psychological dynamics' of slavery rather than on ownership of the self or others (McNay 2008: 15). Slavery is a 'crime of arrogance and social power' (Willett 2001: 16), derived from a sense of superiority through others' degradation. Willett puts hubris at the core of her analysis of slavery in order to de-centre conceptions of freedom that are anchored in property and ownership and in 'the moral attribution of self-control' (2001: 189). Instead, she draws on Frederick Douglass to argue that freedom has a social and ethical force derived from the relations between persons. Slave ethics are rooted in violence. Slave holders developed habits of cruelty and humiliation for pleasure as well as for profit, and slaves who rebelled could also be cruel, although they acted with a limit and a just purpose (2001: 193). Frederick Douglass in his slave narrative declared that: 'A man, without force, is without the essential dignity of humanity' (2001: 201). Human nature, in this account, cannot honour a helpless man, and it is this helplessness that makes a slave a slave, and imprisons them in the absence of their liberty. Slavery, then, was closely connected to hubris for the ancient Greeks, who aimed to break the spirit of the slave not only for economic profit but also for 'perverse psychic and social gain' (2001: 21). This perversity does not remain located within the individual, but moves out into the corruption of ethical bonds through social notions of honour, dishonour and alienation.

Orlando Patterson's analysis of slavery focuses on the concept of 'social death', and the impossibility of slaves acting and living as full social subjects. Slavery, for Patterson, can (and should) be distinguished from other social relationships by its constituent elements of force, dishonour and permanence. Slavery '*is the permanent, violent domination of natally alienated and generally dishonored persons*' (Patterson 1982: 13). Permanence is the key feature that distinguishes slavery from other slavery-like practices such as forced labour or the compulsory recruitment of children for armed conflict. Part of the wound inflicted by slavery is the inheritance of loss: the absence of liberty imprisons not just the individual, but future generations as well. For Patterson, these are all elements of the honour and dishonour that are a universal feature of slavery as an institution and a relationship. As a social system, slavery is characterized for Patterson by marginality and exclusion, dishonour and degradation. In slavery as a concept and a system we can see the harm inflicted by non-recognition, the way it denies a fundamental human need. Within this more relational framework, the lack of recognition at the crux of the slave relation is the key dimension of its injustice, one that is played out through non-recognition and disrespect and so seeps into cultural injustice and a lack of representation.

Rather than taking the liberal focus on ownership of the self, the inherent dishonour of slavery in this account is connected to its origins in defeat and capture, and to its continuing basis in violence. For Hegel, the slave had, by definition, taken life over honour: he had chosen to submit and live rather than to die unvanquished. Honneth's analysis of the struggle for honour is about how it risks the violation of the integrity of the person as a whole, and the goal of this struggle is to provide evidence for the integrity of this person. Both subjects struggle to re-establish their honour by convincing the other that their personality deserves recognition. They are only able to do this by demonstrating to each other that they are prepared to risk their lives. In this reciprocal perception of mortality, subjects perceive each other as 'morally vulnerable persons' and thereby affirm each other in their fundamental claims to integrity (Honneth 1995: 48). Ethical bonds are in part established by the publicly recognized right of the wronged person to redress. When that right to redress is denied, the slave is clearly placed outside the ethical community. Honour, as William Ian Miller argues, is about sensitivity to the experience of humiliation and shame, and the honourable person is 'one whose self-esteem and and social standing is intimately dependent on the esteem or the envy he or she actually elicits in others' (Miller 1993: 84). The violence of slavery, and the slaves' helplessness, place them outside the complex web of esteem, shame and envy that structures social membership and recognition. Slaves have no legitimate witnesses to their struggle for self-consciousness. It is precisely the asymmetry of moral vulnerability in slavery and the absence of legitimate witnesses that mean that the slaves lose their fundamental claim to integrity and so their legitimate claims to intersubjectivity. This is not just about the individual's lack of self-control, but about the reciprocity and the relationships that structure personality and integrity. The perception of mortality and vulnerability is so distorted, and so far from reciprocal, that it cannot form the requisite obligations or a normative core for legal relations (Honneth 1995: 48-9). Instead, outside the web of ethical relations, 'the slave becomes *fixed* in his dependence on the master for his life' (Bernstein 1984: 23).

The fixity of this dependency denies slaves the possibility of weaving themselves into the web of ethical bonds. In the struggle for honour, subjects move from exchange to contracts, where actual acts of exchange are 'replaced by the mutually articulated obligation to do something in the future' (Honneth 1995: 51). This opens up the possibility of breaking your word and violating the law, and also of keeping your word and being recognized as honourable. Once we live within this web of obligations, we can understand ourselves and others as rights-bearers, and so we can offer each other 'recognition respect'. This is a moral respect: 'to recognize every other human being as a person must then be to act, with regard to all of them, in the manner to which we are morally obligated by the features of a person' (1995: 112). The central psychological phenomenon linked to the granting of rights is 'an increase in the ability to relate to oneself as a morally responsible person' and, within that, the possibility of adult subjects seeing their actions as 'the universally respected expression of their own autonomy' (1995: 118). Honneth argues that self-respect in legal relations parallels basic self-confidence in a love relationship. The maintenance of such self-respect requires universal human rights, where rights are granted equally to all persons as free beings. To live without individual rights means living without the chance of developing self-respect (1995: 119). This is the key to how slaves are imprisoned in the absence of their liberty, unable to express their own autonomy and wounded in their basic self-confidence and self-respect. While all of this may be important in understanding the damage done to selfhood by being enslaved, it also raises the problem of how those whose are fixed in their dependence on others can place themselves within the ethical bonds of society. They may not be reduced to objects in the same way as those who are perceived as property, but they are understood to have lost the chance of developing self-respect. In the process of being stripped of their claims to intersubjectivity, it becomes difficult to see them as active agents, involved in weaving their own ethical bonds.

This is an example of the problem identified by Lois McNay, where recognition thinking 'finishes by binding agency too tightly to identity' (McNay 2008: 15), leaving those who are defined as slaves with very little room for manoeuvre or escape. Patterson's other constituent element of slavery, natal alienation, has the effect of binding identity to agency across the generations, isolating slaves from their primordial, genealogical connections. Natal alienation meant living without ties to the past or the future, making slaves unrecognizable (literally, since their names were changed in a radical act of disconnection). Slavery annulled their prior rights and identity, and made them 'shadow members of society' (Patterson 1982: 263). As non-members of a community, recognition respect was impossible and slaves were unable to relate to themselves as morally responsible. Their shadow status was not only about their social invisibility, but also about their own loss of identity and integrity. The relationship between slavery and recognition is all about this kind of psychic loss, and so primarily concerned with 'the subject's very formation and … the external and internal forces that hinder its freedom' (Zerilli 2005: 10).

In Honneth's account, human integrity owes its existence to 'patterns of approval and recognition' (1995: 131). Our moral categories of insult and humiliation point to forms of disrespect, 'that is, to the denial of recognition' (1995: 131). That disrespect and non-recognition means that people's positive, intersubjective understanding of themselves is injured. Honneth carefully anatomizes this disrespect. The first layer is disrespect that affects a person at the level of physical integrity; forcibly depriving someone of their freedom to dispose over his or her own body is 'the most fundamental sort of personal degradation' (1995: 132). Every attempt to gain control over a person's body against their will causes humiliation, a combination of pain 'with the feeling of being defencelessly at the mercy of another subject, to the point of feeling that one has been deprived of reality' (1995: 132). This deprivation brings with it a loss of autonomous control over one's own body and that in turn entails a loss of trust in oneself and the world. The suffering of torture or rape 'is always accompanied by a dramatic breakdown in one's trust in the reliability of the social world and hence by a collapse in one's own basic self-confidence' (1995: 133). For Honneth, this form of disrespect is so damaging to the structure of human beings that he argues that the suffering it entails is not embedded in the process of historical change. Without this form of self-respect, we cannot hope to build the rights of social persons, or to find a footing with others that allows us to spin a web of social obligations.

There is obviously something to this, based as it is on a shared intuition of the psychic damage done to the victims of slavery through their experience of social death. However, there are also dangers in taking this fundamental defencelessness in the face of physical injury as a starting point for understanding slavery. I agree that slavery is clearly a humiliating and insulting denial of recognition, and it is self-evident that it must involve the breakdown of trust, and of psychic integrity. The problem is that as a rhetorical strategy, the equation of slavery with physical injury and psychic damage risks taking it outside of the process of historical change, separating it out from its historical context, and from patterns of approval and recognition. As a rhetorical strategy, it is a crucial component in constituting 'the conditions of political visibility', but it brings with it some unintended meanings and effects (Zerilli 2005: 8). The risk of always and only seeing slavery as an experience like torture or rape is that it makes it difficult to incorporate the survivors into the 'ethical totality' as anything other than victims or as objectified others. The process of becoming visible can end up 'freezing the struggle for recognition perpetually at the point of misrecognition' (McNay 2008: 25).

Honneth's second tier of disrespect is linked to structural exclusion from the possession of certain rights within a society, so that some people are not accorded the same degree of moral responsibility as other members of society. This injures subjects with regard to their self-respect, and this denial of rights is part of the process of historical change. The final layer is the denigration of individual or collective ways of life, downgrading certain forms of life and manners as inferior, and robbing people of every opportunity to 'attribute social value to their own abilities' (1995: 134). Honneth identifies this as a form of cultural degradation, bound up with the process of historical change. All three types of disrespect – physical abuse, the denial of rights and denigration – constitute 'social injuries' to which humans cannot react in emotionally neutral ways. In the impossibility of emotional neutrality lies the potential for 'normative patterns of mutual recognition' to be realized (1995: 138). Slavery involves all these layers of social injury, all entangled with one another, and none of them emotionally neutral. It is important to give the violence and the physical abuse a history: the flogging of slaves in the late eighteenth century, for example, and its representation, can be read as particular moment in the history of racialized sexuality (Favret 1998), and visual representations of the middle passage were crucial in developing and shaping abolitionist campaigns (Wood 2000). If we fail to give pain and the witnessing of others' pain a social and political history, we risk fixing their identity, and reconfiguring the permanence and the alienation of slavery itself by creating a form of recognition that is not mutual, or historically sensitive, or itself a process, but is determined solely by slave status. Focusing on recognition takes us, if we are not careful, into the realms of sentimental and moralized discourse that sets up a dichotomy between normative social actors with the capacity to bestow recognition and empty, deficient, inferior 'others'. The dishonour of the slave gets treated as if it is natural, not provisional or contingent, or deliberately created through branding and marking, and so it becomes essentialized and essentially dehumanizing.

Recognition and Objectification: The Case of Prostitution

In this section, I use the rhetoric surrounding prostitution as a case study of the 'misrecognition of the social relations of oppression' that can result from applying 'the ontology of recognition' to understanding inequalities (McNay 2008: 55). Following McNay's critique of Benjamin's work on recognition and apartheid, we can see how such an analysis can efface specificities, romanticize the oppressed and ignore the struggles and divisions between those who suffer. As Fanon argues about the colonial subject, the status of the prostitute as other 'derives not from misunderstanding but from historically entrenched processes of over-determination' (McNay 2008: 55). In the case of prostitution, we can see how these historical processes, including the structure of the labour market and the gender division of labour, interact with the interpersonal dynamics of power relations and with systematic forms of discrimination to create a culturally specific form of oppression that cannot be reduced to a struggle over identity. At the same time, there is a great deal in the concept of social death and in the politics of misrecognition that can help us to understand that oppression, and the dangers of equating it with slavery. They can illuminate in particular the experience of disrespect, the honour and dishonour, the asymmetric moral vulnerability and the absence of legitimate witnesses that are part of the structure of the prostitution exchange.

Patterson, with his focus on recognition and belonging, offers a nuanced and complex account of what it means to be a slave. For Patterson, and for others, the key is that the slave could not claim or exercise direct powers of property. Even where slaves were understood to own property, they did so without security. Patterson concludes that 'the slave was a slave not because he was the *object* of property, but because he could not be the *subject* of property' (Patterson 1982: 28). It is important in considering the imprisoned absence of slaves' liberty not to assume that by being dishonoured they became objects rather than subjects, or we will find ourselves trapped in the autonomy/dependence binary identified by Willett. Radical feminists from the 1960s and 1970s onwards have argued that prostitution is 'the ultimate in the reduction of women to sexual objects which can be bought and sold' (Jeffreys 2008: 2). For Sheila Jeffreys, for example, prostitution needs to be understood as abuse, founded in violence, so that the man who pays for sex is a perpetrator, a batterer, a rapist, a prostitution abuser who reduces another human being to a sexual object (2008: 5). It sounds like a fundamental dynamic that cannot be given a history, and it also gives injury and pain a central role in maintaining the visibility and credibility of the victim. As Beverley Skeggs argues, the currency of distress, hurt and pain carries with it the assumption that the subject is what she feels and 'she desires recognition of her pain as her primary identity' (Skeggs 2004: 58).

In this sense, some analyses of prostitution begin with physical injury and psychic damage, and move from there to a discourse of objectification that brings together slavery and prostitution. As Martha Nussbaum argues, objectification is 'a relatively loose cluster-term' (Nussbaum 1995: 258). In dissecting its constituent elements, Nussbaum argues that it encompasses the denial of autonomy, lack of agency, fungibility, violability, ownership and the denial of subjectivity, all caught up with one another. That entanglement, though, does not mean that the different threads cannot be separated out. Ownership is not entailed by any of the other items on the list, and does not itself necessarily entail the other elements of fungibility, violability, inertness or instrumentality (1995: 260). Ownership 'probably' does entail lack of self-determination and autonomy 'though an item may certainly lack autonomy without being owned' (1995: 260). This distinction enbales us to think about more nuanced experiences of disrespect and moral vulnerability than the language of human beings being reduced to objects and bought and sold allows.

In teasing out the relationship between slavery, ownership and objectification, Nussbaum argues that slavery as a form of ownership entails a denial of autonomy and the use of the slave as a mere tool, and 'once one treats a human being as a thing one may buy or sell, one is *ipso facto* treating that human being as a tool of one's own purposes' (1995: 264). Again, the point is not that the slave becomes a tool, but that he can be treated as the means to someone else's ends. Slaves are not treated as inert, or necessarily as fungible, although 'the toollike treatment inherent in the institution' at least implies a sort of fungibility in the assumption that a person can be reduced to a set of body parts performing a particular task, and so become replaceable by another similar body or by a machine (1995: 264). This instrumentality and the denial of autonomy are fundamental to slavery, but the slave is not necessarily regarded as violable, or denied subjectivity (Patterson 1982: 23). Treating them as a mere tool leads to a failure of the imagination, imprisons them in the absence of their liberty and denies their rights as a social person, but it does not necessarily turn them into objects. Nussbaum's critique of Andrea Dworkin's and Catharine MacKinnon's analysis is useful here. She points to their failure to sort out and distinguish between the different aspects of the concept of objectification. Instead, they treat inertness, fungibility and ownership as inevitable consequences of the initial denial of autonomy. Dworkin and MacKinnon (and some other abolitionist feminists) see the connections between the elements in the cluster of objectification as ubiquitous, whereas for Nussbaum: 'In the matter of objectification, context is everything' (1995: 271). Her argument is that 'the dehumanization and objectification of persons has many forms' (1995: 288-9).

The identity of 'the prostitute' sometimes gets fixed, by language, discourse and power, as that of a victim or a slave. The way the rhetoric of slavery works in relation to prostitution is to focus intense sentiment on the deserving victims, and in the process to present those victims as incapable of making choices, of controlling their own destiny (O'Connell Davidson 2005: 25-6). They have no chance of developing self-respect or of relating to themselves as morally responsible persons. They are presented as figures 'so thoroughly saturated and determined by power relations' that they have no agency (Lloyd 2005: 10). This is in part because certain strands of feminist discourse assume that the prostitute must have been forcibly deprived of her freedom to dispose over her own body, and so been subjected to the most fundamental sort of personal degradation in Honneth's schema. She has no defence mechanisms against the torture she has experienced, and 'the picture we have is of a body-self that has been so injured that it cannot recognise its true interests' (Wolkowitz 2006: 126). For those, like Kathleen Barry (1995), who equate prostitution with sexual slavery, the body of the prostitute is 'de-selved' and turned into a body-object. This is not the kind of dishonour and disrespect that could provide a motivational basis for agency, but about becoming an object. In other words, women who work as prostitutes are placed outside the process of historical change and no longer treated as subjects with their own histories who can speak for themselves.

These notions of 'de-selving' and of the 'body-object' are complex. They suggest that the prostitute has fundamentally dislocated the connection between her body and her self, and between herself and her property in the person. This seems part of the slave-as-property discourse, but it is also closely tied to the relational account of slavery, and to notions of emptiness that I have explored elsewhere (Brace 2007). Where objectification is treated as if context is not everything, there is a second and related problem identified by Carol Wolkowitz in her discussion of the 'prostitute body'. The essentialist view of the body implied by radical feminist accounts of prostitution presumes an untouched, 'pristine body', uncorrupted by patriarchy (Wolkowitz 2006: 126). It is these pristine bodies that are in need of protecting, saving and rescuing, and for that construction of innocence to work effectively, they have to have been forced or deceived into prostitution, and to have found themselves 'defencelessly at the mercy of another subject' in the process. It is not difficult to see from this perspective why the radical feminist focus tends to be on human trafficking as modern slavery. They work with the idea of women being deprived of reality, of losing trust in themselves and the world and of suffering the total collapse of their basic self-confidence. For radical feminists, this total collapse follows inevitably from involvement in prostitution because sexuality is 'a singular and unique form of embodied interaction' (2006: 127), and so what most defines women as women is what is taken away from them by prostitution. Their security of their person is 'stolen and sold' (MacKinnon 1992). It makes sense, MacKinnon argues, 'to understand prostitution as consisting in the denial of women's humanity, no matter how humanity is defined' (1992). Women are prostituted 'precisely in order to be degraded and subjected to cruel and brutal treatment without human limits' (1992). Prostitution, on this account, is regarded a fundamental sort of personal degradation, based on the psycho-dynamics of power relations between men and women. It reflects the assumption that 'subjectivity is sexuality' (McNay 2008: 47), and these two strands of analysis risk disembedding prostitution from the processes of historical change. By eliding prostitution with slavery, abolitionist feminists return to the question of permanent exclusion. The context of objectification is not treated as fundamental by abolitionist feminists who imagine that 'by requiring a woman to temporarily fix herself as an object, prostitution permanently, completely and literally extinguishes her as a subject' (O'Connell Davidson 2002: 92). The temporary becomes permanent and a prostitute is fixed in her dependency, and confirmed in her status as a shadow.

Responses to this construction of prostitution as slavery are complicated, but I want to try and draw out how some of the critiques of this position illuminate the connections between slavery, recognition and property. In Carole Pateman's classic 1988 account, what is wrong with prostitution is that it commodifies men's sexual access to women's bodies, and allows women's bodies to be for sale in a capitalist market. The sexual contract affirms men's masculinity and women's femininity as political identities based on freedom and subjection. Mastery and subjection are renewed and affirmed through a contract that guarantees men's orderly sexual access to women, so that 'when a prostitute contracts out use of her body she is selling *herself* in a very real sense' (Pateman 1988: 207, emphasis in original). It is this notion of selling the self that supposedly gives prostitution its unique status as a form of slavery and constitutes it as a denial of humanity. Cecile Fabre is careful in her rebuttal, and she resists the objectification behind the argument. Prostitution is not slavery because it 'does not involve selling oneself, procuring human beings for sale, or buying them' (Fabre 2006: 172). For her, there is an integral relation between the body and the self, but the self 'is not reduced to corporeality' (Fabre 2006: 173). There is more to our identity than our sexual construction (such as our moral beliefs, our relationships to our families, our long-term plans and attachments), and if that is correct 'then in selling our body for sex, we only sell a part of what constitutes us as distinct selves' (2006: 173). This is an important corrective to the radical feminist view, helping to restore the dynamics of understanding honour and dishonour and the expression of autonomy within prostitution.

Fabre argues that prostitution is not sexual slavery, where slavery is understood as 'the complete relinquishing of rights over oneself' (2006: 160). The prostitute hires her body out and sells her time and labour, over which she gives her client exclusive but not unlimited rights. Paying for sex is only morally wrong 'where the client regards payment as a means to humiliate and degrade the prostitute' (2006: 164) or the prostitute demands payment to degrade the client. Unlike MacKinnon, she is not arguing that women are prostituted precisely in order to be degraded, and so there is no founding moment in injury and degradation. Fabre's position is closer to Nussbaum's argument that context is everything, and she argues that we have to know the intentions of those involved in the exchange before we can reach conclusions about degradation, humiliation and defencelessness. Where the transaction is about humiliation for either the prostitute or the client, they are treating the other merely as a means to an end, failing to confer proper weight to the fact that the other is a moral and rational agent, 'and thereby deny[ing] them an opportunity for self-respect' (2006: 164). Fabre's argument is that 'although we have the right not to treat ourselves as persons worthy of equal respect, we do not have the power to let ourselves be so treated by others' (2006: 164). While the potential for the denial of the opportunity for self-respect is there, it is not inherent in the encounter itself. The assumption that a woman working as a prostitute has been de-selved and turned into an object is highly problematic. A prostitute may experience her body as commodified in a certain situation, but that does not necessarily entail slavery. Carol Wolkowitz quotes examples from the research of Jo Phoenix and Nanci Scheper-Hughes who both interviewed women working as prostitutes (in the UK and in Brazil) who saw themselves as owners of their bodies, with a degree of control over themselves that enhanced rather than undermined their trust in themselves and bolstered their self-confidence (Wolkowitz 2006: 131). In these contexts, rather than being de-selved, the women use the idiom of owning themselves and a property in their person 'as a support to self-esteem, especially in a society where women have characteristically fewer rights in the person than men' (2006: 131). In acknowledging the flexibility of this discourse, and the uses to which it can be put by prostitutes as well as clients, we can re-embed the question of self-respect, and even of physical integrity, in the processes of historical change, and within social relations of power and the rights of social persons. From here, we can see that it is not easy to move straight from suffering to political agency, and that a convincing account of the relationship between prostitution and recognition needs to explain how individuals understand their own identities in the complex context of objectification (McNay 2008: 154), and how they negotiate honour and dishonour, and the possibility of universally respected expressions of autonomy.

This is not an argument for the idea that prostitution offers a kind of freedom, or for the equation of sex work with other kinds of highly valued work, or for the idea that prostitution is always a free choice, but it is an argument against identifying prostitution too straightforwardly with torture and rape understood outside of their social, political, economic and cultural contexts. Once our understanding of prostitution is embedded in those contexts and in 'embodied social relations' where tensions and conflicts need to be negotiated (McNay 2008: 169), we can see prostitution as a power relation. It is a social transaction that may indeed threaten the physical integrity of the prostitute and her control over her bodily boundaries, and within which the client can exercise powers over a human being that would 'normally be viewed as an illegitimate invasion of her sovereignty' (O'Connell Davidson 1997: 181). It is important to acknowledge that prostitution can often be about disrespect, the exercise of personal power and the evasion of the web of social obligations. Prostitution is not slavery, but it is often structured by misrecognition of the other, and by a powerful sense of 'who belongs'. For some male sex tourists in Thailand, for example, as Julia O'Connell Davidson argues, the point of the transaction is that 'the prostitute who sells this "service" is considered dishonoured, socially dead, and imagined as outside the community' (1997: 181). Clients can treat the prostitute as a sexually objectified body 'without incurring obligations or expectations, and with little threat of any mutual dependency developing' (1997: 183-4). In prostitution as it is currently structured, part of what is paid for is this disregard, this lack of recognition of the prostitute as a subject with her own history (Wolkowitz 2006: 134).

Misrecognition, even where it is a deliberate wound inflicted by the strong on the weak, is not the same as objectification, and to assume that it is would be to miss Nussbaum's point about the importance of context. Fabre argues that it is not inherent in the prostitutional encounter that the client abuses the prostitute, or that he sees her as fungible, or even necessarily that he treats her just as a means, and not as ends as well. Again, context is everything, and it is important to draw out the different strands in the cluster of objectification, and the multiple and varied dimensions of prostitution. Fungibility does not have to imply commodification, and commodification does not necessarily entail fungibility: 'that one can buy something does not mean that one regards it as interchangeable with a similar good, or that one regards the thing's seller as interchangeable with any other seller' (2006: 179). This is a complicated question in relation to prostitution, as O'Connell Davidson has shown in her research on the demand for prostitution in Spain. In interviews, clients made clear that one prostitute is not directly interchangeable with another, since they expressed clear preferences about the 'type' of sex worker they preferred. These preferences were based on a series of stereotypes about groups of women. African workers, for example, were generally thought to have been forced into sex slavery and to be too direct and bad-mannered. As a result, as O'Connell Davidson notes, the African women are 'viewed as standing at the bottom of the prostitution hierarchy', mostly involved in outdoor sex work and offering services at the lowest prices. The negative stereotypes, that African sex workers are liable to be drug-addicted, unclean and uneducated, explain both why some clients choose to avoid paying for their services and why some clients specifically select them. A value attaches to 'sex with the bearer of particular social markings and stereotypes (about market segments as well as race and/or nationality) and [the client] is uninterested in anything that is unique or singular about her as person' (O'Connell Davidson 2010: 10). So, for some clients some prostitutes are fungible (although not any prostitute will do), but as O'Connell Davidson points out, there is no such thing as a typical client, and other research has found clients who seek out particular, individual characteristics in a sex worker, or establish longer term arrangements within which they do not treat the prostitute as fungible. There is not one founding moment of physical injury, or one fundamental interpersonal dynamic that structures all experience of prostitution. It is not always to read the relationships between social forces and psychological conditions, or to disentangle the 'subject question' from the social contexts of power relations (Zerilli 2005: 9).

The argument about objectification centres on whether it is possible to isolate individual prostitutional encounters from prostitution as an institution. For many feminists who argue for the abolition of prostitution, the standard prostitutional exchange between a male client and a female sex worker always involves sex discrimination (and humiliation, degradation and defencelessness), no matter how the individual client behaves within that single encounter. In other words, regardless of the content of their transaction, the exchange itself contributes to reinforcing gender inequalities. In disregarding context, and in assuming that there is something unique about prostitution because it involves the commodification of sexuality, feminist abolitionist arguments take prostitution outside the process of history, and so fail to see the complexity of the exploitation involved. As Fabre argues, the problem with prostitution is not the act of providing sexual services for money; the trouble does not lie within the individual transaction, but in what she calls the 'background conditions under which prostitutes currently have to work' (Fabre 2006: 184). These background conditions include entrenched prejudices against and stigmatization of women and gay people; and the lack of economic and social opportunities for some people that mean that prostitution can sometimes seem 'the best of a bad set of options' (2006: 184). Prostitution takes place against a background of violence, discrimination and inequality, but that is not necessarily inherent in its nature. In this, it is different from slavery because 'while it does not merely consist in selling one's labour, it nevertheless does not consist in selling oneself' (2006: 184).

Slavery, Labour and Property

The case of prostitution allows us to see some of the more complicated connections between embodied identity and agency once we move beyond a unified and undifferentiated idea of identity. Once we understand prostitutes and slaves as social subjects, agency becomes a more 'specific engagement with the world' (McNay 2008: 163). I want to go on to explore some of the specifics of this engagement for victims of slavery who turn out to be doing other things as well as coping with their permanent social exclusion. In Honneth's account of recognition, the individual act of labouring is turned into a form of social activity that no longer serves only one's own needs, but also the needs of others in the abstract. The mutual recognition of the legitimacy of property that has been produced through labour makes legal recognition concrete. The act of commodity exchange confirms not only the exchange value of the object, but also 'the freedom and equality of *subjects* as exchangers' (O'Connell Davidson 2010). The non-recognition at the heart of slavery is not only about violence and dishonour; it is also about not being confirmed as the subject of an exchange. To reiterate Patterson's formulation: 'the slave was a slave not because he was the *object* of property, but because he could not be the *subject* of property' (Patterson 1982: 28). This denial of subjectivity is not so much about the rupture between the self and its objects, but about the relations between social persons. By focusing on being the subject of property, we can move towards an account of recognition that can overcome the problem of objectification. To do so, we need to acknowledge the complexities of slavery, and bring it back into the processes of history by analysing it as an injury that is embedded in the processes of historical change. This is in part about acknowledging that the unique damage of slavery lies in its permanence, but also recognizing its continuities with other kinds of misrecognition. Not only slaves, but also vagabonds and vagrants, the undisciplined, the lazy and the unemployed lived within social relations saturated by violence and structured by relations of dependency. They were degraded and disrespected.

Under the system of indenture in the English West Indies before the 1661 Masters and Servants Act, for example, the labourers signed a formal legal contract that amounted to a slave contract. The alternative to indentured labour was often punishment for vagrancy or vagabondage, and a kidnapping system was well organized (Miles 1987: 77). The indenture system was regarded as indistinguishable from slavery because of the property rights the planters held in their servants, and the ways in which they were treated as fungible, denied autonomy and treated as property: 'Pioneer Barbadian planters quite freely bought, sold, gambled away, mortgaged, taxed as property, and alienated in wills their indentured servants' (Beckles 1996: 575). Servants were required to produce a pass in order to be allowed to leave the plantation, and they had to obtain their master's consent to marry. They could not vote, trade or make cash savings, and they were subject to corporal punishment. These elements of control were part of a wider strategy by the planters 'to demonstrate that the servant was not a free person under contractual obligations, but primarily a capital investment with property characteristics' (1996: 576). This was not permanent exclusion, and it was founded on contract rather than a moment of physical injury or even moral suffering.

The indentured labourer was bound only for a specified period, and as Robert Miles argues, some of them must have chosen to enter these relations 'in the belief that they might realize some benefit from doing so' (Miles 1987: 175). They retained their capacity to exercise independent control over the self and its objects, even as this control was being fundamentally undermined by the possibility of being treated as a capital investment. Unlike slaves, indentured servants kept their status as free individuals 'in abeyance' (Hare 1998: 212). For Beckles, this is an important distinction, and he stresses the unique permanence and inevitability of the slave's status, the fixity of their dependence. Before the 1661 Masters and Servants Act, both servants and slaves were used as property, but slaves 'were seen, like animals, as permanent and self-reproductive' (Beckles 1996: 580). Beckles' conclusion is that the property status is in itself insufficient to allow for a definition of the servant as a slave. We are back to the defining question of permanence, and to the importance of context for understanding objectification. It is important to explore what it means to be an outsider within market society, not permanently excluded or totally objectified, and not unified by experience, but not understood as fully rational social actors either. If we do not think critically about the boundaries of incorporation into existing economic and social structures, then we will decontextualize slavery, and conceal the ways in which prostitutes, low-paid servants and migrant workers interact with a social and political world structured by status and power as well as by ethical bonds. In the same way as choice and consent do not always bring an end to exploitation, exclusion is not only about moral vulnerability and individual integrity (Brace 2004).

Slave operations worked best where slaves were not only punished, but also given incentives to work and granted 'spheres of independence' (Walvin 1996: 136). Slaves were not always deprived of their freedom to dispose over themselves, and some were even able to find a footing with others through their own property relations. James Walvin points to the significance of slaves' own plots, gardens and homes. They spent their free time growing food, tending animals, improving their homes and, crucially, selling, bartering and consuming food, timber, animals and clothes. Patterns of approval and recognition existed for some slaves, and meant that some of them were able to attribute a social value to some of their activities through participation in slave markets and the wider slave economy. They were not entirely imprisoned in the absence of their liberty. However much slaves were constructed as outsiders, as objects of property and dependent consciousnesses, many of them were part of the local cash economy. Walvin points out that in Jamaica in 1774 it was calculated that slaves owned 20 per cent of all the cash in circulation (1996: 147). They were not inert, or entirely de-selved, and they exercised a highly circumscribed degree of self-determination which meant they were not just the tools of others. A theory of recognition that can account for the realities of slavery has to get us beyond the subject/object binary and the dichotomy between autonomy and dependence that structures liberal theory. We need to think carefully about how people, even those most deeply entangled in dependency and inequality, always move within a framework of ethical bonds, and keep on negotiating their own vulnerability, self-respect and trust in the world, rather than finding their identity fixed by the absence of their liberty. This will make visible their own expressions of autonomy, their chances for developing self-respect and their claims to intersubjectivity in contexts where agency and identity are not always fused together.

Conclusion

Where agency is tied too closely to identity, as McNay argues, recognition 'comes close to replicating the very same individualist and voluntarist concepts of subjectivity and action that it originally seeks to dislodge' (2008: 165). An account of slavery and recognition has to resist the temptation to draw bright lines and distinguish too clearly between those with full autonomy and those without. From there, we can begin to recognize that those who are misrecognized or disrespected, whose self-ownership is compromised or whose ethical incorporation is incomplete, need not be reduced to helpless, permanently violated victims or to objects. Honneth's account of misrecognition illuminates the ways in which slavery is the opposite of belonging, and helps us to understand slavery as a relationship, not just a property question. The limitations lie with those who build a rhetorical strategy on the possibility that the slave's unique suffering is a condition of political visibility and can be disembedded from the processes of historical change.

There is something to the idea that slaves can be understood as the prototype for 'outsiders', those who are defined as 'others' by their vulnerability, marginality and incomplete incorporation into the community. On the other hand, there is a danger that this language of being reduced to objects, being bought and sold, of selling the self, of having no identity and no independent existence, risks naturalizing people's status as outsiders and victims, so that we are endlessly having to imagine their rescue and incorporation for them, and never giving them the chance to be subjects with their own histories, actively weaving themselves, their commitments, friendships and sociality into ethical communities. We become more interested in their loss of integrity as an example to us all than we are in acting as legitimate witnesses or in respecting their expressions of autonomy. They remain isolated subjects, rather than social persons, and so the forms of recognition and agency open to them are inevitably distorted. The assumption that they can be detached from history and understood through a single psychological dynamic undermines the possibility of all of us as subjects perceiving each other as morally vulnerable persons, able to affirm each other in our fundamental claims to integrity. Fixing the identity of slaves as hopelessly dependent and women who work as prostitutes as dehumanized undermines the dynamic of Honneth's argument that we are all constituted as persons by the recognition of others, and the possibility of constructing a 'multidimensional model of social relations' that can connect embodied existence to underlying structures of power (McNay 2008: 196).

Acknowledgements

This chapter arose from my participation in the 'Recognition as Love and Care' seminar at the School of Politics, UWE in 2008, organized by Simon Thompson as part of the wider ESRC Seminar Series, 'The Politics of Recognition and the Dynamics of Social Conflict', and a later version was presented to the Politics of Property specialist group at the PSA Conference in Edinburgh in March 2010. I am indebted to participants on these occasions for their helpful comments, particularly Simon Thompson, Majid Yar, Chris Pierson, James Penner, John Salter, Cecile Fabre and Karl Widerquist, and to the reviewer of this chapter. For detailed comments and access to unpublished material, many thanks to Julia O'Connell Davidson. And for knowing more about recognition than I ever will, my thanks to Becky Waghorn.

References

Barry, K. 1995. *The Prostitution of Sexuality*. New York: New York University Press.

Beckles, H. 1996. The Concept of 'White Slavery' in the English Caribbean during the Early Seventeenth Century, in *Early Modern Conceptions of Property*, edited by J. Brewer and S. Staves. London and New York: Routledge, 572-85.

Bernstein, J.M. 1984. From Self-consciousness to Community: Act and Recognition in the Master-Slave Relationship, in *The State and Civil Society*, edited by Z.A. Pelczynski. Cambridge: Cambridge University Press, 14-40.

Blackburn, R. 1988. Defining Slavery – Its Special Features and Social Role, in *Slavery and Other Forms of Unfree Labour*, edited by L. Archer. London and New York: Routledge.

Brace, L. 2004. *The Politics of Property: Freedom, Labour and Belonging*. Edinburgh: Edinburgh University Press.

Brace, L. 2007. Rousseau, Maternity and the Politics of Emptiness. *Polity*, 39(3), 361-83.

Brenkert, G.G. 1998. Self-ownership, Freedom and Autonomy. *Journal of Ethics* 2, 27-55

Coleman, J. 2005. Pre-Modern Property and Self-ownership Before and After Locke. *European Journal of Political Theory*, 4(2), 125-45.

Davis, D.B. 1986. *Slavery and Human Progress*. Oxford: Oxford University Press.

Doezema, J. 2002. Who Gets to Choose? Coercion, Consent and the UN Trafficking Protocol, in *Gender, Trafficking and Slavery*, edited by R. Masika. Oxford: Oxfam GB, 20-27.

Ebbe, O. and D.K. Das. 2008. *Global Trafficking in Women and Children*. Boca Raton, FL: CRC Press.

Fabre, C. 2006. *Whose Body is it Anyway?* Oxford: Oxford University Press.

Favret, M.A. 1998. Flogging: the Anti-Slavery Movement Writes Pornography, in Anne Janowitz (ed.) *Romanticism and Gender.* Cambridge: English Association, 19-43.

Hare, R.M. 1998. What is Wrong with Slavery? in *Subjugation and Bondage: Critical Essays on Slavery and Social Philosophy*, edited by T.L. Lott. Boulder, CO and Oxford: Rowman & Littlefield, 209-28.

Honneth, A. 1995. *The Struggle for Recognition.* Cambridge: Polity.

Jeffreys, S. 2008 [1997] *The Idea of Prostitution.* Melbourne: Spinifex Press.

Kershnar, S. 2003. A Liberal Argument for Slavery. *Journal of Social Philosophy*, 34(4), 510-38.

Locke, J. 1991. Second Treatise, in *John Locke: Two Treatises of Government*, edited by Peter Laslett. Cambridge: Cambridge University Press.

Lott, T.L. 1998. Early Enlightenment Conceptions of the Rights of Slaves, in *Subjugation and Bondage: Critical Essays on Slavery and Social Philosophy*, edited by T.L. Lott. Boulder, CO and Oxford: Rowman & Littlefield, 91-130.

Lloyd, M. 2005. *Beyond Identity Politics.* London: Sage.

MacKinnon, M. 1992. Prostitution and Civil Rights, Speech given at the Michigan Journal of Gender and Law Symposium, revised version available at: http://www.prostitutionresearch.com/mackinnon1.html [Accessed 30 May 2010].

McNay, L. 2008. *Against Recognition.* Cambridge: Polity.

Miles, R. 1987. *Capitalism and Unfree Labour.* London: Tavistock Publications Ltd.

Miller, W.I. 1993. *Humiliation: and Other Essays on Honor, Social Discomfort and Violence.* Ithaca and London: Cornell University Press.

Mills, C.W. 1998. *Blackness Visible: Essays on Philosophy and Race.* Ithaca and London: Cornell University Press.

Nussbaum, M. 1995. Objectification. *Philosophy and Public Affairs*, 24(4), 249-91.

O'Connell Davidson, J. 1997. Does she do Queening? Prostitution and Sovereignty, in *Reclaiming Sovereignty*, edited by L. Brace and J. Hoffman. London: Pinter, 171-87.

O'Connell Davidson, J. 2005. *Children in the Global Sex Trade.* Cambridge: Polity.

O'Connell Davidson, J. 2010. Commodification, Embodiment and Honour: The Fusion of Labour Power and Personhood in Prostitution and Other Forms of Work, unpublished paper.

Patterson, O. 1982. *Slavery and Social Death: A Comparative Study.* Cambridge, MA and London: Harvard University Press.

Skeggs, B. 2004. *Class, Self, Culture.* London: Routledge.

Walvin, J. 1996. *Questioning Slavery.* London: Routledge.

Willett, C. 1998. The Master-Slave Dialectic: Hegel vs. Douglass, in *Subjugation and Bondage: Critical Essays on Slavery and Social Philosophy*, edited by T.L. Lott. Boulder, CO and Oxford: Rowman & Littlefield, 151-70.

Willett, C. 2001. *The Soul of Justice.* Ithaca and London: Cornell University Press.

Wolkowitz, C. 2006. *Bodies at Work.* London: Sage.

Wood, M. 2000. *Blind Memory: Visual Representations of Slavery in England and America, 1780-1865*. Manchester: Manchester University Press.

Zerilli, L. 2005. *Feminism and the Abyss of Freedom*. Chicago: University of Chicago Press.

Chapter 5

Misrecognition: The Unequal Division of Labour and Contributive Justice

Andrew Sayer

Introduction

Studies of public attitudes to economic inequality generally show support for the idea that distribution should be related to what people contribute to society and that 'fair inequality' reflects differences in contribution (Miller 1992, 1999; Joseph Rowntree Foundation 2007, 2009). Such studies also reveal much about recognition, or rather misrecognition, in society. Typically, the public attributes to individual responsibility effects that are largely a consequence of social structures, radically underestimating the extent to which the fortunes of rich and poor depend on the lottery of birth class and the inheritance of economic, cultural and social capital. Thus, one of the most common forms of misrecognition in contemporary society is the underestimation of the extent to which individual and group achievements are dependent not merely on effort and intelligence, but structural inequalities and symbolic domination which give them highly unequal access to practices that are socially valued or recognized. While much of the debate about recognition has been about its relation to distribution (for example, Fraser 1995; Fraser and Honneth 2003), the public also relate it to contribution. Although I shall comment briefly on the relations between recognition and distribution, I want to focus primarily on how what people are allowed or required to contribute in terms of work affects recognition and misrecognition. I shall argue that the misrecognition of what people contribute and achieve through work derives from a tendency to naturalize the 'unequal division of labour', that is the division between jobs of very different quality, offering job holders radically unequal opportunities for self-development and social contribution and the recognition that responds to these. This 'contributive injustice' is rarely noticed and indeed tends to produce dispositions and responses in people that help reproduce that division of labour and make it appear a rational response to differences in ability and effort. While there is much that is fruitful in the debate initiated by Nancy Fraser's seminal paper on the relations between the politics of recognition and distribution, I want to argue that the significance of contributive injustice has been underestimated (Fraser 1995, 2010; Fraser and Honneth 2003).

Together, inequalities in distribution and contribution have a major structuring effect on the social field within which people live and interact, endowing them with different kinds and volumes of economic, social and cultural capital. This 'force field' has a distorting effect on recognition, producing various forms of misrecognition in terms of people's understanding of their own and others' situation. What Bourdieu termed 'class racism' and 'the racism of intelligence' are examples of these. The force field also distorts how acts which signify recognition are *received* by those to whom they are directed. A secondary aim of the chapter is to sketch how this distortion of recognition by the social field works in the case of class. More broadly I hope to show, by reference to class inequalities, how and why misrecognition regarding inequality and its causes is related to misrecognition in terms of the evaluation of persons and groups.

I shall begin by distinguishing two senses of misrecognition: one associated with authors such as Fraser, Axel Honneth, and Charles Taylor, that has a broadly Hegelian ancestry, and one used by Pierre Bourdieu, which is associated with symbolic domination in general. As a further preliminary, I shall then briefly summarize key relations between recognition and distribution, particularly in relation to economic inequalities. I then move to the central topic of the relation between (mis)recognition and contributive injustice, and the latter's origins in unequal divisions of labour. Emphasizing the importance of the kind of work that people do for who they become and how they are regarded by others, I shall go on to argue that the conditions for equal and justified recognition depend not only on a high degree of equality in the distribution of resources, but on a more equal division of labour in which people can contribute a range of work of different skills and qualities, thereby allowing everyone the possibility to develop their capacities. This involves developing both an explanation and a normative evaluation of inequalities in what people contribute through work. I shall then review some of the ways in which the resulting inequalities of the social field tend to engender misrecognition, and conclude.

Preliminaries (1): Two Senses of 'Misrecognition'

There are two forms of recognition or misrecognition involved here. First, in the tradition deriving from Hegel, recognition is of persons and their worth, and concerns relations to others and to self. In appropriate forms, it is necessary for human well-being, both as a condition of our developing a sense of ourselves as subjects at all, and of our psychological well-being. We cannot develop a healthy relation to self without a healthy relation to others. Anyone who meets disrespect and hostility in most of their encounters with others is likely quickly to suffer. Here, 'misrecognition' suggests a denial of recognition to someone or some group, so that they are not treated as equal or independent, but rather as inferior and unworthy of respect or esteem; hence they are "denied the status of a full partner in social interaction" (Fraser 2010: 217; see also Honneth 1995; Schmidt am Busch and Zurn 2010; Taylor 1994). Misrecognition of this kind is both cause and effect of many inequalities. In an unequal society, recognition may be available only from those on the same level or within the same group, while misrecognition characterizes relations with those outside. Typically, misrecognition also provides spurious justifications for structural inequalities, attributing them to differences in individual or group worth.

Within this concept of recognition, following Charles Taylor (1994), we can distinguish between unconditional recognition of others simply as human beings, in virtue of their common capacities and vulnerabilities, and conditional recognition of people in response to their character and how they act. In everyday practice it is evident that not all are given equal unconditional recognition: some lives (and deaths) are regarded as more important than others. The distinction is a good deal more fuzzy in practice than we might wish from a normative point of view: those whose identity, character and behaviour are not valued are typically less valued simply as people. Nevertheless, it will be primarily conditional recognition that will be discussed here.

For Bourdieu, by contrast, "recognition", is not specifically concerned with responses to others but something much more general: "the set of fundamental, pre-reflexive assumptions that social agents engage by the mere fact of taking the world for granted, of accepting the world as it is, and of finding it natural because *their mind is constructed according to cognitive structures that are issued out of the very structures of the world*" (Bourdieu and Wacquant 1990: 168, emphasis in original). The ways of acting are based less on conscious reflection on what is and what could be, and more on an embodied accommodation to the way things happen to be for them, acquired through acting and living in certain conditions; thus, for example, a dominated group may acquire a disposition of deference.[1] Misrecognition here is therefore not so much to do with the valuation of persons as to do with misunderstanding of the nature of social reality. It is particularly associated with relations of symbolic domination, where the misunderstanding is less a result of ideological 'influence' than of the objective situation in which they find themselves. As he put it, "of all the forms of "hidden persuasion", the most implacable is the one exerted, quite simply, by the *order of things*" (Bourdieu and Wacquant 1990: 168, emphasis in original). Further, misrecognition tends to reproduce the conditions – 'misrecognizable' conditions – which make it appear true (Bourdieu and Wacquant 1990: 51).[2] In rejecting the idea of ideology as operating merely at the level of discourse, Bourdieu was, as usual, 'bending

1 Bourdieu also makes extensive use of the term in his discussions of gift relations (see also Bordieu 1990). He refers to a "'common misrecognition' to designate this game in which everyone knows – that everyone knows – and does not want to know – the true nature of the exchange" (2000: 192). I do not think there is this degree of suppressed knowingness about class, but the demands of self-representation can lead to a suppression of acknowledgements of luck in relation to the lottery of birth class (Sayer 2005: Chapter 8).

2 At one point in *The Logic of Practice*, he uses the term 'mis-cognition' (Bourdieu 1990: 141).

the stick' here[3]; we can acknowledge the importance of embodied dispositions attuned to the objective conditions in which they are acquired without denying any influence to discourse and lay reflexivity – for example, to distinctions between the deserving and undeserving poor – and which may sometimes be at odds with our dispositions and inclinations (Sayer 2010).

There is clearly an area of overlap between the two concepts, for misrecognition of others is part of a more general misrecognition of the nature of social reality, and one which tends to support precisely the inequalities and forms of domination that Bourdieu analysed. I shall therefore use *both* of these concepts, showing how and why misrecognition in the Bourdieusian sense regarding class inequalities and their causes is related to misrecognition in terms of the evaluation of persons and groups.

Recognition in both senses is *of* something – something wholly or largely independent of the act of recognition. It is not merely a matter of agreement or collective wishful thinking unrelated to any real qualities that are the object of recognition (Pinkard 2010). The concept of misrecognition implies an objectivist concept of what recognition is of: for us to be capable of mis-recognizing something or someone, that is, to be fallible in our observations and judgements, there must be something independent of those observations and judgements about which we can be mistaken. For instance, for it to be possible for someone to be misrecognized as untrustworthy, their trustworthiness must exist independently of such judgements.

Preliminaries (2): Recognition and Distribution

Recognition (of persons) and distribution tend to be interrelated in several ways:

i. Recognition is not merely a matter of words, but of deeds and circumstances. Pronouncements of equal worth have to be backed by equal treatment if they are not to be dismissed as 'empty words' or hypocrisy. For example, in an organization or society in which people have very unequal resources and opportunities, official statements that 'everyone counts', or is of equal worth, ring hollow. For such statements to be taken seriously, there has to be a significant degree of equality in the living conditions and opportunities within the relevant population. Statements of equal recognition may therefore be confirmed or contradicted through distribution;
ii. Distributional struggles are often motivated by the desire for recognition that improved material circumstances signal, as noted by the historian E.P. Thompson. In organizations, workers often value pay increments more

3 For Bourdieu's reasons for rejecting the concept of ideology see Bourdieu and Wacquant (1990: 250) and Eagleton and Bourdieu (1992).

in terms of the recognition which they are felt to signal than the additional money;

iii. Individuals or groups may pursue recognition either simply in order to be accepted as equal and similar to others, according to shared criteria, or in order to be accepted as different but nevertheless equal in worth, or so as to be accepted as superior to others;

iv. Distributional inequalities are commonly (mis-)read as reflecting differences in individual worth. Hence, as we discuss later, they distort our judgements of self and others, producing, for example, snobbery or a sense of inferiority (Sayer 2005);

v. Nevertheless, distributional inequalities in capitalism are to a significant degree subject to forces which are *un*related to matters of recognition. The market forces and the capitalist strategies which govern employment and pay derive mainly from the pursuit of self-interest. The same goes for consumers: when they change their pattern of demand across different commodities, they generally do so for reasons which have nothing to do with their feelings about the workers who produce those goods and services. For example, the decline in employment in textiles in rich countries has not occurred because customers no longer recognize the workers who produce them, but because they can get cheaper products from elsewhere. Thus while struggles for recognition often take a distributional form, and distributional inequalities are often read as indications of worth, distribution in capitalism is far from merely a consequence of differences in recognition of different groups. Class is not merely a product of 'classism' (Fraser 2010);

vi. Class inequalities produce effects which appear to legitimize them, and underpin the misrecognition of worth. They do this not only because they produce major differences in the distribution of resources, but more importantly because they make people unequal in what they are able and allowed to do and achieve.

This last point leads us to the central proposition of this paper: recognition is related not only to distribution in the sense of resources, or in other words to what people *get*, but to what people do, or are able and allowed to do. Conditional recognition – and misrecognition – are strongly responsive to what people contribute. To explain this, I need to elaborate the concepts of contributive justice and the unequal division of labour.

Contributive (In)Justice and the Unequal Division of Labour

In political philosophy the idea of *distributive* justice is dominant– that is, justice as regards the distribution of resources, or what people *get*. Economic justice in general tends to be equated with this. As the name suggests, contributive justice concerns what people are allowed, expected or required to *do* or contribute (Some treatments of distributive justice define it widely enough to include the distribution of opportunities to contribute, but they rarely examine it in any depth). Although the term 'contributive' justice is unfamiliar – to my knowledge, it was coined by Paul Gomberg in his book *How to Make Opportunity Equal* – what it refers to is thoroughly familiar (Gomberg 2007). For example, arguments within work teams are often not so much about what each team member gets in terms of pay or other reward, but what each person contributes; is everyone 'pulling their weight', or are some 'free-riding' on the work of others? There might also be objections if some team members monopolized all the interesting and pleasant tasks, leaving the less attractive ones to others. Contributive justice can thus be about either the quantity or the quality of the contribution made by people to some project. Similarly, arguments about fairness within households are often not about the amounts of resources that the individual members get, but about their contributions to the running of the household. In particular, arguments about the gender division of domestic labour are about the quantity and quality of such work that men and women do. The contributive *in*justice of the conventional gender division of domestic labour was the focus of an extensive feminist literature (for example, Crompton 2007; Delphy and Leonard 1992; Folbre 1982; Hochschild 1989; Okin 1989; Oakley 1974; Walby 1986, 1990). Men not only do less house work (quantitative contributive injustice), but tend to reserve for themselves the less tedious and more rewarding kinds of task (qualitative injustice).

What people are allowed to contribute, particularly in terms of work, is at least as important as what they get in terms of resources, because the type of work that they do has far-reaching effects on the extent to which they can develop their capacities, and hence on the kinds of people they become. It is a major influence on how they view themselves, and the recognition they get from others, and hence on the quality of their lives. Some work may be a burden and literally 'mind-dulling', but some kinds of work, in appropriate conditions, can be a source of meaning, development and fulfilment – a good or benefit in their own right. Those who do such work also tend to get recognition from others, providing them with a source of self-esteem in addition to that deriving from doing the work itself. In Alasdair MacIntyre's terms, they get not only the internal goods of proficiency in meeting the standards of a complex practice, but also the external goods of recognition (MacInytre 1981).[4] There are many components to good work – interest, variety, complexity, being able to use skill and exercise control and discretion, being trusted and treated with respect, freedom from health hazards, sociability, and so on. These things do not always go together – for example, an unskilled job may offer opportunities for sociability – but neither do they tend to balance out, so that, overall, no job is better than any other. For the purpose of my argument here, it will not make any difference if we lump these qualities together and simply think of a range between 'good' or 'superior' and 'bad' or

4 Note also that these internal goods can be realized regardless of whether their achievement brings external goods.

'inferior' jobs. We can also acknowledge that skill levels are contested, that their very definition frequently involves both deliberate and unintended misrecognition, and that skills involved in work associated with women are typically undervalued. But of course this does not mean that all jobs from cleaning to lawyering are actually equally skilled and merely misrecognized as unequal; in many cases they are correctly recognized as unequal.

Alongside other key activities, work shapes the habitus, and affects the mix and volume of different forms of capital that individuals have. R.E. Lane's major review of research on markets and how they are experienced shows that beyond a certain level of consumption, what people are able to do in terms of work and the quality of their social relations makes a bigger difference to their quality of life than how much they can consume (Lane 1991). Part of the feminist critique of the gender division of labour in the household and in the labour market was that women's unequal share of domestic work (and exclusion from much skilled employment) prevented them from realizing their potential, while men had much greater scope for achieving this. While these concerns about contributive justice are familiar, it is striking that the differences in the quantity and quality of work that people are able or expected to do in the wider division of labour in the formal economy are thoroughly naturalized and rarely seen as problematic – and this, despite the fact that they have such a profound effect on people's lives.[5] What is a common matter of ethical concern in some social spheres is a matter of indifference in others. In effect, feminism draws attention to the *gendered* contributive injustice in this wider division of labour, evident in the vertical segregation of men and women, with men over-represented in high level positions, and women in low level positions. But even if men and women were equally represented at all levels, there would still be contributive injustice of the qualitative kind: part of the workforce would have a disproportionate share of interesting and pleasant work, leaving inferior kinds of work to others.

Gomberg argues that in the context of this unequal division of labour there can at best be merely 'competitive equality of opportunity'. His key point is that as long as the more satisfying kinds of task are concentrated into a subset of jobs, rather than shared out among all jobs (and the less satisfying ones are also concentrated into others), then many workers will be denied the chance to have meaningful work and the satisfaction and recognition that goes with it, regardless of their ability or efforts. With an unequal division of labour, the labour market functions as a zero sum game; the successful are so at the expense of others. This

5 As has been widely pointed out, gender inequalities are reproduced not just in the domestic domain but in all areas of life, so they intersect with, and are reproduced through other axes of inequality, such as the class inequalities associated with unequal divisions of labour; similarly where there are racialized divisions these intersect with class, and indeed Gomberg's primary concern is race rather than class. However, since unequal divisions of labour can exist independently of gender and race divisions, but not class inequalities, and would be problematic even if they were not gendered or racialized, I focus on class.

is commonly spuriously justified by arguing that because success in getting a good job and upward social mobility are possible for some individuals, success must be possible for all individuals simultaneously. This form of misrecognition, involving a 'fallacy of composition', is an important component of meritocratic and capitalist ideology; it is central to the so-called 'American Dream' and a prime target of Bourdieu's critique of the competitions of the social field. According to Bourdieu, most popular responses to the inequalities of the social field operate within its terms. They are limited to 'competitive struggle', that is ' ... the form of class struggle which the dominated classes allow to be imposed on them when they accept the stakes offered by the dominant classes' ... [and] .. 'implicitly recognize the legitimacy of the goals pursued by those whom they pursue ... ' (Bourdieu 1984: 165). They therefore struggle for position, but not to change the nature and structure of positions themselves. More generally, through his use of market metaphors, Bourdieu's analysis of symbolic domination and misrecognition makes much of the fact that while success is portrayed as available to anyone, and indeed to everyone simultaneously, there is actually little room at the top – the most sought-after goods and positions are scarce, and the dominant seek to maintain that scarcity.

Gomberg's critique of the unequal division of labour challenges the structures which produce this contributive injustice. He argues that there can only be equality of opportunity in a meaningful sense if opportunities for good quality work are not scarce, and this can only be the case if as far as possible, complex work is shared out among workers – which of course implies that routine work should be shared out too. In other words, the unequal division of labour would have to be abolished or radically reduced.[6] This, it should be noted, does not require abolishing the social division of labour between quite different kinds of work, such as healthcare, finance, or food processing; rather it requires abolishing or reducing the division between planning and execution, and interesting and boring work *within* particular sectors or organizations (Gomberg 2007). Individuals therefore would not have simultaneously to be a doctor, accountant, or baker (to update Marx's model of the unalienated worker). There could still be a sectoral division of labour, but within any sector, each job could include a mix of tasks with different qualities.[7]

Writing in a US context, Gomberg claims that the education system is adjusted to the unequal division of labour, and is organized to prepare a significant

6 In discussing Hegel's account of recognition in relation to capitalism, work and division of labour, Honneth notes that for Hegel, if the division of labour were to allow workers to be worthy of recognition, the work they are allowed to do would have to be sufficiently complex and visible to warrant it. Where economic developments produced deskilling, then "corporations" or trade associations had a duty "to ensure that the skills of their members received enough care and public attention to enjoy universal esteem in the future" (Honneth 2010: 231).

7 For a discussion of objections to this idea, and possible responses, see Sayer (2009).

proportion of children only for a life of routine labour (Gomberg 2007: 36). Strictly from the point of view of minimizing the economic cost of education and training, it is not worth over-producing highly-qualified workers; it is a waste of resources to train 100 people for 40 skilled posts. Of course, we may want to argue that education should be for life, not just employment, but in the context of such a division of labour, this goal is bound to appear as a luxury. From the point of view of workers, where the division of labour restricts good quality work to a subset of jobs, then many – particularly those who are disadvantaged by class, gender or race – might reasonably consider it not worth the effort of pursuing them. To the extent that the social system, and within it, the unequal social division of labour and the educational system, produces a matching unequal distribution of abilities and aspirations, it encourages misrecognition in the form of self-congratulation in the fortunate, and resignation and self-condemnation in the less fortunate.

Often the division of labour between better and worse quality jobs is defended or explained as the most economically efficient way of doing things. As James Murphy points out, these defences typically lump together two kinds of division of labour – a division between different *tasks* within a given process, and a division between different *workers*, whereby each worker is limited to a single or very small number of tasks – which I have termed an unequal division of labour. The former does not in fact entail the latter, and through various forms of rotation and sharing of attractive and unattractive tasks within a given process, more workers can avoid being restricted to poor quality work (Murphy 1974). However, employers often find it more profitable to create an unequal division of labour and hence confine many workers to low skilled tasks; it reduces their training and operating costs, while the social costs of limiting workers' potential are borne elsewhere (Sayer 2009). It is also often overlooked that the unequal division of labour is partly a product of struggles for power. Those with more power tend to adopt strategies of closure, by hoarding good quality work and offloading inferior work on to others (Tilly 1998). This is central to the rise of professions, occupational demarcation and skills disputes.

But as we noted, there is little public concern about the unequal division of labour. In large organizations, workers in a particular occupation might be upset if a few members of their own rank are given much more pleasant and interesting work than others, but it is less likely to bother them that other occupations are more or less interesting or otherwise desirable than their own. This shows how the reference groups in which people compare their lot with that of others and think about contributive justice are already shaped by the unequal division of labour itself. The parochial character of our concerns about contributive justice in turn enables this division of labour to be normalized, and indeed naturalized. Thus, professional and unskilled workers seem like members of separate castes, not even seeing their contributions as comparable. This is itself a common effect of an unequal division of labour. As Bourdieu argued, the kinds of popular normative thinking and recognition that characterize the social field are themselves patterned and partitioned by it, and this contributes to the efficacy of symbolic domination.

Misrecognition and the 'Racism of Intelligence'

The unequal division of labour is often regarded as an accommodation to differences in people's ability and efforts, and it is in these terms that many would explain and defend it. Gomberg argues that while not all are born equally able, abilities are largely a product of socialization and activities (Gomberg 2007: Chapter 10). In this respect he echoes Adam Smith's view, in *The Wealth of Nations*, of differences in abilities as a product of the division of labour rather than vice versa:

> The difference of natural talents in different men is, in reality, much less than we are aware of; and the very different genius which appears to distinguish men of different professions, when grown up in maturity, is not upon many occasions so much the cause, as the effect of the division of labour. The difference between the most dissimilar characters, between a philosopher and a common street porter, for example, seems to arise not so much from nature, as from habit, custom, and education. (Smith 1776, Bk I, ch.ii: 19-20)

Earlier, having analysed the division of labour in the pin factory, Smith commented:

> The man whose whole life is spent performing a few simple operations … has no occasion to exert his understanding … He naturally loses, therefore, the habit of such exertion, and generally becomes as stupid and ignorant as it is possible for a human creature to become.[8]

Smith believed that the effects of this deskilled, repetitive work would spill over into life outside work, stunting the ability of such workers to participate in the life of the community. Murphy cites empirical research on the relation between the intellectual capacities of workers and the cognitive complexity of the work they do, which shows that over a ten year period the cognitive capacities of workers doing complex jobs developed, while those of workers doing simple and repetitive work deteriorated. Further, as Smith feared, there is evidence that "Workers in mindless jobs not only undermine their capacity for the enjoyment of complex activities at work but also their capacity for the enjoyment of complex activities during leisure" (Murphy 1993: 7 n.19).

However, neither Gomberg's, Murphy's nor Smith's critiques of the unequal division of labour adequately explain how differences in ability, aptitude and aspirations are produced, given that these develop long *before* people are old enough to go into employment. Employment within an unequal division of labour

8 Smith 1776, 2.V.I., art.2 , pp. 302-3.

may make a difference to them and affect their abilities, but young people coming onto the labour market are already unequal.

Research by Leon Feinstein on children's cognitive capacities shows that these develop more slowly in low social class children than high social class children, so that by 120 months, the brightest of low social class children at 22 months are overtaken by the weakest of high social class children (Feinstein 2003). The score at 22 months predicts educational qualifications at age 26 and is related to family background. The children of educated or wealthy parents who scored poorly in the early tests had a tendency to catch up, whereas children of worse-off parents who scored poorly were extremely unlikely to catch up. Feinstein found no evidence that entry into schooling reverses this pattern. Not surprisingly, social mobility in all major capitalist countries is low (Aldridge 2004; Erikson and Goldthorpe 1992).

There appears to be a 'habitus effect' behind this. The unequal division of labour indirectly shapes the next generation's experience and expectations by shaping the circumstances and habitus of their parents. Further, according to Bourdieu, the education system functions as a mechanism for enabling those with inherited (hence undeserved) cultural capital into the merited form of educational capital (qualifications) (Bourdieu 1996; 2008). And, as we saw earlier, from the point of view of workers, many – particularly those lacking economic and cultural capital – might reasonably consider it not worth pursuing good quality jobs. It would be understandable for them to 'refuse what they are refused', and opt for 'the choice of necessity', as Bourdieu often put it.

There is a further form of misrecognition associated with the inequalities that derive from the unequal division of labour, and one which is particularly common in academia and other professions: this is what Bourdieu terms 'the racism of intelligence". He defines this as:

> specific to the dominant class whose reproduction depends, in part, on the transmission of inherited capital that has the property of being an *embodied capital* and thus apparently natural and innate. Racism of the intelligence is racism through which the dominant aim is to produce a 'theodicy of their specific privilege', as Weber put it, that is, a justification of the social order they dominate. It is this that makes the dominant feel themselves to be of a *superior species*. (Bourdieu 2008: 137)

It is evident in the French upper middle-class men interviewed by Michele Lamont who value 'people who can talk about things' and for whom it is no exaggeration to say they regarded themselves as a superior species (Lamont 1992).[9] The theory of contributive injustice and its roots in the uneven division of labour further illuminate the sources of this misrecogntion.

In these ways, through its influence on the acquisition of dispositions, abilities, aspirations and skills, the unequal division of labour produces effects which appear

9 Interestingly, some identified themselves as radicals.

to legitimize it. Hence, this critique " … allows us to *explain the apparent truth of the theory that it shows to be false*" (Bourdieu 2005: 215, emphasis in original).

The Social Field and the Distortion of Recognition

For Bourdieu, the social field is a force field of relations between people, groups and institutions, each having differing degrees of power, depending on the mix and volume of capitals (economic, cultural and social) that they have in relation to others; it is not 'a level playing field'. Thus the dispositions people acquire and which make up their habitus depend on their location within social relations, including relations of domination and subordination. Bourdieu always insisted against 'interactionists', who attempt to explain social action purely in terms of interactions, that the actors bring to their interactions different dispositions and capitals according to their position in the field, and that the interactions themselves are mediated by the force field. Yet while the field is structured, Bourdieu said little about one of its most important structuring forces – the division of labour in society, particularly that which gives people different *qualities* of work. Ironically, even sociology sometimes fails to denaturalize the unequal division of labour and hence expose this misrecognition. Consequently, the social field acts as a force field distorting recognition of self and others. As Adam Smith put it:

> This disposition to admire, and almost to worship, the rich and the powerful, and to despise, or, at least, to neglect persons of poor and mean condition. … is … the great and most universal cause of the corruption of our moral sentiments. (Smith 1759; 1984, I.iii.2.III: 61)

While it is true that this corruption is responsive to differences in wealth, it is also responsive to differences in what people are allowed and able to contribute.

A recent report from the Joseph Rowntree Foundation (2009) on attitudes to income inequality found that most participants positioned themselves in the middle of the income distribution, even though many were not. While they generally viewed those 'above' them favourably,

> (p)articipants' attitudes towards those on low incomes were often more negative and punitive than their attitudes towards those at the 'top'. For example, there was a far greater tendency to ascribe individual responsibility and blame for behaviour towards those at the bottom of the income spectrum than those at the top. Participants routinely drew on negative stereotypes of benefit recipients and often struggled to conceptualize them in positive terms. Whereas they could apparently employ both negative and positive stereotypes of those at the top of the income spectrum, they seemed to be able to draw on only negative stereotypes of those in poverty or in receipt of benefits. (ibid.: 6)

One of the reasons for this was

> a widespread belief about the ready availability of opportunity, resulting in highly individualised explanations of poverty and disadvantage.
>
> For most participants, attitudes to income inequality were expressed within the context of a belief in fair inequality on the basis of desert. As such, participants were not opposed to high incomes they perceived to be deserved. (ibid.: 5; see also Miller 1992; 1999; Joseph Rowntree Foundation 2007)

They tended to "invent or exaggerate the virtues (and therefore desert) of those with high incomes in order to justify existing inequalities" (ibid.: 5).

This accords with the popular 'belief in a just world', according to which the good are rewarded and the bad not, so that failure is taken to be the individual's responsibility. While it is hardly surprising that this idea is an attractive one for the affluent, since it implies their advantages are deserved, the tendency, reported in many empirical studies, of the poor themselves to accept responsibility for their inferior position – unless they happen to be politicized – is perhaps less expected (Lamont 2000; Macleod 1995; Sayer 2005).[10]

In his comments on moral luck, Smith noted the common reluctance to acknowledge that the 'success' of the rich might be undeserved, attributing this to a desire not to be or appear resentful and mean-spirited (Smith 1759 [1984]). The common view that those at the top have worked for it and therefore deserve it seems generous, and likely to win recognition precisely for that generosity and deference. By contrast, justified resentment of contributive and distributive injustice is likely to be misrecognized and condemned as 'envy' by the dominant. For the dominated, as Bourdieu acknowledged, it may therefore be more comfortable to accept domination than to resent and resist it; challenging misrecognition may be painful and invite the disapproval of others, worsening the situation of the dominated.

Infamously, former British Prime Minister Tony Blair, once tried to justify his lack of concern about economic inequalities ("the gap") by saying that:

> What I meant by that was not that I don't care about the gap, so much as I don't care if there are people who earn a lot of money. They're not my concern. I do care about people who are without opportunity, disadvantaged and poor. We've got to lift those people but we don't necessarily do that by hammering the people who are successful. (Blair 2005)

To be rich is thereby portrayed as the fair reward for success, success is a result of merit, and the wealth of the few is unrelated to the lack of wealth of others. This combines misrecognition of the determinants of both distribution and contribution.

10 The just world idea also has more widespread appeal from a normative point of view: who would not want the deserving to be rewarded and the undeserving not to be?

Not all lay views of class position serve to legitimize individuals' position or indeed the inequalities themselves, however, for some are egalitarian. However, in the context of enduring, structural inequalities such as those of class, attempts at recognition between individuals or groups who are differently placed are likely to be unsatisfactory or tokenistic. Those who try to treat both those positioned below and above them as equals are at risk of being suspected of condescension by the dominated, and of being disrespectful and resentful by the dominant. In this way, the unequal social field also distorts the *reception* of acts signifying recognition.

Class denial is another form of misrecognition. It is common for people to avoid acknowledging class, even though they cannot help but be aware of it, and can sometimes 'see someone's class a mile off'. Tacit collusion in the misrecognition of class is a striking feature of all but the most politicized class societies. This is sometimes well-intentioned, sometimes not. People may avoid acknowledging class – particularly the class of those with whom they have to interact – either for 'ethical' reasons: to avoid humiliating members of the subordinate classes or embarrassing the dominant, or, in the case of the dominant classes, instrumental ones: to hide their privilege. Although very different, such evasions may be mutually supportive. The very language of 'working class' and 'middle class' exemplifies this compatibility of ethical and instrumental reasons for class denial: '*working*' avoids the stigmatizing connotations of 'lower', and '*middle* class' for the rest of the population allows those at the top to hide within the middle, thereby reducing resentment and embarrassment. For example, calls for higher taxes for the rich (the upper classes) are routinely denounced in the right wing press as threats to the 'middle' classes, thereby winning over those who really are in the middle and would not be affected by such taxes. As Bourdieu argued, the very meaning of the term class is itself a stake in the class struggle. At the same time, the terminology is flexible enough to mean different things to different people and hence to allow standoffs in this discursive struggle. Thus, middle-class people may sometimes disingenuously claim to be working-class on the grounds that they work, and socialists can value the socialist associations of the term 'working class', even though their constitutive other, the class of capitalists, goes largely unacknowledged in popular discourse. Whatever the reasons for class denial and misrecognition, they depoliticize class and create a space for individualistic and meritocratic explanations of the effects of structural class inequalities.

Yet, while misrecognition of the kinds we have reviewed is a source of much harm, not least to people's self-respect and self-esteem, it is more a response to class inequality than a fundamental cause of it. Merely countering attitudes to others will not have much impact on those inequalities, because they are partly a product of the structural scarcity of good quality jobs. Tilly makes a similar point:

> Mistaken beliefs reinforce exploitation, opportunity hoarding, emulation and adaptation but exercise little independent influence on their initiation ... It follows that the reduction or intensification of racist, sexist, or xenophobic attitudes will

> have relatively little impact on durable inequality, whereas the introduction of new organizational forms … will have great impact. (Tilly 1998: 15)

Getting rid of discrimination against particular groups of workers will not produce genuine equality of opportunity, just more diverse ('representative') groups of winners and losers. Merely reducing class contempt – or 'class racism' as Bourdieu called it – so that different classes are more respectful towards one another will not reduce class inequality; classes will remain as long as the social structures which produce them endure. Misrecognition adds insult to injury, but there are other causes of injury than misrecognition.

Conclusions

Combining concepts of misrecognition of persons with a Bourdieusian concept of misrecognition, I have attempted to show how they interact and how both are encouraged by an unequal division of labour. This major source of inequality makes it inevitable that opportunities for self-development and fulfilment through work, and the recognition that goes with it, are unequally distributed. Further, the cause of the differences in worth of their work is likely to be misrecognized as a product of differences in intelligence and effort, to which the unequal division of labour is seen as merely a response. This misrecognition may be reinforced by the thought that those who get the better jobs deserve this through having done better than others in a seemingly meritocratic competition for qualifications or educational capital. Not only is the unequal division of labour misrecognized but so too are the processes by which differences in ability and ambition are produced through the socialization of children in different parts of the social field. Further, the unequal division of labour helps to produce an unequal social 'force field', which distorts people's assessments of themselves and others.

Finally, many would regard this radical critique of the unequal division of labour, and its implication that good and bad quality work should be equally shared, as hopelessly idealistic. How could we expect to do so in a modern world? While I think some forms of expertise might be lost if workers were not able to devote most of their time to it, for example, brain surgery or scientific research, I would argue that it would be possible to significantly reduce the unequal division of labour. Nevertheless, I acknowledge that it is tempting to dismiss the whole theory because its implications are so radical. To do so on those grounds would be fallacious; it would be like deciding that because it is hard to imagine changing ways of life and economic organization in developed countries to make them carbon-neutral, we should reject the evidence that global warming is anthropogenic. That it is difficult to imagine a much more equal division of labour does not mean that the unequal division of labour is unimportant in producing major inequalities in life chances and recognition. Its importance is another 'inconvenient truth'.

References

Blair, T. 2005. Blair does mind the wealth gap. *The Guardian* [Online 24 March]. Available at: http://www.guardian.co.uk/politics/2005/mar/24/uk.election2005 [accessed: 10 May 2010].

Bourdieu, P. 1984. *Distinction*. London: Routledge.

Bourdieu, P. 1993. *Sociology in Question*. London: Sage.

Bourdieu, P. 1996. *The State Nobility: Elite Schools in the Field of Power*. Cambridge: Polity.

Bourdieu, P. 1998. *Practical Reason*. Cambridge: Polity.

Bourdieu, P. 2000. *Pascalian Meditations*. Cambridge: Polity.

Bourdieu, P. 2008. *Political Interventions: Social Science and Political Action*. London: Verso.

Bourdieu, P. and Wacquant, L.J.D. 1992. *An Invitation to Reflexive Sociology*. Chicago: Chicago University Press.

Crompton R. 2007. Gender Inequality and the Gender Division of Labour, in *The Future of Gender*, edited by J. Browne. Cambridge: Cambridge University Press, 228-49.

Delphy, C. and Leonard, D. 1992. *Familiar Exploitation: A New Analysis of Marriage in Contemporary Western Societies*. Cambridge: Polity.

Eagleton, T. and Bourdieu, P. 1992. Doxa and Common Life. *New Left Review*, 1(191), 111-21.

Feinstein, L. 2003. Inequality in the Early Cognitive Development of British Children in the 1970 Cohort. *Economica*, 70, 73-97.

Folbre, N. 1982. Exploitation Comes Home: A Critique of the Marxian Theory of Family Labour. *Cambridge Journal of Economics*, 6, 317-29.

Fraser, N. 1995. From Redistribution to Recognition?: Dilemmas of Justice in a Post-Socialist Age. *New Left Review* I(212), 68-93.

Fraser, N. and Honneth, A. 2003. *Redistribution or Recognition?: A Political-Philosophical Exchange*. London: Verso.

Fraser, N. 2010. Rethinking Recognition, in *The Philosophy of Recognition: Historical and Contemporary Perspectives*, edited by H-C. Schmidt am Busch and C.F. Zurn. Lanham: Lexington Books, 211-22.

Gomberg, P. 2007. *How to Make Opportunity Equal: Race and Contributive Justice*. Oxford: Blackwell.

Hochschild, A.R. 1989. *The Second Shift: Working Parents and the Revolution at Home*. London: Piatkus Ltd.

Honneth, A. 1995. *The Struggle for Recognition: The Moral Grammar of Social Conflicts*. Cambridge: Polity.

Honneth, A. 2010. Work and Recognition: A Redefinition, in *The Philosophy of Recognition: Historical and Contemporary Perspectives*, edited by H-C. Schmidt am Busch and C.F. Zurn. Lanham: Lexington Books, 223-39.

Joseph Rowntree Foundation. 2007. *Understanding Attitudes to Tackling Economic Inequality*. Available at: http://www.jrf.org.uk/sites/files/jrf/attitudes-tackling-economic-inequality-full.pdf [accessed: 10 May 2010].

Joseph Rowntree Foundation. 2009. *Political Debate about Inequality: An Information Resource.* Available at: http://www.jrf.org.uk/sites/files/jrf/political-debate-economic-inequality-full.pdf [accessed: 10 May 2010].

Lamont, M. 1992. *Money, Morals and Manners: The Culture of the French and American Upper-Middle Class*. Chicago: Chicago University Press.

Lamont, M. 2000. *The Dignity of Working Men: Morality and the Boundaries of Race, Class and Imagination.* New York: Russell Sage Foundation and Harvard University Press.

MacIntyre, A. 1981. *After Virtue*. London: Duckworth.

Macleod, J. 1995. *Ain't No Makin' It: Aspirations and Attainment in a Low Income Neighbourhood*, 2nd edn. Boulder, CO: Westview Press.

Miller, D. 1992. Distributive Justice: What the People Think. *Ethics*, 102: 555-93.

Miller, D. 1999. *Principles of Social Justice*. Cambridge, MA: Harvard University Press.

Murphy, J.B. 1993. *The Moral Economy of Labor*. New Haven: Yale.

Oakley, Anne. 1974. *Housewife*. London: A. Lane.

Okin, S-M. 1991. *Justice, Gender and the Family*. New York: Basic Books.

Pinkard, T. 2010. Recognition, the Right and the Good, in *The Philosophy of Recognition: Historical and Contemporary Perspectives*, edited by H-C. Schmidt am Busch and C.F. Zurn. Lanham: Lexington Books, 129-51.

Sayer, A. 2005. *The Moral Significance of Class*. Cambridge: Cambridge University Press.

Sayer, A. 2009. Contributive Justice and Meaningful Work. *Res Publica*, 15(1), 1-16.

Sayer, A. 2010. Reflexivity and the Habitus, in *Conversations about Reflexivity*, edited by M.S. Archer. London: Routledge, 108-22.

Schmidt am Busch, H-C. and Zurn, C.F. (eds). 2010. *The Philosophy of Recognition: Historical and Contemporary Perspectives*. Lanham: Lexington Books.

Smith, A. 1759[1984]. *The Theory of Moral Sentiments*. Indianapolis: Liberty Fund.

Smith, A. 1776[1976]. *An Inquiry into the Nature and Causes of the Wealth of Nations*, edited by E. Cannan. Chicago: University of Chicago Press.

Taylor, C. 1994. The Politics of Recognition, in *Multiculturalism: Examining the Politics of Recognition*, edited by A.Gutmann. Princeton, NJ: Princeton University Press, 25-74.

Tilly, C. 1998. *Durable Inequality*. Berkeley, CA: California University Press.

Walby, S. 1986. *Patriarchy at Work*. Cambridge: Polity.

Walby, S. 1990. *Theorising Patriarchy*. Cambridge: Polity.

Chapter 6
Disability and Misrecognition[1]

Gideon Calder

This chapter considers the politics of disability in light of concepts of misrecognition. While the parallels between the two seem evident enough, it is curious that they are rarely dwelt upon. This is all the more striking because of the rising profile of disability politics, and the shapes that it has taken. In the past 40 years or so, disability has become a political issue in fresh, pressing, impactful ways. This has reconfigured quite profoundly how it is viewed and treated, particularly by social institutions. Where once 'disability issues' would have occupied a peripheral, occasional place in the structures of those institutions, now they will be wired in at the core. Among all kinds of service providers, there are new and prominent commitments to place sensitivity to diversity, and the promotion of equality, at the heart of institutional practice. In the United Kingdom, this reflects a series of deliberate legislative moves – of which the Equality Act 2010 is the latest example[2] – designed to refine and integrate the law around different potential forms of discrimination. Disability occupies a central place in such legislation. In a sense, this is a kind of victory for the political theory of recognition, or at least a sign of its momentum and influence. We find a 'normalization' of concerns about difference and its social implications (or the attempt at this, at any rate) and an acknowledgement of the nuances that such concerns involve. And with disability in particular, we find an acceptance that tackling the forms of disadvantage with which it is associated means identifying their causes not in *individual* incapacity, but in *social* barriers to which misrecognition can be seen as a key contributing factor.

These changes – in the law and in wider social orientations – originate in the campaigning work of grassroots organizations, engaged in a 'new disability politics' emerging in the 1970s. The tone of that work is helpfully captured by Colin Barnes and Geof Mercer. While, historically, disabled people had been

---

1 I am grateful to Simon Thompson and an anonymous referee for comments on an earlier draft of this chapter.

2 Previous stages in the legislative process include the Disability Discrimination Acts of 1995 and 2005, and the Equality Act 2006, which saw the abolition of the six-year-old Disability Rights Commission (along with the Commission for Racial Equality and the Equal Opportunities Commission) and its replacement by a single Equality and Human Rights Commission, launched in 2007.

primarily subject to control and treatment, and regarded as passive recipients of pity or strategies for cure,

> [d]isabled people now highlighted their everyday familiarity with social and environmental barriers, restricted life chances, and negative cultural representations. This required a re-evaluation of their individual and collective support needs and rights. It encompassed a critique of the regulation of disabled people's lives by a diverse group of health and welfare professionals. Disability activists did not deny the positive potential of appropriate medical and allied intervention. Rather, they challenged those professional experts who equated disability solely with functional limitations and concentrated service provision on individual rehabilitation and adjustment. (Barnes and Mercer 2010: 2-3)

'Expertise', along with wider, informal presumptions about disability, has been duly challenged. Within an impressively short space of time, this critique has informed and transformed institutional practice, and changed the shape of legislation, to a striking extent. Of course, this does not necessarily mean that such legislation 'gets it right', or that institutions translate it successfully into duly nuanced forms of practice. Nor is there any guarantee that formal changes in the law, or in rules in other spheres, lead to substantive improvements of the kinds their designers – let alone the disability rights movement – may hope for. But still, the politics of disability has been both reoriented, and in important ways mainstreamed.

As such, this movement seems a prime example of a recognition-centred politics that – in clear, exceptional ways – has 'worked' in terms of making an impact and (however incompletely) achieving goals. Viewed one way, the disability rights movement has prioritized displacing the historical patterns of misrecognition and non-recognition experienced by disabled people, and staking a claim for what Axel Honneth calls 'a positive understanding of self' (1992: 189), free of the tendencies towards prejudice, insult, belittlement and disrespect typical of historically dominant views of the disabled. Moreover, its aims seem broadly consonant with those identified by Nancy Fraser under the heading of 'participatory parity'. She has developed this as a kind of normative standard by which to evaluate claims for recognition. For claims to be justified, for Fraser, 'claimants must show that current arrangements prevent them from participating on a par with others in social life' (Fraser 2003: 38). The new politics of disability has had precisely this aim as an undercurrent. To the extent that it has been successful, it has shown with great force that precisely such impediments persist in current social arrangements. Again, and as we shall see, this makes it an especially good example of a certain kind of recognition politics in action. A substantial part of the target of the disability rights movement has been constituted by systematic misrecognition of a particularly stark kind.

These considerations make it all the more striking that disability has not been at all prominent in the recognition literature. We find there, of course, a great amount of critical attention to the nature and scope of identity and difference, and their implications for theories of social justice. But as I have remarked elsewhere, we find very little on disability itself (2008), even (indeed especially) in some of the 'keynote' treatments of difference as a social justice issue. It is a case where political philosophy lags conspicuously behind politics itself. This applies not just in the liberal tradition (exemplified, of course, in Rawls 1971, 1993), but in those veins of theory for which liberalism itself is insufficiently alert to difference. Thus keynote works in recognition theory simply tend not to devote space to disability: see Fraser (1997); Fraser and Honneth (2003); Honneth (1995); Taylor (1992); Young (1990; 1997).[3] Across the works just mentioned, there is a single mention of disability between them, and this in a footnote. The same is broadly true of critiques of recognition theory, whether sympathetic (for example, Markell 2003 – no mention at all) or hostile (for example, Barry 2000 – some coverage, though cursory and in passing). Other examples of differentiation always feature first, and usually exclusively: culture, ethnicity, gender, sexuality, language, religion. Disability, seemingly so neatly fitted within the politics of recognition, slips out of view in the mainstream of its theoretical treatment.[4]

I will not, in this chapter, seek to offer any deep explanation of this discrepancy. Rather, I want to explore the extent to which disability highlights strengths and weaknesses of recognition politics – and specifically, the location of mis- or non-recognition at the heart of injustice. The discussion has three main stages. In the next section, I outline the 'social model' of disability, a key component of the recent transformation of disability politics. In these terms, disability is an aspect of relations – between individuals, and between individuals and their environments – and, as I shall argue, a site of misrecognition in all the standard senses. In the following section, I consider some pros and cons of the social model, from both political and theoretical points of view. While its progressive political value has been widely affirmed, it has been sympathetically criticized for involving certain ontological deficits and simplifications – particularly around the connections between bodily impairment and disability. In the section following that, I relate these pros and cons back to critical reception of the political theory of recognition – and specifically to Fraser's elaboration of the notion of participatory parity. And in concluding, I argue that considering disability vis-à-vis participatory parity suggests that Fraser is correct in famously suggesting that when it comes to social justice, misrecognition is not the only game in town: it risks an overemphasis on culture at the expense of other dimensions of oppression and disadvantage. But departing from Fraser, I suggest that 'participatory parity' has further preconditions

3 Iris Young does make mention of disability in her *Inclusion and Democracy* (2000), but sporadically – and not specifically in relation to recognition *per se*.

4 For a rare exception, see Ikäheimo (2010) for an illuminating treatment of disability deploying the wider theoretical toolbox of recognition politics – specifically, vis-à-vis notions of personhood and social inclusion. These themes run in a kind of parallel to many of those addressed here – and the very force of Ikäheimo's case highlights how odd it is that recognition theorists have not had more to say about disability.

than just redistribution and recognition. I suggest that a capabilities-based approach is well-placed to tackle the particular political-theoretical challenges which emerge with the new politics of disability.

Misrecognition and the Social Model

We have seen that even in the mainstream of institutional practice, disability has come to be regarded as a social condition, rather than something simply inherent in the individual. This is all the more striking because of the durability of that 'commonsense' conception of disability for which it is a *distinctly* individualized kind of problem – a shortcoming, perhaps a tragedy, attaching to the bodies and/or minds of an unfortunate minority. On this view disability consists in the absence of a capacity or ability considered to be part of a normally functioning life. To their critics, such presumptions have served to medicalize the 'condition' of disability in a way which disempowers those who come to be regarded as 'patients', while simultaneously empowering those credited with the expertise to identify their problems and needs, and the prospects for their rehabilitation. This general understanding of disability as deficiency/tragedy will be readily confirmed, as Barnes and Mercer put it, 'by its pre-eminent medical diagnosis [in industrialized Western societies] in terms of individual pathology, and associated deficits, abnormalities and functional limitations' (Barnes and Mercer 2010: 1). From this angle – labelled by critics as the 'medical model' – to be disabled is to possess such deficiencies. A disability is a lack or malfunctioning either to be 'cured', or accepted as untreatable and accommodated in the confirmed role of a 'dependent' – someone incapable of self-sufficiency, economic productivity, full agency, and 'normal' participation in social life. For its critics, the medical model, and the association of disability with tragedy, weakness, helplessness and lack of full personhood are themselves the source of oppression, stigma, and disempowering perceptions of the disabled – and thus, we may say, of misrecognition. They are themselves disabling.

For the 'social model', on the other hand, to be disabled is to inhabit a certain kind of social world. Here disability is conceived as arising not from physical, sensory or cognitive impairment, but from discrimination, exclusion, and other features of one's lived environment. To be specific: it is not the impairment itself which disables, but society. As an oft-quoted statement by the Union of the Physically Impaired Against Segregation put it: 'Disability is something imposed on top of our impairments by the way we are unnecessarily isolated and excluded from full participation in society' (UPIAS 1976: 14). The distinction between impairment and disability is crucial. Phillip Cole helpfully refines the definition:

> a disability is an inability that is related to an impairment of the body, but disabilities are always primarily social in that they only have form and content in a particular social context: a disability is the exclusion from an action or ability

> which the social framework makes possible for others, but impossible for the disabled. Whether or not that social framework can be altered, it is the primary factor, not the bodily impairment. (Cole 2007: 172)

Disability is thus a form of *social* oppression. As Mike Oliver characterizes the social model, the causes of disability lie not in the individual, nor in biological pathology, but 'squarely in society and social organisations' (Oliver 1990: 11). It is not impairments themselves which oppress, but the particular form of misrecognition represented by 'disablism': presumptions, negligences, barriers deliberate or otherwise, prejudices, lack of forethought, and default assumptions about 'normality' which exclude those with impairments.

There are nuances of difference in these definitions, to which we will return later. For now, what is important is the ostensible fit between disability as viewed via the social model, and the notion that it is a kind of exclusion through the misrecognition, or non-recognition, of identity.[5] For Taylor, in a key text in the inauguration of contemporary discussion on these lines:

> a person or group of people can suffer real damage, real distortion, if the people or society around them mirror back a confining or demeaning or contemptible picture of themselves. Nonrecognition or misrecognition can inflict harm, can be a form of oppression, imprisoning someone in a false, distorted, and reduced mode of being. (Taylor 1992: 25)

Consider Taylor's account alongside this characterization of the impacts of the deficiency/tragedy model…

> The long-term physically impaired are neither sick nor well, neither dead nor alive, neither out of society nor wholly in it. They are human beings but their bodies are warped or malfunctioning, leaving their full humanity in doubt. … They are neither fish nor fowl; they exist in partial isolation from society as undefined, ambiguous people. (Murphy 1987: 112)

… or this diagnosis of the impact of the social model…

---

5 In saying this, I should note that Oliver (1990, 2010) and others instrumental to the generation of the social model of disability operate within an explicitly historical-materialist framework, for which the philosophical tenor of recognition politics may be overly Hegelian/idealist. As it happens I see no incongruity between understanding disablism in terms of misrecognition, and the wider backdrop of Marxist social theory. The causes of misrecognition itself can certainly, in principle, be located in the economic mode of production – and indeed, Oliver's work itself offers a strong case along these lines, even if it is not explicitly couched in the normative terms of recognition.

> Disability was exposed as a form of social oppression that should not be tolerated, analogous to already recognized oppressions associated with gender, race, class and sexuality. Once this understanding of disability is adopted, the manifestations of disablism can be readily observed: a wheelchair user or a person with visual impairment cannot access public transport systems, or is not able to obtain a quality education that would enable them to compete for well-paid jobs in the labour market, or is represented as a person of lesser value in films and other media. The disabling 'social barriers' in the lives of people with impairments can be identified *and challenged* because socially created barriers can be dismantled. (Thomas 2004: 20, emphasis in the original)

...and it is clear that part of the political force of the social model lies precisely in its consonance with critiques of misrecognition. That is to say, what is wrong in the deficiency/tragedy model, in its most forceful articulations, is its contribution to the 'imprisonment' of people with impairments within, to use Taylor's phrase, a 'false, distorted and reduced mode of being'.

In its place, proponents of the social model have sought a positive affirmation of disability, in terms of particular qualities of life associated with living with impairments which are either hidden from view in generalized accounts of well-being, or downgraded by them. The rejection of that presumptive downgrading amounts to a struggle for the recognition of a particular form of identity. As French and Swain put it, recounting the experiences of people with various impairments who have come to regard them as enhancing, and not something to wished away:

> Nobody can predict the amount of tragedy or happiness a person will experience in life and yet people feel confident to make such predictions about disabled people. The inherent assumption is that disabled people want to be other than as they are, even though this would mean a rejection of identity. (French and Swain 2004: 38)

For many proponents of the social model, it is that 'identity' which it is the goal of disability politics to retrieve and affirm. Here we find a definite attempt to constitute 'the disabled' as a political community, and precisely to shift analysis from (medical, individualized) questions of 'what' impairment consists in, to (structural, relational) questions of how disability itself is socially constituted, and the possibilities for an 'identity politics' of disability. Thus, as Honneth puts it: 'While groups such as ... the disabled previously defined their own identities through concepts of sexual or biological deviation, so that they had to understand themselves as contingent collections of individuals, today they characterize themselves to a much greater extent as culturally integrated communities with a common history, language and sensibility' (Honneth 2003: 162). Understood as a group in this way, the disabled might seem obviously to share an interest both in reforming a physical environment configured without due regard for the needs of disabled people, and in challenging the social construction of the disabled in mainstream discourse and policy (Smith 2005: 554-6). We find invoked 'a positive, collective, aesthetic expression of self-recognition that constitutes a "great refusal" to accept discrimination and second-class citizenship' (Paterson and Hughes 2000: 43).

Sticking-Points with the Social Model: Normative and Ontological

Yet, as elsewhere, such appeals to 'group-ness', 'collective expression' and shared identity are problematic and contested. As soon as it arises, there comes the obvious response that the lives of 'the disabled' are defined as much by differences – in the experience of impairments, but also along lines of class, gender, race, religion and ways of life – as by the commonalities to which Honneth refers (Scott-Hill 2004). A challenge which comes with this territory is to achieve inclusivity in the construction of a given identity without hypostatizing or 'freezing', as Iris Young puts it, 'both the identity of that group and its relations with other groups in the polity' (Young 2000: 149). Even if there is a generalized misrecognition of the disabled as such (which itself is debatable), it is not clear that emancipation from this lies in the affirmation of an alternative *shared* identity. Essentialism, even of a purely strategic kind, seems to many to be false, but also counterproductive in that it risks an alternative over-generalization no less problematic than disablism itself. While the social model in its explanatory mode directs us towards an open-textured, non-reified, contextually sensitive conception of what 'counts' as disability, the politics of identity construction may seem to push in opposite directions, generating, as depicted by Fraser in characterizing the identity politics model of recognition, 'moral pressure on individual members to conform to a given group culture' (Fraser 2000: 112). The point has been made that those most active in disability politics, and investing most heavily in the notion of a disabled identity, do not themselves constitute some demographically representative group. Working class people, older people, younger people, those from minority ethnic groups, lesbian, gay, bisexual and transgender people, people with learning difficulties, and those in the mental health system have all, say critics, been disproportionately minor voices in the movement (Barnes and Mercer 2003: 129-30; Shakespeare 2006: 72-6). Any 'identity politics' which requires of its operative identities stability, homogeneity, closure, pre-ordained boundaries and in general a neat, fixed self-coherence will come unstuck just because any imaginable such political identity, to put it no more technically, will have none of those features (Calder 2006). To this extent, the obstacles to invoking 'the identity of the disabled' are just the obstacles in connection with invoking *any* identity as a political vehicle.

Yet in some ways, the risks of over-generalization about 'the disabled', and of the elision of differences within that designated group, are *especially* stark. 'Disability' covers a wide range of conditions, across the categories of physical, cognitive and sensory impairment. While a sense of oppression may be shared across those 'impairment groups', this by no means implies that the nature of that oppression, or the experience of it, is consistent between those with markedly different impairments – say, those with a spinal cord injury and those with learning difficulties. Here, the political force of the social model is designed to shift focus from the particularities of individuals' impairments to the wider sphere of social responses to the impaired, which is where the sources of disability are deemed to lie. But here, too, it is not clear that the dynamics of disablism will work in consistent patterns among all those identified (by themselves or others) as disabled. And again, while this will apply with all purported identity groupings, along lines of race, class, gender or otherwise, it seems especially pointed in the case of disability. Bickenbach et al. press hard on this point:

> Not only are the social responses to different forms of mental and physical impairments vastly different, from the other direction there is almost no commonality of experience, or feelings of solidarity, between people with diverse disabilities. There is no unifying culture, language or set of experiences; people with disabilities are not homogenous, nor is there much prospect for transdisability solidarity. (Bickenbach et al. 1999: 1181)

Thus to return to Murphy's phrase, the *ways* in which different people with different impairments are located 'in partial isolation from society as undefined, ambiguous people' may be radically divergent, even if the state of marginalization itself is a shared condition.

The workings of misrecognition – its nature, scope and impacts – will diverge too. And so, accordingly, will the ways in which it might be counteracted. Is there a 'mode of being' (in Taylor's words) which is distorted in the same way for all those oppressed by disablism? Is there an alternative, shared, non-distorted, 'true' mode of being which might be recognized aright? To neither question is there an obvious affirmative answer. And even seeking one might risk a form of oppression in itself. One way around this problem would be to include among 'the disabled' only those self-identifying as such. This might offer the possibility of avoiding imposing some notional 'true mode of being' on those who, for whatever reason, might resist it. But this, as Tom Shakespeare points out, risks a problematic voluntarism. The notion that 'you are disabled if you say you are' would, as he puts it, 'include some people who happen to like the idea of being members of a disabled minority group, but in objective terms are not oppressed in any way' – and also 'exclude some people who may objectively experience oppression, but subjectively refuse to identify themselves as oppressed' (Shakespeare 2006: 77). And it may also include people 'who may experience oppression based on physical difference, but would not traditionally be seen as disabled' – for example, the very overweight, or the anorexic.

So when it comes to appeals to a shared state of misrecognition among disabled people, we find a kind of pincer movement between two kinds of problem. One is that 'the disabled' are neither an internally homogenous nor a sociologically separate group – and that the appeal to such a group identity is itself a potential form of misrecognition. The other is that the matter of who is included in the category is itself up for question, in ways which – given the claims and parameters of the social model – seem problematic to resolve either in voluntaristic or objectivized terms. To some critics – Shakespeare prominent among them, but see also, *inter alia*, Abberley (1987), French (1993) and Terzi (2004, 2010) for other lines of sympathetic critique – all of this serves to highlight severe limitations with the social model. On the normative side, the emancipatory potential of mobilizing a 'disabled' identity brings as a counterpart the threat that heavy invocation of such an identity might itself be coercive and exclusionary. But there are also ontological problems with an explanation of disability solely in terms of social barriers. The political power of the social model lies in large part in the directness of its message and its rejection of two accounts of the relationship between disability, impairment and society…

i. *impairment* → *disability* (an individual's impairment causes their disability)
ii. *impairment* = *disability* (an individual's impairment *is* their disability)

… and the replacement of these by a third (borrowing here from Thomas 1999: 14):

iii. *social barriers* → *disability* (social barriers cause the individual's disability)

In fact, in the reception and development of the social model, we find a fourth alternative: [6]

iv. *certain relationships between impairment and social barriers* → *disability*

Politically as well as philosophically, much hinges on the distinctions between (iii) and (iv), and the relative persuasiveness of each position. In support of (iii), Mike Oliver insists that 'disability is *wholly and exclusively social*… disablement is *nothing to do with the body*' (Oliver 1996: 41). In tune with (iv), Sally French (1993) and Lorella Terzi (2004) among others have suggested ways in which certain disabling impairments would remain even in some notional state where all disabling social barriers had been removed. For proponents of (iv), (iii) over-

6 For some commentators on the social model, the very distinction between disability and impairment is itself unstable. It 'concedes' impairment to medicine, and the biologistic model, in a way that rules out the possibility of a sociological understanding of impairment itself. In this light, a possible position (v) might be: *disability is caused by barriers and impairments, both of which are social and political 'all the way down'.* A version of this position emerges in the work of Cole (2007) and Oliver (2009) . But both present it as a political strategy, rather than a philosophical stance – 'a practical tool … not a theory' (Oliver 2009: 57).

socializes disability. By locating the causes of disability entirely on the social side, it neglects the personal, the psychological – and the *embodied* experience of disability. Against (iii), Shakespeare suggests that '[s]ocial model theory enables disabled people to deny the relevance of their impaired bodies or brains, and seek equality with non-disabled people on the basis of similarity' (Shakespeare 2006: 80). Thus social perceptions, and the forms of exclusion which result from them, are the cause of disability. Enablement, it follows, will result from changing social perceptions, in the direction of a more inclusive society. To some of its critics, the problem with this position is a kind of sociological imperialism. This consists in the assumption that social perceptions – cultural meanings, in broad terms – are where all the action is, in both explaining and redressing disadvantage. Viewed this way misrecognition, by itself, is the source of disablement, and recognition, by itself, will be the source of enablement. Disability politics is thus altogether a *politics* of recognition.

One thing that seems problematic about this view is precisely the assumption that social perceptions, in the form of prejudicial or negligent assumptions, are the source of all barriers which the disabled might encounter. The urge to avoid biological reductionism pushes in the direction of cultural determinism (Thomas 2004). The fear of admitting qualities to our embodied experience which are not wholly socially constructed leads to a picture in which an arguably distinct ontological level – that of the impairment itself – drops out. The fear here, as Thomas and others have argued, seems to have its source in the presumption that the medical model has got impairment right. On the medical model as painted by its opponents (and in fact it is hard to find proponents of it, as such), an impairment is a kind of objectified, inert feature of the self which is treatable in separation from it. There is a resolutely Cartesian picture of the mute, luggage-like, cumbersome body as opposed to the agentive, versatile, life-shaping mind (see Calder 2005). In the grip of this picture, to allow impairment 'back in' when considering the sources of disability is to surrender the appeal to agency which is so crucial to the project of transforming the (self-)image of disabled people. 'Do not reduce me to my impairment' is of course a vital slogan in any such project. But a slogan which runs 'do not consider my impairment for fear of reducing me to it' seems to presume that, as for Descartes, we need to drive a wedge between our (independent, free, rational) mind and our (determined, vulnerable, impulse-driven) physiology, our senses, our materiality, in order to preserve a sphere in which agency can do its stuff. We are all, as Vic Finkelstein (2004: 20) notes, 'weak, vulnerable, physically imperfect and socially dependent'. As Alasdair MacIntyre (1999) argues similarly and at length, in moral terms we neglect our definitive, embodied vulnerability – the characteristic disability typical of extensive parts of the lifespan for all humans – at our peril.[7]

---

7 Difficulties in incorporating human beings' characteristic *lack* of ongoing autonomous self-sufficiency into frameworks of recognition are captured neatly in the 'trilemma' described by Arto Laitinen (2006): (i) all human beings deserve equal respect on

Disability, Misrecognition and Participatory Parity

The patterns of contention here mirror debates among recognition theorists about the place and scope of misrecognition vis-à-vis social injustice in general. They find a particularly resonant echo in the debates between Nancy Fraser, and in the other corner Iris Young and Axel Honneth, about whether (mis)recognition is prior to, and encompasses, other putative forms of social (in)justice. For Young (1997) and Honneth (2003), any distinction between the cultural and the material is definitively unstable – and so Fraser's (1997) distinction between (cultural) misrecognition and (economic) maldistribution as alternative sources of injustice must itself be unsustainable. As Fraser characterizes this distinction more recently:

> In my conception … misrecognition is an institutionalized social relation … analytically distinct from, and conceptually irreducible to, the injustice of maldistribution, although it may be accompanied by the latter. Whether misrecognition converts into maldistribution, and vice versa, depends on the nature of the social formation in question. (Fraser 2008: 58-9)

Young and Honneth, from different theoretical directions, dispute the distinctness and irreducibility of these two factors. The twists and nuances of these debates are well-covered elsewhere, and this is not the place for further commentary on them. My point here is briefer, and simply for the sake of argument. If indeed cultural determinism is problematic, such that it is worth distinguishing between different aspects of injustice rather than subsuming everything within the rubric of recognition, then Fraser's case seems to 'speak to' option (iv) above, in so far as it defends an analytical distinction between separate levels in the contribution to social disadvantage, and avoids reduction to either. Granted, as points of contrast with the impact of culture, impairment (on the one hand) and economic maldistribution (on the other) are clearly distinct. But the tenability of (iv), like Fraser's contrast between recognition and redistribution, depends on the feasibility of identifying non-cultural contributory factors to disadvantage. It also suggests that there are places which a politics of recognition cannot, conceived exclusively as such, reach.

---

the basis of equal moral status; (ii) our worthiness of respect depends on the possession of certain features associated with personhood; (iii) not all human beings have those features all of the time. The problem on these terms is how to invoke a universal norm ('to recognize every other human being as a person') which depends for its purchase on the presence of features which are themselves variable between people, and across the lives of individuals. Difficulties on this score lead some to frame the issue in more negative terms, that is, that recognition is inevitably oppressive, and an instrument for reinforcing the dominant culture whether within groups or in society as a whole, and requiring of the individual subject that they establish their personhood in line with that culture – see for example, Oliver (2001).

Interestingly, some equivalent version of (iv) is implied in the United Nations definition of disability as 'a function of the relationship between disabled persons and their environment', issuing in 'the loss or limitation of opportunities to take part in the life of the community on an equal level with others' (United Nations 2006). Disadvantage here is couched in terms of lack of opportunity for participation, but in ways which proponents of (iii) will find problematic, precisely because of the operative distinction between impairment and social environment as separate contributors to disability. As mentioned earlier, participation, and the opportunities to attain it on equal terms, are central to the normative dimension of Fraser's politics. One barrier to participation is misrecognition:

> To be misrecognized, in my view, is not simply to be thought ill of, looked down on, or devalued in others' conscious attitudes or mental beliefs. It is rather to be denied the status[8] of a full partner in social interaction and prevented from participating as a peer in social life – not as a consequence of a distributive inequity (such as failing to receive one's fair share of resources or "primary goods") but rather as a consequence of institutionalized patterns of interpretation and evaluation that constitute one as comparatively unworthy of respect and esteem. When such patterns of disrespect and disesteem are institutionalized, for example, in law, social welfare, medicine, and/or popular culture, they impede parity of participation, just as surely as do distributive inequities. (Fraser 2008: 58)

Again, the 'fit' between the focus of disability politics and Fraser's account of misrecognition is striking. Indeed this passage provides a particularly good encapsulation of what a good proportion of the recent work of the disability rights movement has been directed towards. Yet, of course, part of Fraser's purpose in distinguishing between this and economic forms of injustice is to insist that both are impactful, but differently. In originally proposing the distinction, she gives as examples of socioeconomic injustice:

---

8 Fraser's account here is explicitly wedded to a Weberian understanding of the status group, which contrasts with what Simon Thompson calls the 'identity model' of recognition proposed by Taylor and Honneth – see Thompson (2006: 78-9) for an illuminating discussion of the contrast and its link to the norm of paritipatory parity. The avoidance of the 'identity model' is arguably, for the reasons discussed earlier in this chapter, a further commendation of Fraser's approach vis-à-vis disability politics. It avoids reifying culture and essentializing identities; recognition does not attach to a distinct, group-specific identity, but to the status of individual group members. On the other hand, the 'status model' itself, if endorsed wholesale, would direct attention away from certain psychic harms which will be regarded as important in any understanding of disablism as misrecognition. I am grateful to Simon Thompson for raising this point, which will be important to pursue in any overall appraisal of the relevance of Fraser's work for a recognition-centred account of disability politics.

> exploitation (having the fruits of one's labor appropriated for the benefit of others); economic marginalization (being confined to undesirable or poorly paid work or being denied access to income-generating labor altogether), and deprivation (being denied an adequate material standard of living). (Fraser 1997: 13)

Economic marginalization, especially, has been the target of much work done in the service of the disability rights movement.[9] While it is certainly not the case that all impairments will, for example, be seen as reducing productivity and so employability, there is legitimate scope for Oliver to claim that the continuing exclusion of disabled people from the world of work 'is the most important factor in what happens to us and the way we are treated by society' (Oliver 2009: 159; cf. Oliver 1990). The sphere of work has been a primary focal point of recent UK legislation on disability discrimination, and of incremental successes for the disability rights movement. The point need not be further laboured: there are clear cultural and economic dimensions to disability politics. Ruth Lister has written that this politics 'provides a perfect example of the two-dimensional social justice claims' which Fraser depicts (Lister 2007: 161). This makes the absence of disability at a discussion-point in Fraser's work all the odder. Arguably, of the currently prominent approaches taken in recognition theory, hers is especially well-placed to deal with the dimensions of subordination along the lines of disability.

Might then the goal of participatory parity, on Fraser's terms, provide an adequate frame for that politics? I would suggest that it might, but not by itself, and not solely on Fraser's own terms. For Fraser, the norm of parity of participation 'requires social arrangements that permit all (adult) members of society to interact with one another as peers' (Fraser 2003: 36). Consistent with her delineation of distinct forms of injustice, she identifies two conditions which must be satisfied in order for such parity to be possible – neither being sufficient on its own. One is the preclusion of impeding 'forms of and levels of economic dependence and inequality'. The other is that 'institutionalized patterns of cultural value express equal respect for all participants and ensure equal opportunity for achieving social esteem' (2003: 36). In the context of disability politics, these conditions correspond to those associated with the goal of 'independent living', as promoted by Shakespeare, Jenny Morris and others – with this conceived in terms of parity for disabled people facilitated through the service environment, and an escape from the asymmetrical power relations associated with the 'care' relationship. Much has been said about whether 'independence' as a goal is possible, or indeed desirable.[10] Yet as a goal, it is directly related by its proponents to the right of the disabled to 'take their place in society', and to 'fully participate' in it (Morris 1993: 7, 8). And its preconditions are typically conceived to equate to those which Fraser identifies

9 See Roulstone (2004) for an overview.

10 See, for a critical discussion, Smith (2001).

in connection with participatory parity: both a matter of material resources, and of the recognition of disabled people's right to autonomy.

This parallel is worth drawing because in both cases – participatory parity and independent living – we might question whether Fraser's economic and cultural conditions are sufficient, by themselves, to bring about the goal in question.[11] On the one hand, as already noted, disabled people have certainly, clearly, been disadvantaged along the lines of both kinds of impediment to parity. But whether due attention to these two dimensions would secure parity by itself is another matter.

As we saw earlier, one objection (emerging from debates within disability politics) to exclusively cultural accounts of oppression is that they cannot account for the specifics of embodied experience, and of the body – construed broadly, as including motor, cognitive and sensory aspects – as an ontologically distinct dimension of what it is to be disabled. One might apply a similar objection to a dual consideration of economic and cultural factors when seeking to explain and address disability. Both will avoid problems around biological reductionism, and crass methodological individualism. But even operating in tandem, they seem not to cover important aspects of the conditions of disability. These might include phenomenological factors, to do with the individual's perception of their own bodies, their experience of proprioception, of interaction with others and their environments. They might also include brute physiological factors which condition or inhibit or enhance or anyway influence the playing-out of a particular impairment, and its impact on the life of the person concerned. One way of putting this general line of objection is that, like much normative theory (see Calder 2008), Fraser's dualistic tack is insufficiently nuanced in its social ontology. Thus rather than denying or bracketing biology, we might do better to incorporate it within an account of disability which stresses the interplay between (i) the biological conditions of impairment, (ii) social and economic institutions and structures, and (iii) cultural intersubjectivity. As Scambler and Scambler (2003) put it, the individual is a complex, dynamic mix of psycho-organic and socio-cultural properties. To think about disability without factoring in this complexity – as arguably both the social model and Fraser's approach would recommend – is thereby going to miss out on important levels and aspects of disability, and of the injustices associated with it.

To help flesh out these points, it is worth considering the following table, offered by Berth Danermark and Lotta Coiavitis Gellerstedt in the course of a discussion of issues related to this chapter. The table outlines not two, but five 'analytical levels' applicable in disability research, in relation to employment but also wider social contexts:

---

11 For further discussion of this and related points in connection with the goal of participatory parity see Olson (2008); Calder (2010). It is important to note that Fraser herself has since acknowledged the need to include the political as a third dimension of justice – see Fraser (2005).

Table 6.1 Analytical Levels in Disability Research

Levels	Examples of mechanisms	Examples of contexts	Examples from a particular context: a specific work site	Examples of negative outcomes
Culture	Negative evaluation of a characteristic	Law	Employment procedures	Denigration, exclusion
Socio-economic	Profit, exploitation	Labour market	Organization of work tasks	Unemployment, slimmed organizations
Psychosocial	Relation-to-self	Social interaction	Relations in work team	Lack of self-esteem
Psychological	Feelings of pride and shame	Communication	Conversation during breaks	Withdrawal
Biological	Genetic factors	Noisy surroundings	Shop floor	Sensorioneural hearing loss

Source: Danermark and Gellerstedt (2004): 350

What the authors intend by this table is not some comprehensive account of everything disability 'is', but a more modest, preliminary point: that 'injustices to disabled people can be understood neither as generated by solely cultural mechanisms (cultural reductionism) nor by socio-economical mechanisms (economic reductionism) or by biological mechanisms (biological reductionism)' (ibid). Rather, to analyse disability we need to take into account a range of different levels, mechanisms and contexts. It is not just that it is 'safe' in normative terms to allow the personal and the bodily 'back in', alongside the now well-established social and economic factors. It is also, I would suggest, required in order to offer a fully adequate account of how it is that impairments come to be disabling, what disability is like, and how it links up with wider debates about social justice. The conditions of participatory parity are not just cultural and socio-economic; they are also psychosocial, psychological, and biological.

Conclusion: Capability and Participation

This chapter has developed a series of points. First: recent disability politics has to a great extent taken on the character of a struggle for recognition, and has developed a critique of the impacts of particular kinds of misrecognition. It is odd that those in the disability rights movement do not say more about recognition – and even odder that theorists of recognition say so little about disability. Second: the strengths and limitations of the social model of disability in many ways mirror those of recognition as a vehicle for politics. There are areas in which the social model, and recognition politics, can achieve far more than other theoretical approaches. But both can be over-extended; neither should be relied on exclusively, as a catch-all framework for the promotion of social justice. Third: Nancy Fraser's dualism between economic and cultural factors helps avoid a kind of 'cultural monism' which can be seen as damaging and delimiting both as a general normative/explanatory stance, and as a particular 'take' on the politics of disability. There are non-cultural dimensions both to the condition of disability, and to any satisfactory normative response to it. But fourth: we need to add in further dimensions too. Maldistribution and misrecognition do not, between them, 'cover all the bases' when it comes to accounting for disability as a social justice issue – that is, what is wrong about the forms of disadvantage associated with it, and what might count as adequately addressing those wrongs.

At this point, it is important to consider how we might best cover those bases, and incorporate those extra dimensions. I would suggest that a capabilities-based approach, along the lines of that developed by Amartya Sen (*inter alia* 1992, 1999) and Martha Nussbaum (*inter alia* 2000, 2007), offers much in this regard. I say along those lines, because for my money neither of those theorists themselves gives an adequate account of the issues covered in this chapter. But it seems to me that the capabilities approach points in that direction. It emerges, in Sen's work, as part of a critique of welfarist and resourcist approaches to distributive justice. For Sen, neither equality of welfare nor equality of resources are adequate in accounting for egalitarian concerns. We need more than an equal distribution of resources, because individuals differ in their capacity to turn resources into well-being. Resources are valuable not in themselves, but in so far as they enable us to function in certain ways. Welfarists focus instead on the satisfaction of preferences. But what we value in goods is separate from, and ranges wider than this. As Alexander Kaufman puts it, 'Tiny Tim may be happier and more satisfied with his share of goods than Scrooge is with his share, but this fact should not lead an egalitarian to redistribute goods from Tiny Tim to Scrooge' (Kaufman 2006: 1-2). The capability approach appeals to an alternative indicator of social justice: what human beings are actually able to do and be (Berges 2007: 16). For Sen, 'what matters to people is that they are able to achieve actual functionings, that is the actual living that people manage to achieve' – and so what is crucial is 'the freedom to achieve actual livings that one can have a reason to value' (Sen 1999, 74, 73).

What seems appealing about the capability approach, in the context of our discussion here, is the added range and depth of its focus, in addressing the scope for extending social justice. Thus to address the preconditions of 'achieving actual functionings' – which in my view must include participatory parity along the lines invoked by Fraser – will inevitably involve consideration of the multiple levels identified by Danermark and Gellerstedt. Capability can be fully afforded neither by redistribution (as Sen argues), nor by recognition, nor by a combination of the two. As Elizabeth Anderson argues, herself drawing on the capabilities approach,

> [T]o be capable of functioning as an equal citizen involves not just the ability to effectively exercise specifically political rights, but also to participate in the various activities of civil society more broadly, including participating in the economy … To be capable of functioning as a human being requires effective access to the means of sustaining one's biological existence – food, shelter, clothing, medical care – and access to the basic conditions of human agency – knowledge of one's circumstances and options, the ability to deliberate about means and ends, the psychological conditions of autonomy, including the self-confidence to think and judge for oneself, freedom of thought and movement. (Anderson 2004: 174)

Here we find the multiple dimensions just referred to. We also find, in my view, a fuller account of the particular complexity of the goals of disability politics than a recognition-centric approach would be able to provide. Fraser herself is resistant to invoking thick notions of 'the good life', and would find the capability approach too thick, too Aristotelian, for comfort. How justified this wariness might be is a topic for another day. And the claim that factoring in capability, along with further dimensions of analysis, might 'round out' Fraser's own approach and make good its promise, obviously needs further development to carry weight. I hope to have shown here that such further work is worth considering, and would enhance our understanding of the scope and aims of disability politics.

References

Abberley, P. 1987. The concept of oppression and the development of a social theory of disability. *Disability, Handicap and Society*, 2(1), 5-19.

Allen, B. 1999. Disabling knowledge, in *The Ethics of Postmodernity*, edited by G.B. Madison and M. Fairbairn. Evanston: Northwestern University Press, 89-103.

Anderson, E. 2004. Against luck egalitarianism: what is the point of equality?, in *Social Justice*, edited by Matthew Clayton and Andrew Williams. Oxford: Blackwell.

Barnes, C. and Mercer G. 2003. *Disability*. Cambridge: Polity.

Barnes, C. and Mercer, G. 2010. *Exploring Disability*. 2nd edition. Cambridge: Polity.

Berges, S. 2007. Why the capability approach is justified. *Journal of Applied Philosophy*, 24(1), 16-25.

Bickenbach, J.E., Chatterji, S., Badley, E.M. and Ustun, T.B. 1999. Models of disablement, universalism, and the international classification of impairments, disabilities and handicaps. *Social Science and Medicine*, 48(9), 1173-87.

Calder, G. 2005. Post-Cartesian anxieties: embodied subjectivity after the linguistic turn. *New Formations*, 56, 83-95.

Calder, G. 2006. Soft universalisms: beyond Young and Rorty on difference. *Critical Research in International Social and Political Philosophy*, 9(1), 3-21.

Calder, G. 2008. Ethics and social ontology. *Analyse & Kritik*, 30(2), 427-43.

Calder, G. 2010. Pragmatism, critical theory and democratic inclusion. *Etica & Politica*, 12(2), 52-67.

Cole, P. 2007. The body politic: theorizing disability and impairment. *Journal of Applied Philosophy*, 24(2), 169-76.

Danermark, B. and Gellerstedt, L.C. 2004. Social justice: redistribution and recognition – a non-reductionist perspective on disability. *Disability and Society*, 19(4), 339-53.

Finkelstein, V. 2004. Representing disability, in *Disabling Barriers – Enabling Environments*, edited by J. Swain, S. French and C. Barnes. 2nd edition. London: Sage, 13-20.

Fraser, N. 1997. From redistribution to recognition?, in *Justice Interruptus: Reflections on the 'Postsocialist' Condition*. London and New York: Routledge, 11-40.

Fraser, N. 2000. Rethinking recognition. *New Left Review* series 2(3), 107-21.

Fraser, N. 2003. Social justice in the age of identity politics, in *Redistribution or Recognition? A Political-Philosophical Exchange*, by N. Fraser and A. Honneth. London: Verso, 7-109.

Fraser, N. 2005. Reframing justice in a globalizing world. New Left Review series 2, 36, 1-19.

Fraser, N. 2008. Heterosexism, misrecognition, and capitalism, in her *Adding Insult to Injury*, edited by Kevin Olson. London: Verso.

French, S. 1993. Disability, impairment or something in between, in *Disabling Barriers, Enabling Environments*, edited by J. Swain, S. French, C. Barnes and C. Thomas. London: Sage, 17-25.

Honneth, A. 1992. Integrity and disrespect: principles of a conception of morality based on the theory of recognition. *Political Theory*, 20(2), 187-201.

Honneth, A. 1995. *The Struggle for Recognition*. Cambridge, MA: MIT Press.

Honneth, A. 2003. Redistribution as recognition, in *Redistribution or Recognition? A Political-Philosophical Exchange*, by N. Fraser and A. Honneth. London: Verso, 110-97.

Ikäheimo, H. 2010. Personhood and the social inclusion of people with disabilities, in *Arguing About Disability: Philosophical Perspectives*, by K. Kristiansen, S. Vehmas and T. Shakespeare. London: New York, 77-92.

Kaufman, A. 2006. Introduction, in *Capabilities Equality: Basic Issues and Problems*, edited by A.A. Kaufman. London: Routledge.

Laitinen, A. 2006. *Mutual Respect*. Paper to the Social Ethics Research Seminar, University of Wales, Newport, 22 May.

Lister, R. 2007. (Mis)recognition, social inequality and social justice: a critical social policy perspective, in *(Mis)recognition, Social Inequality and Social Justice*, edited by T. Lovell. London: Routledge, 157-76.

MacIntyre, A. 1999. *Dependent Rational Animals: Why Human Beings Need the Virtues*. Chicago: Open Court.

Markell, P. 2003. *Bound by Recognition*. Princeton: Princeton University Press.

Morris, J. 1993. *Community Care or Independent Living*. York: Joseph Rowntree Foundation.

Murphy, R. 1987. *The Body Silent*. London: Phoenix House.

Nussbaum, M. 2000. *Women and Human Development*. Cambridge: Cambridge University Press.

Nussbaum, M. 2006. *Frontiers of Justice*. Cambridge, MA: Harvard University Press.

Oliver, K. 2001. *Witnessing: Beyond Recognition*. Minneapolis: University of Minnesota Press.

Oliver, M. 1990. *The Politics of Disablement*. Houndmills: Macmillan.

Oliver, M. 1996. Defining impairment and disability: issues at stake, in *Exploring the Divide: Illness and Disability*, edited by Colin Barnes and Geof Mercer. Leeds: The Disability Press, 29-54.

Oliver, M. 2009. *Understanding Disability: From Theory to Practice*. 2nd edition. Houndmills: Palgrave.

Olson, K. 2008. Participatory parity and democratic justice, in *Adding Insult to Injury* by Nancy Fraser. London: Verso, 246-72.

Paterson, K. and Hughes, B. 2000. Disabled bodies, in *The Body, Culture and Society* by P. Hancock et al. Buckingham: Open University Press.

Rawls, J. 1971. *A Theory of Justice*. Oxford: Oxford University Press.

Rawls, J. 1993. *Political Liberalism*. New York: Columbia University Press.

Roulstone, A. 2004. Employment barriers and inclusive futures?, in *Disabling Barriers – Enabling Environments*, edited by J. Swain, S. French and C. Barnes. 2nd edition. London: Sage, 195-200.

Scambler, G. and Scambler, S. 2003. Realist agendas on biology, health and medicine: some thoughts and reflections, in *Debating Biology: Sociocultural Reflections on Health, Medicine and Society*, edited by S.J. Williams, L. Birke and G.A. Bendelow. London: Routledge, 53-66.

Scott-Hill, M. 2004, Impairment, difference and 'identity', in *Disabling Barriers – Enabling Environments*, edited by J. Swain, S. French and C. Barnes. 2nd edition. London: Sage, 87-93.

Sen, A. 1992. *Inequality Reexamined*. Oxford: Oxford University Press.

Sen, A. 1999. *Development as Freedom*. Oxford: Oxford University Press.

Shakespeare, T. 1992. A response to Liz Crow. *Coalition*, September, 40-42.

Shakespeare, T. 2006. *Disability Rights and Wrongs*. London: Routledge.

Smith, S.R. 2001. Distorted ideals: the 'problem of dependency' and the mythology of independent living. *Social Theory and Practice*, 27(4), 37-54.

Smith, S.R. 2005. Equality, identity and the disability rights movement. *Critical Social Policy*, 25(4), 554-76.

Swain, J., French, S. and Cameron, C. 2003. *Controversial Issues in a Disabling Society*. Buckingham: Open University Press.

Taylor, C. 1992. *Multiculturalism and the Politics of Recognition*. Princeton: Princeton University Press.

Terzi, L. 2004, The social model of disability: a philosophical critique. *Journal of Applied Philosophy*, 21(2), 141-58.

Terzi, L. 2010. What metric of justice for disabled people? Capability and disability, in *Measuring Justice: Primary Goods and Capabilities*, edited by Harry Brighouse and Ingrid Robeyns. Cambridge: Cambridge University Press, 150-73.

Thomas, C. 1999. *Female Forms: Experiencing and Understanding Disability*. Buckingham: Open University Press.

Thomas, C. 2004. Disability and impairment, in *Disabling Barriers – Enabling Environments*, edited by J. Swain, S. French and C. Barnes. 2nd edition. London: Sage, 21-7.

Thompson, S. 2006. *The Political Theory of Recognition*. Cambridge: Polity.

United Nations 2006. The United Nations World Programme of Action Concerning Disabled Persons. Available at: http://www.un.org/esa/socdev/enable/diswpa01.htm [accessed: 7 March 2008].

UPIAS 1976. *Fundamental Principles of Disability*. London: Union of the Physically Impaired Against Segregation.

Young, I.M. 1990. *Justice and the Politics of Difference*. Princeton: Princeton University Press.

Young, I.M. 1997. Unruly categories: a critique of Nancy Fraser's dual systems theory. *New Left Review*, 222, 147-60.

Young, I.M. 2000. *Inclusion and Democracy*. Oxford: Oxford University Press.

Chapter 7
"And Every Cruelty Will Cloud It"[1]: On Love, Damaged Selfhood and Criminal Harm[2]

Majid Yar

Introduction

Axel Honneth has developed, over a number of years, a distinctive theory of recognition, one that innovatively combines insights drawn from Hegelian philosophy, political theory, sociology and psychoanalysis (Honneth 1995, 1996, 2002, 2007). While this project has generated a not insignificant amount of critical commentary and engagement, such interventions have tended to focus on the more explicitly political dimensions of his work (see, for example, Thompson 2006; van den Brink and Owen 2007). In particular, attention has been directed to the question of whether recognition, as a foundation for moral-political life, can be analytically or practically distinguished from issues of material redistribution (see Fraser 1997; Yar 2001; Honneth 2001; Fraser and Honneth 2003; Thompson 2005). Considerably less attention has been devoted to one of the more intriguing dimensions of his theory, namely its 'philosophical anthropology' of moral development (what in the context of this article I call the 'ontogenetic thesis'). This component of Honneth's account deploys a developmental account of how individuals come to acquire the capacity to relate to others as moral subjects in their own right, thereby enabling them to engage with those others on a basis of mutual respect and affirmation. Drawing upon the relational psychoanalysis of D.W. Winnicott and Jessica Benjamin, Honneth situates the initial development of recognitive capacities in relations of 'love', those inter-personal and intimate interactions with parents and

1 This quote is taken from the song 'How Men Are' by Scottish New Wave group Aztec Camera, which appeared on their 1992 album appropriately entitled *Love*. I express my enduring gratitude to its writer, Roddy Frame ('the Scottish Bob Dylan') for inspiration over more years than I care to remember.

2 My thanks for comments and feedback to David Gadd, Natalia Hanley, and all those who participated in the ESRC Workshop on 'The Politics of Recognition and the Dynamics of Social Conflict', at the University of the West of England, in January 2008. The usual caveat nevertheless pertains, and any errors and shortcomings in this chapter are the responsibility of the author alone.

friends. Such development, Honneth postulates, provides the foundations for the individual's ability to form mutually affirmative relations in the wider spheres of intra-group belonging ('solidarity') and political citizenship ('rights'). However, this developmental account, for all its supposed significance, remains relatively under-explored in Honneth's writings, and its foundational contribution to public and political recognition remains under-analysed. Moreover, beyond general references to psychoanalytic studies, Honneth offers no empirical evidence to support the connection between early inter-subjective development and the adult's ability to recognize others as subjects worthy of moral consideration (as opposed to objects to be subordinated in pursuit of the self's desires). This chapter, drawing upon empirical research in criminology, aims to fill this gap, and to support (in a qualified manner) the claim that inter-personal experiences in the formative stages of childhood can and do exercise significant influence over the modes of moral engagement we favour as adults. Specifically, I will seek to demonstrate how the absence of 'love' (through neglect, abuse, and other similar harms) manifests itself in later dispositions to harm others, thereby empirically connecting misrecognition across the spheres of love, solidarity and rights. By proceeding in this way, I hope to demonstrate the value of Honneth's tripartite theorization of recognition, and to extend and enrich this theoretical model through empirical application.

The chapter is organized into three substantive sections. The first offers a brief analytical reconstruction of the basic 'ontogenetic' thesis about moral development in Honneth's work. Drawing upon relational psychoanalysis, I will postulate the mechanisms through which a 'distorted' development of selfhood can manifest itself in the truncation of individuals' ability to relate to others in a manner consistent with mutual recognition. The second section will review research findings relating to the social backgrounds of convicted offenders, in order to demonstrate the prima facie plausibility of a connection between harms experienced in childhood and harms inflicted in adulthood. In other words, misrecognition of the self in childhood can and does shape misrecognition of others in adulthood. The third section, building further this argument, will draw upon the psychosocial criminology of Gadd (2000, 2003, 2006), Jefferson (1998, 2004) and Gadd and Jefferson (2007a, 2007b) in order to demonstrate how such connections between the absence of 'love', the damage to selfhood, and the capacity to inflict criminal harm, become apparent in the psycho-biography of violent offenders. I conclude that empirical investigation of inter-personal relations in this way can illuminate the centrality of 'love' in the formation of moral subjectivity.

Inter-Subjective Moral Development and the 'Ontogenetic Thesis'

The starting point for Honneth's moral theory is a Hegelian critique of the foundations of liberal-individualist thought. From Locke to Kant (all their differences notwithstanding), liberal theorists have viewed the individual as a self-subsistent entity, 'always already' fully constituted as it enters the world. The moral and political problem thus becomes one of mediating, reconciling or balancing individual wills such that can each realize their autonomy and independence without interference from others (through a social contact in Locke's case, and through the promulgation of a universal moral will in Kant's). Against this 'monadic' ontology, Hegel argues that what he calls the 'independent consciousness' (equivalent to the sovereign individual of liberal theory) in fact exists in a paradoxical state of essential *dependence* upon others (Benjamin 1992: 189-90; also Gerson 2004). The individual comes to know himself, to recognize himself as a being with particular attributes or properties, through the acknowledgement conferred by an other. An individual's sense of worth remains mere 'subjective self-certainty', and hence uncertain of itself, unless that sense of worth (or 'idea-of-self') is affirmed by others (Kojève 1969: 11; also discussion in Crossley 1996: 16-21). This position is exemplified in Hegel's famous exposition of the 'Master-Slave Dialectic' in the *Phenomenology of Spirit* (Hegel 1977). Hegel hypothesizes a scenario in which a seemingly autonomous subject (the Master) enjoys unrestricted acknowledgement of his freedom from the other. The other (the Slave) exists in order to answer the desires and affirm the authority of the Master. However, in the very moment of his 'triumph' (the apparent realization of his self-conception as an autonomous, free individual), the Master is undone. Firstly, because his autonomy is non-autonomous, insofar as he can only come to experience himself as such through a relation of dependence on the Slave. The Master is in a reversal of positions, the Slave of the other because of this need, and the Slave is in fact the Master in that he enjoys the power to arbitrate or mediate recognition. Secondly, and of crucial importance, there is the 'incompleteness' or 'hollowness' of the self-affirmation that the Master experiences, in that the Slave is *compelled*, by virtue of his subordination, to recognize the Master. The Slave's recognition is *coerced*, forced from him through the basic asymmetry of his relationship of servitude to the Master. As Kojève (1969) notes, this is the essence of the Master's 'tragedy', that recognition of his value or worth can only be experienced as meaningful or 'real' if it is granted *freely* (rather than forced) from another who is simultaneously recognized as free in his own right. In other words, we only value recognition if it comes from who we deem worthy of granting it, and who can choose to do otherwise if they did not feel such esteem. The upshot is this analysis is twofold. Firstly, it demonstrates that self-realization cannot be anything other than an inter-subjective endeavour, and that the forging of a coherent sense of selfhood (self-esteem) is dependent upon recognition from others. Secondly, it shows that for recognition to work it must of necessity be a *mutual* relationship, one in which each recognizes the other's autonomy, freedom and human value. It is from this grounding that Honneth (along with other contemporary theorists of recognition, such as Charles Taylor (1994)) derives a moral-political vision for a just society, one in which public institutions mediate something akin to universal recognition of all by all, a mutually self-sustaining relationship of affirmation.

Honneth further develops his theory of recognition through a reading of Hegel's *Philosophy of Right* (1991). In particular, Honneth (1996) discerns three distinctive social modes or levels of recognition, each corresponding to a different institutionalization of social and political relations.[3] At the level of formal political systems (coincidental with Hegel's notion of the state), we find the institutionalization of respect, the universal recognition of value appropriate to membership of the human community as such. In practical terms, respect is mediated through legal rights in which are embedded fundamental principles of mutual regard. At the level of intra-group solidarity (continuous with Hegel's formulation of civil society), we find recognition in the form of solidarity, mechanisms of mutual esteem that acknowledge the value of shared cultural characteristics and social identities. At the level of intimate relations (corresponding to the Hegelian family) we find love, which is to be understood as 'referring to primary relationships insofar as they – on the model of friendships, parent-child relationships, as well as erotic relationships between lovers – are constituted by strong emotional attachments among a small number of people' (Honneth 1996: 95). In relations of love, one is recognized not as a rights-bearing subject equivalent to all others, nor as the holder of common traits shared with other members of a social group, but in one's particularity, by virtue of traits and characteristics that are unique to oneself. Honneth is careful to analytically and practically distinguish these different levels of recognition, and to identify the appropriate social spheres in which they are to be satisfied. Thus, for example, it would be a mistake to model a political-democratic project upon the recognitive vectors of intimacy, seeing the polity as a gesture of love 'writ large' (as would be the case if we derive a political imperative from the Christian imperative to 'love thy neighbour'). Love, by its nature, is exclusive and particular, and cannot be indefinitely extended (at least the intimate, inter-personal conception of love that is under consideration here). Likewise, it warns us of the dangers inherent in using group solidarity and cultural specificity as the basis of political life, in that such commonalities necessarily exclude others who do not share that group's defining traits (as, for example, when religious identities or ethnic backgrounds are promulgated as the grounds of national membership). It also rejects the notion that a political order founded on formal rights alone suffices, seeing a rights-only conception of the political as deracinated and excessively 'thin' in substantive ethical commitments.

For Honneth, the three spheres of recognition co-exist, each satisfying an essential dimension of our need for affirmation from others. However, it can be argued that love (despite the supplemental or background role it plays in

3 The question of whether in fact Honneth follows Hegel in assigning different modes of recognition to distinct spheres has divided his readers. For example, Thompson (2006: 25) claims that 'he rejects the idea that each particular mode of recognition can be experienced only in a particular institutional location'. In contrast, I take Honneth to largely defend such a differentiation, based upon the sociological insight that different forms of social action are functionally, practically and normatively associated with different social sub-systems (cf. Parsons 1982; Alexander 1992; Luhmann 1996).

Honneth's theory) enjoys a kind of primacy vis-à-vis its counterparts (solidarity and respect). This is, firstly, because love temporally precedes the others; it is the first form of recognition for which we strive, corresponding to the earliest stages of life. Secondly, and perhaps more importantly, it takes ontological precedence insofar as it is the experience of recognition-as-love that forms the bedrock of our selfhood and establishes the basic affective and behavioural disposition that we later take out into the wider world. Honneth (1996: 38-9, 103-4) acknowledges this role when he talks of love as imparting 'basic self-confidence', the core of a healthy, 'undistorted relation to self' (107-8). In other words, we can suggest that the experience of recognition (and just as significantly misrecognition)[4] in formative inter-personal relationships exercises a powerful influence over the extent to which we learn to realize our selfhood through mutual recognition of others. This is what I call the 'ontogenetic thesis', the putative role played by love in the genesis of the morally responsible and responsive social subject. The precise mechanisms through which such capacity might be acquired are outlined below.

Honneth's understanding of recognition-as-love is derived from a reading of D.W. Winnicott's 'object-relations' approach to psychoanalysis, alongside Jessica Benjamin's explicitly Hegelian and inter-subjective recasting of this tradition. The classic Freudian model treats the psychic subject as a self-contained entity (Benjamin 1992: 184), and the psychodrama of development comprises a conflict between internal or intra-psychic elements (id, ego, superego). Insofar as external others play a role, it is as contingent objects onto which internal desires and strivings are projected through the play of fantasy (Bienenfeld 2005: 73-4):

> In the traditional psychoanalytic view, human psychology is driven by the impulse to express instinctual drives, and it is in order to do this successfully that relationships with others are formed. In object relations theory, this order of events is reversed, Freud's instincts being replaced by an assumption that humans are fundamentally relationship-seeking creatures ... libido is object-seeking rather than pleasure-seeking (Frosh 1987: 96)

Thus Winnicott breaks with the Freudian formulation in at least three important respects. Firstly, others become real agents who interact with the individual and crucially shape his development through such interaction (Phillips 1988: 7-9).

4 An analytical distinction must be drawn here between non-recognition and misrecognition. The former entails an absolute refusal to acknowledge the existence of the other as a human subject, while the latter entails an act of recognition that is 'distorted' or 'incomplete' in the sense that it fails to constitute the other in accordance with either their fundamental human needs and/or their self-conception as a fully constituted social subject. However, in practical terms, almost all instances of what we might call 'a refusal of recognition' in fact take the form of misrecognition: a subject is recognized in some sense or other, but not in a manner consistent with the requirements of a full and complete affirmation of a subject.

Secondly, the Freudian focus upon libidinal drive is displaced by an associational impetus, a desire to connect with others as the fundamental imperative that moves human individuals. Thirdly, Winnicott focuses upon the pre-Oedipal stage; prior to any sexual drama in which desire confronts the symbolic father, we see the developing individual's relationship with the mother/carer as of fundamental importance for self-constitution.

Winnicott identifies a number of developmental stages through which the individual self takes shape in the context of the dyad of the 'nursing couple'. In the earliest stages of infancy, the self (as a distinct entity differentiated from the environment outside itself) has yet to form. The infant experiences its environment as an undifferentiated field, continuous with itself, rather than as an independent external realm. The infant, experiencing its environment in this way, makes incessant demands and expects its desires (for comfort, food, etc) to be instantaneously gratified (a situation akin to Freud's formulation of 'primary narcissism'). The role of the mother-carer at this point is to subordinate herself to these demands, so that the developing infant can experience a reality that is amenable and responsive to its needs. However, a point is reached in the developmental movement in which the child begins to undergo separation-individuation, that is to experience itself as a bounded entity apart from its environment, and to experience the environment as an independent reality with its own properties that cannot simply by subordinated or transformed by the child through the act of will. It is at this point, with the loss of 'illusory omnipotence' (Frosh 1987: 106), that a fundamental difficulty comes to the fore. If the environment, including the mother-carer, is independent, then the child is vulnerable to that environment, insofar as it may not answer the child's needs. As Benjamin (1992: 190) puts it, 'she or he can move away from mother – but mother can also move away from her or him'. This occasions a powerful anxiety, the fear that the other will not answer the child's needs, the fear of abandonment. If the mother-carer responds appropriately, the child will develop its sense of individuality safe in the knowledge that the other can be trusted to provide the care and nurturing it needs; while mother is a separate subject with an independent will of her own, she chooses to recognize the child's needs and responds to them. This is the basis of what Honneth calls 'basic self-confidence', the normalized expectation that one's fundamental needs will be met. It is also the basis of self-confidence, the realization that others love the individual sufficiently to care, and that the individual is deserving of such responsiveness. One comes to experience oneself through the eyes of others, and if that experience is one of care and nurture, then the self experiences itself (through reflexive self-understanding) as fundamentally whole. This situation constitutes a balance of independence and dependence – one is able to experience one's dependence on others as safe and pleasurable, thereby freeing oneself be a confident individual without being immured in anxiety about one's vulnerability in an otherwise potentially hostile world. The emergence of such a self furnishes the basis of all subsequent inter-subjective encounters, and thus provides the template of a positive relation-to-self and relation-to-other.

However, the failure to find a healthy inter-subjective settlement, the balance of dependence and independence through relations of mutual recognition, can have profoundly pathological consequences for the individual's selfhood. This occurs when the environment does not respond to the child's needs, when it comes to be experienced not as benign and reliable, but as hostile or indifferent. This can happen when the mother-carer withdraws from the child (either through her prolonged physical absence, or through her emotional unavailability). Equally, it occurs when the child's expressed needs are met not with appropriately caring gestures, but with violence, retaliation and punishment. In all such instances, the child cannot find a path out of its anxiety, as its worst fears about its vulnerability and dependence upon others are confirmed. In such a situation, trust in others and basic self-confidence cannot emerge, as the child experiences others as inimical to its well being, and itself as unworthy or worthless in the eyes of others. The inability to find a healthy and self-assured form of separateness and independence consequently manifests itself in a range of pathological symptoms. For example, the child's neglected or abused body comes to stand as an unbearable and anxiety-provoking form of weakness, from which he seeks to dissociate himself. 'The psyche attempts to disown the body which, due to maternal neglect, is felt to be a persecutor' (Phillips 1988: 95-6). The body, as the mark of perceived weakness and vulnerability, must be eliminated, resulting in destructive forms of self-harming. Equally, the inability to accept the environment as trustworthy and reliable produces a pathological pattern of 'reality-testing', in which the child incessantly provokes others, as he cannot come to accept that it will not ultimately let him down by withdrawing or retaliating. This, for Winnicott, is the source of much supposedly 'delinquent' and 'anti-social' behaviour observed amongst 'troubled' children (17, 68-9). Finally, if the child experiences himself as worthless in the eyes of others, that despised self become subject to an operation of defensive splitting and projection. The individual separates from himself that 'worthless' element and projects it outwards onto others. Self-loathing is thus transformed into a pathological loathing of others, misrecognition of self becomes an entrenched pattern of refusing to recognize others who 'stand in the place of' the damaged self that is too painful to acknowledge. Winnicott is at pains to stress that such behavioural pathologies are a form of 'attempted self-cure' by the individual concerned (1988: 50), the attempt to master and manage the anxiety set in place by the failure to develop an appropriate and secure form of 'dependent independence'.

The forgoing discussion is intended to establish the *prima facie* plausibility of connecting early experience of care, nurture and love to the emergence of a capacity to engage in relations of mutual recognition. The viability of such an explanation of moral development (the genesis of moral ontology, or ontogenesis) can, I argue, be empirically validated, rather than remaining a plausible (yet defeasible) hypothesis. One way in which this can be done (and will occupy the rest of this chapter) is to examine those individuals who refuse recognition to others through the perpetration of criminal harms, and attempt to trace this pattern of misrecognition to a 'damaged selfhood' which emerges from formative experiences of inter-subjective encounters. However, a significant caveat must at this point be noted. It would be all too easy to take this developmental hypothesis as a linear and rigid chain of causation, such that all instances of misrecognitive disposition could clearly find their singular causal antecedent in childhood. However, we must acknowledge that such a mono-causal explanation is unsustainable, as many and varied contingent factors can intervene and mediate between formative development and adult behaviour. We can certainly envisage situations in which those deprived of early experiences of love-as-recognition nevertheless become adults who are capable of demonstrating considerable sensitivity to the needs of others. Indeed, psychotherapeutic interventions and the establishment of loving relations in later life can do much to repair damaged and fractured selves, offering a path out of pathological patterns of attempted resolution. In short, the social and psychological biographies of individuals are too complex and multi-faceted to sustain any reductionist causality where it comes to moral development. Nevertheless, I would support the claim that childhood experience of love (and its absence) can and do play a significant role in moral socialization. Therefore, what is defended here is an amended and more modest ontogenetic thesis, one that supports connections between childhood and adult experience, but does so in acknowledgement of other intervening variables that can exercise significant influence. Ontologically and epistemologically, this approach is consistent with a critical realist standpoint that sees human behaviour as an emergent property of complex, multi-causal interactions and combinations of elements, such that no empiricist and reductive postulations of causality are possible (Sayer 1999: 13-16).

Offenders' Experiences of Neglect and Abuse: The Criminological Case

I have elected to focus here upon those convicted of criminal harms because the perpetration of such acts against others stands as an exemplar of misrecognition (be it in the form of love, solidarity or respect). In harming others in this way, individuals inevitably deny others proper recognition of their status as autonomous and esteem-worthy beings deserving of respect and solicitude. Indeed, as Honneth (1996: 20) notes, Hegel had already made the connection between crime and the refusal to recognize others as bearer of legitimate rights and entitlements. This is not to say that all actions dubbed 'crimes' entail misrecognition in this way; indeed, given that the power relations sustaining inequality often shape what is considered as 'crime', criminalization itself can be seen as a form of misrecognition (an obvious case here would be the historic criminalization of sexual minorities such as homosexuals, who have found themselves refused recognition – in terms of love, rights and esteem – precisely because their identities and actions have been deemed criminal). However, I take as my focus here the specific subset of crimes that deal with violent harm, and treat them as legal prohibitions that formalize the moral intuition that subjecting others to such harm is a violation of their rights and autonomy. To this extent, we can treat crime as a form of misrecognition.

The field of developmental criminology focuses upon the underlying or primary developmental processes of offending behaviour, which are often examined through broad-based cohort studies that seek to uncover the experiential and social correlates of criminal behaviour. A proportion of such studies have examined the prevalence of childhood experiences of physical punishment, neglect, violent maltreatment, and sexual victimization amongst offender populations (for example, Malinosky-Rummell and Hansen 1993; Ferguson and Lynskey 1997; Siegel and Williams 2003). Given the limitation of space available, a systematic survey of this literature is not possible within the present piece. Therefore, I will confine myself to some indicative research findings that bear most directly on the propositions under examination.

With respect to childhood sexual abuse, the relationship with a propensity to offend (particularly violent offending) is contested. Some studies (for example, Reich and Gutierres 1979; Zingraff et al. 1993) found no statistically significant correlation between self-reported sexual victimization in childhood and the likelihood of violent offending (as measured through formal arrest rates). In contrast, Baskin and Sommers' (1998) study of convicted violent female offenders found that 36 per cent of the sample (n.170) self-reported having been sexually abused by an immediate family member, while 26 per cent reported abuse at the hands of someone from their extended family. The correlation becomes more consistent and clear when we expand our view beyond childhood sexual victimization to also examine other forms of violent abuse and neglect. In their review of the research literature, Malinosky-Rummell and Hansen (1993: 70) report that 'adolescents who exhibit aggressive and violent behaviours, including extrafamilial and dating violence, demonstrate higher rates of maltreatment than do the general population'. Similar patterns are apparent amongst adult offenders. For example, Sack and Mason (1980) found that men convicted for violent offences (including sexual offences) had much higher rates of childhood physical abuse than non-convicted male control groups (similar conclusions were reached by McCord (1983) who found significant connections between violent offending and parental aggression). Loeber and Stouthamer-Loeber (1986) reviewed the significance of familial factors as predictors of adult offending and found the most important to include 'poor parental supervision, parental rejection of children … low parental involvement with children, parental conflict and antisocial parents' (Farrington 2002: 669). Family breakdown (and the breakdown of normalized trust, care and reciprocity that this might entail) has been consistently correlated with offending; Morgan (2002: 1138) reports that 23 per cent of incarcerated offenders (and 38 per cent of those under 21 years of age) have previously been taken into care as children.

While the foregoing research data is certainly suggestive of a link between childhood maltreatment and later dispositions to commit harms, it must be understood as inconclusive for a number of reasons. Firstly, such studies encounter perennial problems of sampling and the biases that might arise from its selectivity. Only a small proportion of those who perpetrate offences (including violent offences and sexual crimes) will actually be prosecuted and convicted; therefore, research based upon known offender populations tells us nothing about those others who have not been convicted, and whose salient social and personal characteristics may be significantly different from those studied. Moreover, given that participation in retrospective studies is voluntary, the significant proportion of those approached who decline participation can further result in an unrepresentative sample. As Young (2004) concludes, the selectivity of sampling can all too readily skew research findings, presenting a distorted picture of the actual experiences prevalent amongst any notional population. Secondly, the self-report nature of these studies (in which participants are invited to reveal their childhood experiences of neglect and abuse) raises significant questions about truth telling. There may be a complex range of factors that variously incline respondents to under- or over-report such experiences. For example, respondents may make recourse to narratives of abuse as a way in which to deflect responsibility for their own harmful behaviour, and/or to deal with the feelings of guilt and shame their own behaviour may occasion – what Sykes and Matza (1957) term 'techniques of moral neutralisation'. Conversely, feelings of shame and self-recrimination may make it difficult for respondents to share details of traumatic and emotionally charged childhood experiences with researchers. Finally, and perhaps most fundamentally, all such studies are basically limited since, while they can demonstrate correlation between two variables (in this case childhood neglect/abuse and later criminal dispositions), they cannot demonstrate causation (that is, that the latter behaviours are the causal consequences of the former experiences) (Malinosky-Rummell and Hansen 1993: 68). Indeed, such correlation studies are notoriously weak when it comes to offering plausible explanatory hypotheses; where they are attempted, they all too often take the form of rather psychologically crude and reductive propositions such as reasserting 'a sense of power believed to have been lost as a result of the victimization' or 'a misplaced expression of anger' (Siegel and Williams 2003: 85). For all of the above reasons, such findings must of necessity be supplemented by more careful study that explores in detail the possible causal connections between formative absences of love-as-recognition and the later moral non-responsiveness to others.

Psychosocial Criminology: Offender Psycho-biography and the Experiential Roots of Harm to Others

Psychosocial criminology is an innovative approach for analysing and explaining offending, developed largely through the work of criminologists David Gadd (2000, 2003, 2006) and Tony Jefferson (1996, 1998, 2004) (see also Gadd and Jefferson 2007b for a systematic overview of the psychosocial approach). The approach differs from much conventional criminological research in that it goes beyond identifying correlations between offending and social characteristics (class, gender, ethnicity, locality, etc.) and seeks to understand the complex psychic worlds of offenders themselves. Unlike the traditions of cognitive, behavioural, or evolutionary psychology, it views human actions as embedded in self-understandings that emerge from relational interactions and encounters in social life. Crucially, individuals are viewed as 'defended subjects' who are fragmented and 'anxiously managing (repressing, splitting and projecting) thoughts, feelings and memories that threaten the integrity of the self' (Gadd 2000: 430). This conforms to the view, expressed earlier, that 'pathological' psychic strategies for managing anxiety are likely in response to traumatic experiences in which love-as-recognition is not available. Methodologically, the psychosocial approach eschews quantitative data collection in favour of detailed psycho-biographical narratives unearthed through the technique of Free Association Narrative Interviewing (FANI) (see Hollway and Jefferson 2000 for a detailed explication of this method). Where such access through research interviews is not possible, the approach makes recourse to existing (secondary) biographical and documentary sources. Through such research it attempts to uncover the psychodynamics that shape individuals' understanding of self and others, and which furnish the essential emotional contours of experience and action. Below I shall draw upon a number of salient examples of such psychosocial analysis (in the form of abbreviated case-studies) in order better to support empirically the ontogenetic account of moral capabilities, and specifically the importance of childhood experiences of love-as-recognition for shaping adult conduct.

Case 1: 'Gary'

Gadd (2000) presents a case study of 'Gary', a 26-year-old white male undergoing counselling as a result of repeated violent assaults upon his girlfriend. Gadd invites Gary to share his earliest memories. Salient here is that he reveals his confusion when, aged 4, his parents separated and his father found a new partner. As a result of now having a 'step mum', he was told he now could no longer address his mother as 'mum':

> I can…remember being told that I wasn't allowed to call me mum, 'me mum' anymore. I had to call her 'Aunty Emily'. Which really confused me at times, coz I didn't understand why…I knew she were me mum. (432)

He goes on to recount 'feeling really like lonely', 'not really bothering to try and make friends with anybody else', and running out of school early to meet his mother (434).

When he goes on to talk about his violence towards his girlfriend, 'Rebecca', the experiences of childhood reappear in his narrative. Violence is triggered when

Rebecca (at least in Gary's view) refuses to accept his statements or assertions at face value. Gary narrates his reaction thus:

> And I'd just get so frustrated and angry because when I were younger a lot of the time I seemed to be, just not believed by my parents…They'd just not believe me. So I'd get really frustrated. The same thing, I'd get really frustrated by the fact that somebody wouldn't believe me. I'd just get unbelievably angry about it. And I'd just start screaming and shouting and throwing things around. Just like basically having a tantrum….just like completely lose it, and go completely over the top. Like breaking things and chucking things and punching holes in stuff and hurting Rebecca. (435-6)

What are we to make of this 'not being believed', and its wider place in the aetiology of Gary's violence? I would suggest that the childhood experience of 'not being believed' is fundamentally problematic for Gary in that such experience amounts to not being recognized by those who matter most to him in terms of shaping his self-understanding. Such understanding has already been undermined by the loss of his mother. Gadd (439) further argues that Rebecca's non-recognition of Gary's views (echoing his childhood experiences) is perceived as a threat of her separation, withdrawal, or independence from him. For Gary, independence means maternal withdrawal, and withdrawal is synonymous with abandonment, the disappearance of love and care. Moreover, we can suggest that the early experience of his mother's disappearance from the childhood scene is doubly problematic, as he is denied the ability to even communicatively sustain their bond – 'I wasn't allowed to call me mum, "me mum" anymore'. Also significant here is that Gary not only harms others, but has a history self-harm including two suicide attempts (438). Taken together, we can read his violence-against-self and violence-against-others as symptoms of the same psychodynamic of splitting and projection. Gary, unable to accommodate or integrate his experiences of anxiety attending his childhood loss of love and care, splits off the part of his self that suffers such weakness and projects it elsewhere. His own (unloved, unheld) body becomes associated with weakness and he attempts to eradicate it through alcohol, drugs and suicide. Equally, this weak self is projected outward onto his partner, who comes to 'stand in for' the unbearable feelings of un-acknowledgement, which he then attempts to eradicate through violence.

Case 2: Mike Tyson

Jefferson (1996, 1998) offers a fascinating psychosocial reading of the 'criminal career' of Mike Tyson. Lacking access to Tyson himself, Jefferson makes recourse to a wide range of journalistic and biographical sources, alongside interviews with individuals who encountered Tyson (such as his appellate lawyer, Alan Dershowitz) (Jefferson 2004: 36). The question Jefferson sets out to answer is how did 'a millionaire boxer with the world apparently at his feet manage[d] to "blow it" so comprehensively?' (Ibid.). Why did he end up in a destructive downward spiral resulting accusations of sexual assault and domestic violence, culminating in a prison sentence for rape? The answer is, Jefferson argues, to be found in Tyson's biography, whose psychosocial reading I suggest can offer fruitful insights into the connections between childhood experience and adult violence.

As is widely documented, Tyson grew up in profoundly inter-personally and socially dislocated circumstances. His father left Tyson's mother prior to his birth, and he grew up in extreme deprivation in the 'ghetto' of Brownsville, Brooklyn. His alcoholic mother, Lorna, was repeatedly brutalized by a series of boyfriends, and died when Tyson was aged 16 (Saraceno 2005). The environment outside the home offered little respite, as Tyson found himself victimized by others, mocked as a 'little fairy boy' because of his soft-spoken lisping. Thus he was 'poor, abandoned, neglected, unsettled, odd and bullied' (Jefferson 1986: 155). Tyson developed into a passive child, a disposition that only earned him further victimization. While this passivity earned him appellation as a 'good boy', Jefferson suggests that 'inside' he felt anything but. From our perspective, Tyson's emerging selfhood was scarred and assaulted by repeated deprivation of the love and care needed to form basic confidence in self and trust his environment (it is no surprise that, to this day, he is dogged by perpetual feelings of worthlessness and insecurity – 'I'll never be happy. I believe I'll die alone. I would want it that way. I've been a loner all my life with my secrets and my pain. I'm really lost…I'm really a sad, pathetic case' – Saraceno 2005). However, at some point in his life this apparent passivity was transformed into outwardly expressed rage and violence, manifest through participation in a street gang, repeated run-ins with the law, followed by periods of incarceration in juvenile detention. The story of the 'turning point' has, as Jefferson (1996: 159) notes, become part of the 'Tyson myth' (as with other African-American boxers, such as Muhammad Ali and the story of the 'stolen bicycle'[5]). However, what matters most here is the transformation itself. One psychosocial reading of this change is that Tyson, unable to contain the feelings of anxiety and shame induced though misrecognition, internalized the overwhelmingly negative responses of others and identified with them. Others' denigration of weakness and effeminacy ('little fairy boy') was adopted as his own subjective standpoint. That part of Tyson that was the target of these symbolic and physical violations was split-off from his self and projected outwards onto others. Thus internalized self-hatred

5 This is the oft-told (and retold) story of how as a 12-year-old Ali (then Cassius Clay) came to learn to box. There are a number of variants, but the basic details remain the same. As a young boy his bicycle was stolen, and he reported this to Joe Martin, a police officer who just happened to run a boxing gym on a part-time basis. Ali vowed that he was going to 'whup' whoever was responsible. Martin advised the furious boy to learn about boxing before trying to take on anyone in a fight, and invited Clay there and then to come to his gym (an invitation that, of course, was accepted, and which set the stage for a rise to fame as one of the greatest ever professional boxers) (Hauser 2004: 18).

became hatred towards others, and violence against his 'abandoned, neglected and bullied' self was transformed into an attempted resolution through the bullying and violation of others. Ray et al. (2004) likewise note this pattern of shame, projected outward as rage, in their study of perpetrators of racist violence). This is nowhere more apparent than in Tyson's violent and violating relationships with women. The effeminate 'fairy boy' he perceived himself to be through the eyes of others was simultaneously loathed and denied, resulting in a misogynistic rage directed towards women who represented everything dangerous for his ramshackle attempts to forge an indestructible 'hyper-masculine' self, a self invulnerable to his hostile environment.

Case 3: 'Toby'

Our final vignette is drawn from Erwin James' 'prison notebook', *A Life Inside* (2003). James, who served 20 years in prison for a life sentence, offers an insightful viewpoint not only upon the British penal system but also a view into the subjective experiences and social biographies of its inhabitants. The particular individual concerned here is a young man James identifies as 'Toby'. Incarcerated at 17, he progresses through a series of maximum-security custodial institutions over the next 14 years. His patterns of violent behaviour are a marked feature of his time in prison, including 15 assaults against prison officers. James (2003: 44) notes that Toby 'certainly hated all forms of forms of authority figures', even adopting as his "surrogate family" political prisoners from the IRA (Irish Republican Army). In James' view 'being seen to "side" with the "Irish cause" was his way of demonstrating his utter contempt and loathing for "the system"'. However, James judges that 'behind the aggressive body language and big talk he was a vulnerable, emotionally stunted adolescent' (44). This damage and vulnerability is horrifyingly clear when Toby demonstrates what he calls his 'party trick' to fellow inmates, pulling down his pants and setting his pubic hair afire with a lighter (60).

The key insight into the connection between Toby's emotional vulnerability, self-harming and his propensity for violence (especially directed towards 'authority') emerges some time later:

> There was a knock on my cell door and Toby pushed it open. "I need to talk" he said. "I've just been in the governor's office. The police are coming to see me. It's about what happened to me when I was a kid in the home … One of the other lads who's my age has made allegations about some of the care staff and the police want to interview us to see if it happened to anyone else".
>
> Toby sat with his head bowed as he told me this. He started to tell me more, then his upper body began to shudder and I realized he was crying. I understood immediately that those tears had been a long time coming. I placed my hand lightly on his shoulder, and I cried too'. (Ibid.: 61-2)

While we are told nothing about the circumstances under which Toby was first taken into care, it is reasonable to conclude that a fairly fundamental breakdown of his family circumstances must have occurred in order to necessitate intervention by the state. Here, then, is his first experience of loss, the rupturing of the child-parent bond. As Winnicott notes in his study of wartime evacuee children, such separation is profoundly disruptive for the individual's developing sense of trust and self-confidence. Yet it can be managed if the replacement environment offers 'good enough' reassurance through sympathetic engagement on the part of carers, including a sense of continuity of care through the otherwise traumatic changes being experienced (Phillips 1988: 63-4). Alas in Toby's case, we see that the opposite occurred: his needs for care and reassurance to help him manage loss of parenting went not only unanswered, but his trust in the environment and others was shattered through subjection to sexual abuse by his putative 'carers'. We can suggest that his behaviour in adolescence and adulthood are (ultimately doomed and destructive) attempts to manage the feelings of anxiety, weakness, self-loathing and rage induced by the experience of childhood neglect and abuse. It is no coincidence that his self-harming is directed towards the genitalia; given the sexual abuse inflicted upon him, this part of his body becomes associated with weakness and vulnerability, something he must disown and attempt to eradicate. Similarly, his unremitting hostility to 'authority figures' indicates a displacement of affect developed in the context of institutional abuse. 'Authority' is associated not with legitimacy but with suffering, and as the source of this suffering it must be assaulted until the feelings it evokes recede. Toby's association with the IRA prisoners, we can suggest, is contingent, in that it does not indicate any political affiliation on his part. What matters is that these men stand in an analogical relationship to authority with himself: he and they (the abused child, the Irish) are both the powerless victims of a dominant authority (abusive 'carers', the British state).

It is further important to note that, according to James (2000: 62-4), Toby's demeanour undergoes a 'dramatic change' in the weeks after his confessional encounter with James and subsequent visits from the police. His normally erratic, volatile and violent behaviour gives way to a much calmer, considered and conciliatory disposition; talk rather than explosive violence becomes his means for dealing with conflict with prison staff and fellow inmates. It is not unreasonable to suggest that Toby's exchanges with James function for practical purposes as a kind of therapeutic encounter. After decades of splitting and projecting from himself the vulnerable child who was helpless in the face of his abusers, he finally acknowledges that child as himself, and starts down a path of self-healing by reintegrating that disowned element. 'Taking possession' of himself in this way forecloses the need to project his anxiety and sense of weakness outward onto others. Others start to become subjects in their own right, rather than readily available objects upon which he can project feelings and experiences that he cannot bear to accept as his own. In James' phrase, Toby has started to 'lay his ghosts to rest'.

Conclusions

This chapter's starting point was a sympathetic reception of Axel Honneth's tripartite model of inter-subjective recognition. I sought, firstly to elaborate the connections between these modes, specifically the importance of early experiences of love-as-recognition for the development of moral capabilities in adult life. Following Honneth's cues, I made recourse to relational psychoanalysis in order to unpack the role played by formative psycho-relational encounters in this regard. Secondly, I sought to furnish some empirical evidence that supports this 'ontogenetic' hypothesis. Drawing upon development criminology, I have suggested that we can observe such connections at work in the over-representation of abused and neglected children amongst violent offender populations. Going further, I have drawn upon the psychosocial criminology of Gadd and Jefferson to offer psychoanalytically informed readings of individual offender case studies. What these readings suggest is that the inability or unwillingness to relate to others as independent subjects deserving of recognition can be fruitfully explained (at least in some cases) through appreciation of the psychic processes set in play as a result of the formative absence or loss of love-as-recognition. Misrecognition of the self in childhood forecloses the capacity to relate to others in a way that balances independence and dependence, translating vulnerability and anxiety into domination and violence. In this dynamic we begin to see clearly how love furnishes the basic architecture of moral sensitivity, and the key role it plays in the wider configuration of public life. The implication for social and political theory is that it must needs look beyond the sphere of political socialization and education in its search for the roots of injustices; it must look beyond the 'public' realm to the domain of 'private' relationships if we are to better grasp how and why individuals come to refuse recognition to others, and how we might better set about formulating meaningful strategies for rectifying such problems.

References

Alexander, J. 1992. *Theoretical Logic in Sociology: Modern Reconstruction of Classical Thought: Talcott Parsons* v. 4. Berkeley: University of California Press.

Baskin, D.R. and Sommers, I.B. 1998. *Casualties of Community Disorder: Women's Careers in Violent Crime*. Boulder, CO: Westview.

Benjamin, J. 1992. Recognition and Destruction: An Outline of Intersubjectivity, in *Relational Perspectives in Psychoanalysis*, edited by N.J. Skolnick and S.C. Warshaw. Hillsdale, NJ and London: Analytic Press, 61-117.

Bienenfeld, D. 2005. *Psychodynamic Theory for Clinicians*. Philadelphia, PA: Lippincott Williams and Wilkins.

Crossley, N. 1998. *Intersubjectivity: The Fabric of Social Becoming*. London: Sage.

Farrington, D.P. 2002. Developmental Criminology and Risk-Focused Prevention, in *The Oxford Handbook of Criminology*, 3rd edition, edited by M. Maguire, R. Morgan and R. Reiner. Oxford: Oxford University Press, 657-701.

Ferguson, D.M. and Lynskey, M.T. 1997. Physical Punishment/Maltreatment During Childhood and Adjustment in Young Adulthood. *Child Abuse & Neglect*, 21(7), 617-30.

Fraser, N. 1997. *Justice Interruptus: Rethinking Key Concepts of a Post-socialist Age*. London: Routledge.

Frosh, S. 1987. *The Politics of Psychoanalysis: An Introduction to Freudian and Post-Freudian Theory*. Basingstoke: Macmillan.

Gadd, D. 2000. Masculinities, Violence and Defended Psychosocial Subjects. *Theoretical Criminology*, 4(4), 429-49.

Gadd, D. 2003. Reading Between the Lines: Subjectivity and Men's Violence. *Men and Masculinities*, 5(4), 333-54.

Gadd, D. 2006. The Role of Recognition in the Desistance Process: A Case Analysis of a Former Far-right Activist. *Theoretical Criminology*, 10(2), 179-202.

Gadd, D. and Jefferson, T. 2007a. On the Defensive: A Psychoanalytically Informed Psychosocial Reading of The Jack Roller, *Theoretical Criminology*, 11(4), 443-67.

Gadd, D. and Jefferson, T. 2007b. *Psychosocial Criminology: An Introduction*. London: Sage.

Gerson, G. 2004. Object Relations Psychoanalysis as Political Theory. *Political Psychology*, 25(4), 769-94.

Hauser, T. 2004. *Muhammad Ali: His Life and Times*. London: Robson Books.

Hegel, G.W.F. 1977. *Phenomenology of Spirit*. Oxford: Oxford University Press.

Hollway, W. and Jefferson, T. 2000. *Doing Qualitative Research Differently*. London: Sage.

Honneth, A. 1995. *The Fragmented World of the Social: Essays in Social and Political Philosophy*. New York: SUNY Press.

Honneth, A. 1996. *The Struggle for Recognition: The Moral Grammar of Social Conflicts*. Cambridge: Polity.

Honneth, A. 2001. Recognition or Redistribution?: Changing Perspectives on the Moral Order of Society. *Theory, Culture & Society*, 18(2-3), 43-55.

Honneth, A. 2002. Grounding Recognition: A Rejoinder to Critical Questions. *Inquiry*, 45, 499-520.

Honneth, A. 2007. *Disrespect: The Normative Foundations of Critical Theory*. Cambridge: Polity.

Jefferson, T. 1996. From "Little Fairy Boy" to the "Complete Destroyer": Subjectivity and Transformation in the Biography of Mike Tyson, in *Understanding Masculinities: Social Relations and Cultural Arenas*, edited by M. Mac and Ghaill. Milton Keynes: Open University Press, 153-67.

Jefferson, T. 1998. Muscle, "Hard Men" and "Iron" Mike Tyson: Reflections on Desire, Anxiety and the Embodiment of Masculinity, *Body & Society*, 4(1), 77-98.

Jefferson, T. 2004. From Cultural Studies to Psychosocial Criminology: An Intellectual Journey, in J. Ferrell, K.J. Hayward, W. Morrison and M. Presdee (eds) *Cultural Criminology Unleashed*. London: GlassHouse Press, 29-40.

Kojève, A. 1969. *Introduction to the Reading of Hegel*, A. Bloom (ed.). New York: Basic Books.

Luhmann, N. 1996. *Social Systems*. Palo Alto, CA: Stanford University Press.

Malinosky-Rummell, R. and Hansen, D.J. 1993. Long-Term Consequences of Childhood Physical Abuse. *Psychological Bulletin*, 114(1), 68-79.

McCord, J. 1983. A Forty Year Perspective on the Effects of Child Abuse and Neglect. *Child Abuse and Neglect*, 7, 265-70.

Morgan, R. 2002. Imprisonment: A Brief History, The Contemporary Scene, and Likely Prospects, in The *Oxford Handbook of Criminology*, 3rd edition, edited by M. Maguire, R. Morgan and R. Reiner. Oxford: Oxford University Press, 1113-67.

Parsons, T. 1982. *On Institutions and Social Evolution*. London: University of Chicago Press.

Phillips, A. 1988. *Winnicott*. London: Fontana.

Ray, L. Smith, D. and Wastell, L. 2004. Shame, Rage and Racist Violence. *British Journal of Criminology*, 44, 350-68.

Reich, J.W. and Gutierres, S.E. 1979. Escape/Aggression Incidence in Sexually Abused Juvenile Delinquents. *Criminal Justice and Behaviour*, 6, 239-43.

Sack, W.H. and Mason, R. 1980. Child Abuse and Conviction of Sexual Crimes: A Preliminary Finding. *Law & Human Behaviour*, 4, 211-5.

Saraceno, J. 2005. Tyson: "My Whole Life has been a Waste", *USA Today* [Online, 13 June] Available at: http://www.usatoday.com/sports/boxing/2005-06-02-tyson-saraceno_x.htm [Accessed 4 January 2008].

Sayer, A. 1999. *Realism and Social Science*. London: Sage.

Siegel, J.A and Williams, L.M. 2003. The Relationship Between Child Sexual Abuse and Female Delinquency and Crime: A Prospective Study. *Journal of Research in Crime and Delinquency*, 40(1), 71-94.

Sykes, G. and Matza, D. 1957. Techniques of Neutralization: A Theory of Delinquency. *American Sociological Review*, 22, 664-70.

Taylor, C. 1994. *Multiculturalism: Examining the Politics of Recognition*, Amy Gutman (ed). Princeton, NJ: Princeton University Press.

Thompson, S. 2005. Is Redistribution a Form of Recognition? Comments on the Fraser-Honneth Debate. *Critical Review of International Social and Political Philosophy*, 8(1), 85-102.

Thompson, S. 2007. *The Political Theory of Recognition: A Critical Introduction*. Cambridge: Polity Press.

Van den Brink, B. and Owen, D. 2007. *Recognition and Power: Axel Honneth and the Tradition of Critical Social Theory*. Cambridge: Cambridge University Press.

Yar, M. 2001. Beyond Nancy Fraser's "Perspectival Dualism". *Economy & Society*, 30(3), 288-303.

Young, J. 2004. Voodoo Criminology and The Numbers Game, in J. Ferrell, K.J. Hayward, W. Morrison and M. Presdee (eds) *Cultural Criminology Unleashed*. London: GlassHouse Press, 13-28.

Zingraff, M.T., Leiter, J., Myers, K.A. and Johnsen, M.C. 1993. Child Maltreatment and Youthful Problem Behaviour. *Criminology*, 31, 173-202.

Chapter 8
Recognition and Esteem: A Case Study of the Struggles of People Affected by Leprosy[1]

Ricardo Fabrino Mendonça

The concept of recognition has fostered a deep renewal in critical theory. Faithful to the Frankfurtian legacy, it offers fine-grained analytical tools for the comprehension of injustices and for the ongoing quest to surmount them. In this sense, the notion of misrecognition is a key dimension of the framework advanced by Honneth, Taylor and Fraser. Misrecognition is constitutive of recognition to the extent in which it functions both as a problem to be overcome and as an engine that propels conflicts over moral grammars. The study of recognition necessarily involves paying attention to misrecognition.

If misrecognition may steer the advancement of recognition, the opposite also seems to be the case. Some scholars have argued that struggles for recognition can promote new forms of misrecognition, thus obstructing justice (Fraser 2003; Markell 2003; Mendonça 2011). Most of these criticisms are mainly concerned with the importance Honneth attributes to social esteem. According to him, the permanent attempt of presenting oneself as valuable and worthy of esteem helps to promote social bonds, fostering broad solidarity in complex societies. The role of esteem for social justice is, nevertheless, highly controversial. Some fear that demands for esteem may reify collective identities, generating more oppression (Fraser 2003; Markell 2003). Others argue that some demands for esteem may lead to harmful social competition that grounds new sorts of misrecognition (McBride 2009; Seglow 2009).

I claim, however, that this does not have to be the case. Struggles over the realm of social esteem do not necessarily lead to misrecognition. Actually the kernel of the criticisms directed at recognition are based on the interpretation that struggles for esteem are battles for the positive reception of collective identities. Such an interpretation does not do justice to Honneth's notion of esteem. The importance of social esteem for self-realization should not be reduced to the idea of valuing specific group attributes.

---

1 A version of this chapter has originally been published by *Political Studies.* Article first published online: 17 January 2011 (p. 1-19).

In this chapter I want to evince this point and to illustrate it through a case study, analysing the struggles of people affected by leprosy. Obviously, former patients do not seek the appreciation of their disease. Individuals that have had leprosy do not aim at promoting some sort of admiration for their shared attribute. And yet, esteem is a central dimension of their struggles against misrecognition.

The chapter is divided in two main parts. In the first one, I will support a Honnethian definition of social esteem that does not reduce recognition to *identity politics*. I will also point out some controversies within Honneth's definition, drawing insights especially from Jonathan Seglow (2009). In the second part of the chapter, I will analyse how esteem permeates the struggles against misrecognition of people affected by leprosy in Brazil. This analysis is based on focus groups held in former Brazilian Hansen's Disease[2] colonies and in a newsletter published by Morhan (Movement for the Reintegration of People Affected by Hansen's Disease). The analysis reveals, first of all, that esteem is at the heart of what these individuals see as justice. It also reveals that there are several ways of struggling for esteem that do not reinforce misrecognition.

The Role of Esteem in Recognition

Axel Honneth (1996) argues that a sufficiently differentiated notion of recognition is the best theoretical tool for the interpretation of social struggles and for the contestation of disrespect. Placing self-realization at the heart of justice, the German philosopher claims that three realms of interaction have become essential in contemporary western societies: 1) primary relationships provide the necessary emotional support that grounds the emergence of self-confidence; 2) legal relations provide a universal sort of respect that allows individuals to build self-respect; 3) communities of values foster social esteem, which is at the heart of the possibility of self-esteem. This article is particularly concerned with the third realm of recognition.

Based on both Hegel and Mead, Honneth (1996: 121) claims that 'in order to be able to acquire an undistorted relation-to-self, human subjects always need – over and above the experience of affectionate care and legal recognition – a form of social esteem that allows them to relate positively to their concrete traits and abilities'. Different from legal respect, which does not accept degrees or differentiations, social esteem allows individuals to be valued in their specificities. 'Persons can feel themselves to be 'valuable' only when they know themselves to be recognized for accomplishments that they precisely do not share in an undifferentiated manner with others' (Honneth 1996: 125).

Individuals' traits and abilities are evaluated daily according to the way they are seen as contributing in some sense to the accomplishment of collective goals. The

2 The use of the term leprosy has been legally banned in Brazil since the 1970s. It has been replaced by Hansen's Disease (*Hanseníase*).

thing is that some individuals face a situation of permanent misrecognition. Their attributes or ways of life lead to *a priori* denigration, no matter what they do. They cannot be seen as contributing to society because they are not perceived as worthy of social esteem. Some individuals may be always perceived as filthy, immoral, ignorant or unimportant. Misrecognized from the start, some may even be seen as a burden to society.

However the values that steer these evaluations are historical and, thus, susceptible to change. Individuals that feel that their traits and abilities are often belittled may struggle for the transformation of socially shared patterns of interpretation. According to Honneth, struggles for esteem are important for the moral development of society, because they foster the idea that every individual should have the chance to be seen as valuable. In doing so, these struggles promote social solidarity. If esteem is symmetrical, every person can be seen as contributing to societal goals in a certain way. This process is important for binding people together in contemporary societies, as it promotes 'that kind of special consideration we owe to each other insofar as we participate jointly in the realization of a project' (Honneth 1997: 32).[3]

It is important to highlight that Honneth's definition of esteem does not imply everyone should be esteemed equally, nor that individuals should be esteemed because they share a specific collective attribute. Thompson (2006: 74) points out that, for Honneth, persons 'are not esteemed simply because they are associated with a particular culture or because they have a particular social identity, but rather because they possess specific features which distinguish them as unique individuals'. Honneth (1996: 29-130) himself has highlighted that symmetry of esteem does not mean everybody should receive the same amount of social esteem. Essentially, it means that nobody should be denigrated on the basis of their identity.

It is thus incorrect to associate struggles for social esteem with battles for the positive evaluation of one's identity. However, this sort of association is very frequent. It emerges, for instance, on the trivalent framework used by Feldman (2002) to analyse disrespect. In distinguishing maldistribution, misrecognition and political exclusion, he clearly links misrecognition to a cultural evaluation of identities.[4] The association also grounds the arguments of some scholars who claim that struggles for esteem foster new types of misrecognition.

Nancy Fraser (2003) and Patchen Markell (2003) are interesting examples in this sense. The former claims that Honneth empties the notion of esteem by advocating esteem should be equally distributed.[5] She believes that the quest for collective

---

3 For a clear explanation of this argument, see Smith (2009: 56).

4 The trivalent approach presented by Feldman (2002) anticipates the ideas developed by Fraser in her recent publications.

5 I am referring here to a very specific point of Fraser's critique to Honneth. The debate between them is obviously more complex. Fraser (2000; 2001; 2003) proposes a significant shift in the notion of recognition, by advocating a *status model* steered by the idea of *parity of participation*. She is mainly concerned with a theory of justice that thinks of disrespect

admiration can reify identities and hinder the contestation of injustices. In the same direction, Patchen Markell (2003) equates the idea of recognition to a struggle for self-affirmation, assuming Honneth advocates some sort of public approval for collective entities. From Markell's perspective, the theory of recognition could only produce more oppression because it is based on a will to sovereignty. As explained by him, one of his central arguments

> is that the politics of recognition is characterized by central important misrecognitions of its own – not misrecognitions of identity, but failures to acknowledge one's own basic ontological conditions – and that these arise from the fact that the pursuit of recognition expresses an aspiration to *sovereignty*. (Markell 2003: 10)

However, as long as esteem is not equated to the affirmation of difference, Markell's and Fraser's fear seems unwarranted. In attempting to show that these criticisms do not do justice to his ideas, Honneth has further clarified his definition. His replies to the critics emphasize that esteem should be thought of in terms of *achievement*, and not in terms of collective attributes (Honneth 2001; 2003). He argues that the emergence of capitalist societies has created the conditions for an individuation of esteem, in which esteem is distributed 'by individual achievement within the structure of the industrially organized division of labor' (Honneth 2003: 140). Prestige started to be awarded on the basis of merit, according to standards of productivity.

The problem, nonetheless, is that what is characterized as 'important work' ends up undervaluing other social activities, such as those of the housewife or mother. One of the problems of capitalist societies is that they have a severely restricted conception of 'valuable contribution', which does not consider contributions that are not located in the labour market (Honneth 2003; Hartmann and Honneth 2006). In an interview given to Anders Petersen and Rasmus Willig (2002: 273), Honneth states, for instance, that he considers outrageous the fact that our societies cannot make persons with disabilities feel socially needed. Individuals who are not seen as productive or whose productions are not valued by contemporary capitalist frameworks have their contributions undervalued or misrecognized.

From this perspective, struggles for esteem challenge this sort of misrecognition. They are attempts to change the patterns of distribution of both prestige and the resources associated to it. As explained by McBride and Seglow (2009: 8-9), 'for Honneth, the primary terrain on which struggles for particular esteem recognition takes place is the economy which ostensibly distributes social esteem according to

---

not in terms of negative impacts to self-formation but in terms of hindrances to parity of participation. Fraser claims that recognition and redistribution are both essential for the promotion of justice, and policies that target disrespect should be built deliberatively in the public sphere. I have dealt with this debate in detail in another paper (Mendonça 2009b). My point here is simply that she misinterprets Honneth's understanding of social esteem.

the "achievement principle"'. Hence, struggles for esteem should not be understood as competitions to show oneself as better than others. They should be thought of as fostering a process of reciprocal understanding in which individuals 'learn to understand themselves as subjects possessing abilities and talents that are valuable for society' (Honneth 2003: 142). Through esteem, individuals do not seek to be recognized as members of a cultural group, but as cooperative members of society.

If Honneth (2003: 168) has made it explicit that social esteem is not directed at cultural groups, his definition is still broad enough to encompass different meanings. Several scholars point out that the notion remains somehow imprecise in his work. Geoff Boucher (2004), for instance, notices that esteem could be distributed by division of labor, by abstract societal goals or by concrete attributes of individuals. He argues that Honneth has changed his mind, even if he does not acknowledge it. This shift would become evident in the replacement of *solidarity* by *merit* and *achievement* in Honneth's recent formulations (Boucher 2004; Cooke 2008: 94).

Seglow (2009) suggests that, more than a shift, Honneth's conception of esteem would carry two different meanings. On the one hand, social esteem could be granted according to personal achievements. On the other hand, social esteem could be distributed on the basis of the contributions that individuals offer to society. For Seglow (2009), there would be a tension between these two definitions:

> On the achievement view, individuals are focused on individual striving [...] There may be difficulties in fostering a common ethos. On the contribution view, by contrast, society regards itself as a community of members, each of whom is able in some way to satisfy common needs and interests. [...] Solidarity is more easily explained on this later view. (Seglow 2009: 70)

Seglow's point is that merit and contribution are not synonyms. According to him, the latter would be compatible with solidarity, but struggles are often based on claims of achievement that challenge social cohesion. Struggles for esteem might, therefore, stimulate a competitive sort of politics that does not lead to a 'common ethos'. Such competition may lead to new forms of injustice and misrecognition, affecting the way people treat each other and, consequently, the structure of individual psyches.

This point is also made by McBride (2009), according to whom the struggle for esteem may be a dangerous political enterprise. Citing Rousseau, he claims that this type of struggle 'has a dynamic that always risks turning a reasonable concern with *amour propre* into an unreasonable compulsion to hierarchically distinguish ourselves from others' (McBride 2009: 106). It is important to highlight that McBride acknowledges that esteem recognition should not be eradicated, because it is important for the emergence of stable personalities (2009: 104). However, he argues that esteem should not be seen as the focus of the politics of recognition, especially if we are to think of policies implemented by the state. 'While the pursuit of esteem may be relatively harmless at the individual level [...], at the collective level it risks pitching us into a morally unacceptable and politically destabilizing politics of competition and hierarchy' (McBride 2009: 107).

If Seglow and McBride accurately point out a tension within Honneth's conception of esteem, they somehow seem to simplify the effects of this tension. The public exhibition of one's achievements does not necessarily lead to destabilizing social competition, although this may be the case. Showing one's achievements may also be a way to confront taken-for-granted meanings that reduce one's existence to useless (or harmful) survival. If the *unreasonable compulsion to hierarchically distinguish ourselves from others* may indeed lead to new forms of misrecognition, the act of showing one's achievements may also ground deep challenges to existent injustices.

An analysis of the struggles of people affected by leprosy in Brazil reveals exactly this point. It also reveals that social esteem should not be equated to the affirmation of differences. Struggles for esteem play an important role even when the appreciation of a shared attribute is definitely not at stake. These struggles can be seen as attempts to challenge the symbolic patterns that prevent these individuals from being seen and regarded as estimable. More than a quest for public approval, it should be seen as a quest for the contestation of misrecognition.

Case Study: The Struggles of People Affected by Leprosy

Leprosy is a chronic illness 'that mainly affects the skin, the peripheral nerves, mucosa of the upper respiratory tract and also the eyes, apart from some other structures' (World Health Organization 2009). The initial symptoms of leprosy are patches on the skin that have a loss of sensation to heat, touch or pain. As the disease evolves, nerve damages and disabilities are also frequent. It is mainly transmitted through long and intimate contact with an ill person who has not undergone treatment. However, more than 80 per cent of human beings are believed to be resistant to *Mycobacterium leprae*.

Leprosy has been a curable disease since the early 1940s. It has been eliminated as a public health problem for most countries.[6] In spite of that, around 240 thousand cases are diagnosed every year, according to the latest statistics of the World Health Organization (WHO 2010). India and Brazil are responsible for approximately 70 per cent of these cases.

Besides this problem, one cannot talk about leprosy without referring to its history of stigma. Throughout centuries, and based on different justifications, persons affected by the disease have been segregated and systematically disrespected (Gould 2005; White 2001; Gussow 1989). They have been seen as challenges to: the idea that men were made according to God's image; the anthropocentric ideals of sovereign men; the civilizing process; and the aesthetic and productive ideals

6 The elimination of leprosy as a Public Health Problem is achieved once the prevalence rate of a country is less than one case per 10,000 persons.

of contemporary societies (Mendonça 2007). This complex web of meanings that constitute the stigma has generated a variety of social practices, including exclusion from communities, symbolic funerals and massive segregation.

The history of leprosy is therefore constitutively marked by experiences of misrecognition, since the conditions for the formation of healthy self-relationships have been systematically denied to most patients. Injustice, disrespect and structural oppression were and are central features of millions of lives, thus hindering the possibility of self-realization. Honneth's tridimensional approach to disrespect seems to apply perfectly to this case, as the misrecognition of former patients involves: 1) the impossibility they have faced to freely dispose of their own bodies according to their will; 2) the recurrent denial of certain rights; and 3) the systematic and aprioristic depreciation of their value as individuals.

The first form of disrespect becomes clear if one pays attention to the frequent physical abuses to which they were subjected: collective drownings, incinerations, imprisonments, sterilizations and "scientific" experiments were recurrent. There are several narratives about the transportation of patients in sealed railway wagons in the early 1900s, as well as stories about children taken away from their parents as soon as they were born. Physical punishment was "therapeutically" adopted in most colonies, assuring order within these institutions.

The second form of disrespect is also very clear in the history of leprosy. Richards (1993: 159) recalls that, in the Middle Ages, the exclusion of a diseased person changed her/his status: the individual "became a non-person, unable to bequeath or inherit property, to defend his claims in court etc.". Béniac (1997: 136) also points out that leprosy "conferred to its victims a special legal status". More recent examples of the denial of rights may be found throughout most of the 20th century in the form of compulsory hospitalization, which led to the loss of several civil liberties, such as the right to come and go and to self-expression. Isolation also abolished any effective possibility of participation in society, and imposed severe restrictions on the experience social rights. Many leprosy patients were forbidden to study, removed from their jobs and conveyed to institutions in which they were compelled to work under the justification of *labour therapy*.

The third form of disrespect to illustrate the misrecognition of leprosy patients is evident in the lasting *stigmatization* of the disease. Tied to moral impurity since ancient times, leprosy has always been associated with degrading meanings. In these imaginaries – permanently updated through discourses and social practices – recurring myths speak of a disease that causes the decay of life, also bringing up images of hordes of mendicant lepers. Ugliness, unproductiveness, dehumanization and filthiness are constant elements when thinking of leprosy.

If misrecognition is so strong in the history of leprosy, it is also important to note the existence of practices through which people have struggled against it. There are several occasions in which individuals collectively sought to rectify historic and symbolic values that have denied them the possibility of self-worth. It is important to mention here the successful struggle of former Japanese patients for financial compensation in the early 2000s. Long before that, between 1930 and 1960, the

American national leprosarium of Carville had witnessed a powerful political struggle led by Stanley Stein (Gussow 1989: 160; Gould 2005). The United States has also been the stage for the work of civic associations, such as the American Legion which gathered war veterans who had acquired the disease overseas. One of these veterans, John Early, was considered a pioneer of leprosy activism, engaging with the issue in the beginning of the 20th Century (Gussow 1989: 145). Even before that, in 1870, Hawaiian patients and family members had violently risen up against insular isolation (Gussow 1989: 100).

Brazil has also had its history of struggles. It is worth mentioning the diligent work of Alice Tibiriçá in the first half of the 20th century and Abrahão Rotberg's international campaign to change the name of leprosy to Hansen's Disease in the 1970s. In contemporary Brazil, there are also associations concerned with people affected by leprosy. The most active and representative of them is Morhan (Movement for the Reintegration of People Affected by Hansen's Disease), which was founded in 1981. Morhan has 62 branches spread throughout Brazil, involving roughly two thousand activists. Since its creation, Morhan has fought for the elimination of leprosy and for the reintegration of those affected by it. The movement has managed significant accomplishments, including participation in several governmental bodies. In 2007, it promoted a series of demonstrations aimed at supporting a bill that would compensate individuals who had been compulsorily segregated. The bill was transformed into a Presidential Decree and it was later approved in both legislative houses. The Law 11.520 has already benefited more than 5,800 former patients.

Morhan's claims can be conceived of as struggles for recognition. Its demands include struggles for love, rights and social esteem, in an attempt to assure the possibility of self-realization for those affected by leprosy.[7] It proposes new moral grammars that seek to alter patterns of behavior and intersubjective relationships. The social movement thus provides interesting data for the analysis of struggles for social esteem.

In order to collect this data, I have observed meetings, seminars and events organized by Morhan during a period of four years, besides conducting several non-structured interviews. More importantly, for this article, I have read and summarized the stories published in all the 45 issues of the movement's newsletter (*Jornal do Morhan*). I have paid particularly close attention to the 20 issues published between 1988 and 2007.

The dimensions of recognition (love, rights and esteem) were coded every time they emerged in texts. This process of coding did not aim at comparing,

7 Morhan's struggles for love include demands related to the situation of children who were separated from their parents; claims for relatives not to abandon patients; campaigns to alter the relationship between physicians and patients; and arguments about the importance of touching. Struggles for rights involve civic, political and social rights, which aim at guaranteeing equality and dignity in society. Struggles for social esteem will be the focus of my analysis.

quantitatively, the significance of each realm of recognition for Morhan. It was used to identify how each realm of recognition was discursively presented by the movement's official newsletter.

It would be a mistake, nevertheless, to restrict the struggles of people affected by leprosy to the demands presented by a social movement. Citing Bourdieu, Honneth (2003: 118) points out that 'the overwhelming share of cases of everyday misery are still to be found beyond the perceptual threshold of the political public sphere'. Misrecognition often remains invisible. In order to collect the more imperceptible demands for recognition, I have conducted twelve *discussion groups* in former leprosy colonies situated in three Brazilian states: Acre, Ceará and Minas Gerais. These groups were audio-recorded and the tapes were transcribed. The transcriptions have been coded according to the dimensions of recognition.

In what follows, I present an analysis of different ways in which the dimension of social esteem emerges in the struggles of people affected by leprosy. This analysis combines the data collected in Morhan's newsletter with the data collected in conversation groups. I seek to map how the realm of social esteem permeates claims, so as to show that there are several ways of struggling for it that do not aim to affirm difference. Struggles for social esteem do not necessarily create new forms of misrecognition. The demonstration of one's achievements does not necessarily foster destructive social competition.

The Struggles for Social Esteem of People Affected by Leprosy in Brazil

The data analysed points to the existence of three main ways of struggling for social esteem. The first one, very important in the context of leprosy, refers to the contestation of negative meanings that undervalue individuals *a priori*. The second way of struggling for social esteem is to show how former patients contribute to important social goals, such as public health. The third way is to challenge the crystallized idea that leprosy patients are useless through the demonstration of personal achievements.

Confronting stigma

The contestation of negative meanings and metaphors that define leprosy is a key element of the struggles of people affected by the disease. Former patients realize that prejudice severely reduces their chances to be esteemed, since it frames them as despicable, disgusting and unproductive. Stigma grounds misrecognition and challenges the symmetry of esteem, because it places these individuals at the bottom of social hierarchies, also depriving them of the possibility of being esteemed.

The centrality of stigma becomes evident in the way injustice is defined. Several narratives point to the existence of disrespectful practices, as shown by the examples below:

> **Eduardo (Group 12)**: I suffered when I tried to get a professional driver's license. I felt embarrassed, because they said I couldn't. They told me I was incapable, because of the disease. I felt humiliated.

> **Osmar (Group 6)**: it would be better to be an outlaw, a thief… anything bad. At least, we would be healthy and we wouldn't be stigmatized. If we were arrested, we would be able to come back after a while. But the Hansen's disease patient will never be able to say he was… He is! He is a leper! He can never say he no longer is. […] No compensation can pay for the dreams I had. I wanted to be something. I wanted to grow up and to build something.

These fragments show how individuals use stigma to define injustice. Stigma creates significant hurdles to their aspirations, contradicting normative expectations of fair treatment. It continuously indicates their situation of misrecognition. In the second statement, Osmar claims that stigma attaches its connotations to individuals, depriving them of their singularities. People always tend to see the stigmatized attribute, further attaching depreciated identities to subjects. This process would hinder individuals that wanted 'to be something', 'to grow up' and 'to build something'. It prevents them from being perceived as valuable and estimable.

Although former patients are highly skeptical about the possibilities of actually overcoming stigma, they have proposed some strategies that may be capable of diminishing the strength of such stigmas. Several comments made by them suggest the need to establish a continuous conversation with society that would demystify the disease. Health campaigns are an important part of this conversation, as they would enlighten society about the scientific and biological dimensions of the disease.

> **Ana (Group 1):** If people know and have information, especially the right information about Hansen's Disease, their prejudices will diminish.

Morhan is deeply engaged in this process of demystification. It constantly publishes bio-medical information about the disease and relentlessly states that 'Hansen's disease is curable'. Besides its newsletter, the movement produces 'textbooks, cartoons, books, folders and advertisements'.[8] An influential activist recalls that 'the elimination of prejudice requires the clarification of this pathology to society'.[9] Seeking to amplify social conversation, the movement highlights the importance of debating leprosy 'with schools, churches, physicians, associations and the media'.[10] It suggests including the issue in school curricula,[11] and it has

8 *Jornal do Morhan* (*JM*), n.40, 2004, p. 12.

9 *JM*, n.39, 2004, p. 10.

10 *JM*, n.30, 1999, p. 6.

11 *JM*, n.25, 1998, p. 13.

established partnerships with several universities.[12] Broad and diffuse conversation is considered essential because the 'diminishment of stigma is related to an effective transformation of societies' ethical and cultural standards'.[13]

The media can also play an important role in this process. Morhan dedicates several articles of its newsletter advising its activists how to deal with media professionals. It highlights that journalists can become extremely important allies.[14] Celebrities could also be significant actors in the struggle against stigma. They can shed light on issues that have been invisible, 'since a famous person advocating something is more newsworthy than you or I doing so' (Parkinson 2003: 147). In Brazil, several musicians and television stars have supported Morhan.

Besides lending their visibility to the issue, celebrities may also contribute in attaching positive meanings to leprosy, as explained by a colony resident:

> **(Group 10) Nair**: Label is what matters, my friend. It is the label! Do you understand? [...] So, if a famous person [hugs Carolina] 'Oh, I will hug Carolina; Carolina has Hansen's disease, but I will hug her, because that famous guy has hugged her'.
>
> **Carolina**: Solange Couto [renowned Brazilian actress] has taken a picture with her, so I want one too'. [laughs]
>
> **Nair**: The label of someone with leprosy is rotten! Our label is rotten, because the word in itself says everything. It reproduces the stigma. [...] I think we should mobilize these famous people. [...] People like things that have media, fame, status, you know?

In this conversation, two women suggest that celebrities might be able to link the disease to positive images therefore contesting their ('rotten!') label. As celebrities express some of society's ideals and projections, they can help in challenging the stigma of leprosy.

The importance attributed to the media and to its celebrities can also be seen in the continuous work of *media watch*. In many occasions, colony dwellers and Morhan activists have denounced newspapers and broadcasters for reproducing stigma. They mainly criticize the use of the word 'leper', the publication of jokes about the disease and the association of the illness to images related to 'pieces falling apart' or to some sense of incapacity. Most of the time, they say that their complaints are not heard. When they feel they have affected media narratives, however, they celebrate it.

A story told by Carolina illustrates this point. She sent several letters to a broadcasting company, complaining about the existence of prejudice in a soap

---

12 *JM*, n.39, 2004, p. 5.

13 *JM*, n.27, 1999, p. 2.

14 *JM*, n.28, 1999, p. 7/*JM*, n.30, 1999, p. 12.

opera. She was already skeptical about the fruitfulness of this strategy, when she noted that the characters of another soap opera had raised the issue of leprosy in a non-stigmatized fashion.

> **Carolina (Group 10):** At that point, I felt like a winner! Because if I had not complained, they wouldn't have contradicted what they had said in the other soap opera.

The way activists and colony residents emphasize the relevance of information and the role of the media against stigma evinces their belief in the potential of broad and diffuse social conversations in challenging degrading notions. Clearly, this battle against stigma can be thought of as part of a larger struggle for esteem. If the negative meanings attached to the disease are contested, it will become possible for these individuals to be perceived as estimable. Confronting stigma is a powerful way to foster the symmetry of esteem and to overcome one of the bases of their misrecognition. It is thus evident that the search for esteem may not be based on the affirmation of differences. Esteem is sought here through challenges to *a priori* denigration.

Protecting society: some contributions of persons affected by leprosy

A second way of struggling for esteem consists in showing that persons affected by leprosy offer important contributions to society. The struggle moves one step forward here as activists and colony residents claim they can help society to achieve some of its goals.

The statements analysed suggest that the major contribution persons affected by leprosy claim to offer society is their persistent effort for the elimination of the disease. Medical information abounds in Morhan's newsletter, and the movement is constantly engaged in campaigns for early diagnosis. Morhan often presents its actions and strategies aimed at eliminating the disease. It claims to help when advising governmental actors; when divulging information; when keeping governmental authorities accountable; and when articulating different social actors. In all the issues of Morhan's newsletter, there is news about the movement's branches and their strategies to confront leprosy, ranging from concerts[15] to cycling events,[16] and including theatre productions.[17]

Morhan argues that it 'is doing its part; and hopes the government will do the same'.[18] An activist points out, in a letter published by *Jornal do Morhan*, that

15 *JM*, n.28, 1999, p. 5.
16 *JM*, n.33, 2000, p. 10.
17 *JM*, n.44, 2006/2007, p. 11.
18 *JM*, n.27, 1999, p. 2.

anybody that knows the movement's work 'will understand immediately its social importance to the world'.[19]

Honneth (1997: 30) argues that, in the realm of social esteem, 'the individual is recognized as a person whose capabilities are of constitutive value to a concrete community'. Similarly, Seglow (2009: 68) points out that: 'Social movements' battles to get their esteem-worthy achievements on the public agenda evince their belief in the normative power of a community of esteem'. If that is so, the best way Morhan could claim to be esteem-worthy is by defending values taken as unquestionable, such as public health. In an editorial, the national coordinator of Morhan tries to convince other activists about the need to struggle against the disease:

> At this moment, we are deeply involved in accelerating the pace towards the elimination of Hansen's disease in our country. Grass-root activists must follow this strategy, seeking uniformity and the quality of our actions. We need to struggle for the rights of people affected by the disease. But how can we achieve this in a country in which the great majority of the population does not fully exert citizenship? The movement's struggle is thus broader, advocating citizenship and health to everybody.[20]

The text justifies the importance of struggling for the elimination of leprosy and it requires activists to act in this direction. Morhan's coordinator argues that the struggle for citizenship depends on the universality of the right to health. In doing so, he states that the movement's struggle is socially relevant and aims at the construction of a better society. Curiously, a claim for citizenship can be a part of the struggle for social esteem. This is why Morhan's coordinator argues, in the same text, that 'every day we will feel prouder for being at Morhan'.

More than propelling self-interest, these persons would be fighting for justice and social well-being. This explains, for instance, their articulation with several struggles in the field of health, including those related to HIV/AIDS, tuberculosis and thalidomide.[21] Instead of affirming the differences of people affected by leprosy, the movement broadens the scope of its political goals, claiming to be committed to society's objectives (Alexander 1996; Barnes et al. 2006: 201; Melucci 1996). The health discourse helps the movement to show its value.

This is not, however, the only contribution that people affected by leprosy claim to offer society. An entirely different way to show their value is related to their past experiences. Several individuals in conversation groups argue that their entire lives have been sacrificed to protect society from the disease. They argue they have lost their freedom, their rights and their families so as to allow society to accomplish modernity's cleansing goals. They have had their houses burned and their families

19 *JM*, n.33, p. 2000, p. 11.

20 *JM*, n.28, 1999, p. 2.

21 *JM*, n.28, 1999, p. 3/*JM*, n.30, 1999, p. 5.

destroyed for the sake of public health. Based on these arguments, they affirm society owes them:

> **Osmar (Group 5)**: Society has a duty towards patients, you know? […] It has the obligation of receiving us, because we came from it and we are here because of it!

This sort of argument emerges frequently in the struggle for compensation of those that have been compulsorily segregated. Several individuals claim that the sacrifice of their lives for the sake of societal goals has been misrecognized. It is important to mention that my data was collected in a period marked by a debate in the Brazilian National Congress over a bill to compensate former patients. In most conversation groups, the bill was mentioned. People often supported it with arguments grounded on the idea that the lives of individuals segregated were sacrificed to promote a common good.

> **César (Group 7):** You were placed here against your will […] If you had remained in society you could have infected other people. So, they pushed you into this colony without asking you. Against your will, splitting families, sons and mother […]. I look at my mother's case and many other persons' stories. I think this compensation is more than fair. And it shouldn't be small. It should be even higher, because they are already at the end of their lives.

From César's perspective, persons who have been segregated deserve a high compensation, because they were pushed into colonies to avoid contamination. Their contribution would be manifest in their own biographies and the hurdles they had to face so that society could achieve its goals.

Personal Achievements

A third way of struggling for social esteem involves the demonstration of personal achievements. This third type of struggle is particularly targeted by the critics of Honneth who fear that the quest for social esteem may lead to new forms of injustice and misrecognition. In the data analysed for this article, several individuals attempted to show they were not incapable or unproductive. They often deny, for instance, anything that associates leprosy to panhandling, as such association may corroborate the idea of uselessness.

> **Raimundo (Group 3):** Ask him for how long I have worked with this bike? Always selling bread. He mentioned the possibility of begging … The beggar should feel ashamed.

> **Esmeralda (Group 2):** Morhan struggled a lot against panhandling, you know? It helped in showing that patients are capable; they can work and improve their conditions.

Work is a way of showing oneself as productive and capable. If work is clearly a way to claim one's social contribution, in this case it is also a way to show one's personal achievements, due to the severe hindrances these individuals had to face in order to work.

> **Eduardo (Group 12):** I am a professional driver. And why do I say I am professional? Because I can work exactly in the same way as those that have their hands and feet in perfect conditions. [...] I worked for several years as a nurse, receiving half of a minimum wage. But, as a leprosy patient, I was proud to be working and to be financially independent.

> **José (Group 5):** I was very demanding as a construction worker [...] Every detail had to be done perfectly [...] God gave me the gift of working. I started when I was five years old, when I lost my father. [...] I can't stand still. As the sun goes up, I feel like doing something.

In both utterances, individuals state they are able to work and express their pride in being able to financially sustain themselves or in having 'the gift of working'. Effort and work ground self-esteem, as individuals claim they are not a burden to society. On the one hand, this perspective challenges the stigma of incapacity. On the other hand, it corroborates the idea that individual effort is a fair way evaluate human beings. The statements dispute the connection between leprosy and worthlessness, but not the broader understanding that ties social value to work. This broader understanding is, nonetheless, at the basis of contemporary stigma around leprosy, thus feeding individuals' persistent misrecognition (Bakirtzief 1994; Mendonça 2009a).

Hartmann and Honneth (2006) point out the dangers of meritocratic societies when they discuss the paradoxes of contemporary capitalism. If the principle of achievement has an emancipatory dimension, it has led to an overestimation of the role of market success, transforming it into 'the sole criterion for rewarding achievement' (Hartmann and Honneth 2006: 54). This process has led to the misrecognition of other forms of achievement, which can create a sense of inner emptiness and absence of purpose (Honneth 2004: 467).

In this sense, there are other sorts of achievement claimed by persons affected by leprosy which seem to be more displacing than the capacity to work. Two of them must be noted here: 1) activist engagement; and 2) the arts of everyday practices.

Several activists display their engagement as an important source of achievement. They try to show themselves as leaders of important victories.

> **Nair (Group 10):** many Hansen's disease patients were leaving the colony and they came to me. That is how this neighborhood was formed. I was always organizing projects. I sent one to Brasília during the government of President Sarney [requesting resources] so that we could construct houses. And we have received 105 houses. And we built these houses in a time when there were no roads. We were in the dirt, carrying wood on our shoulders. My shoulder was injured and I have photographs to prove it. But we have accomplished it. We built 105 houses in 11 days! That is why I say I can walk with my head held high. I know I have paid my duties to society!

> **Claudia (Group 12):** I was engaged with several popular movements. I was one of the founders of the Labor's Party. I have walked through 80 suburbs, and I was the only one with Hansen's disease. Then, I went to work with the basic ecclesiastic community. I became the coordinator. After that, I worked in the church. I have done many things. I have given 17 years of my life to communities and popular movements. […] And then we founded Morhan. If you look at the initial meeting minutes, my name is there, as one of the founders of Morhan. […] I was also in the feminist movement. I arrived there as an activist and I became president.

Both Nair and Claudia seek to show how they have been active in their communities. Nair emphasizes the effort required to build 105 houses for former colony residents, which allows her to feel proud. Claudia highlights her history of struggles in civil society. These examples clearly show how personal achievements and social contributions can be thought of as intertwined in certain cases. These women state they have devoted their lives to the improvement of their communities. Their personal achievements are also social contributions.

Similarly, Morhan's newsletter shows how activism is simultaneously seen as a source of personal achievement and as a form of social contribution. Several stories point to important accomplishments obtained by activists. Bacurau, the founder of Morhan, has received many international awards and has also met with the Pope.[22] Even after his death, 'he is remembered in the entire world', as shown by visits to China[23] and Italy.[24] Antônio Borges, another highly ranked Morhan activist, has also been granted many awards.[25] He has been in New York for a United Nations meeting[26] and has written an autobiography about his accomplishments.[27] A third

22 *JM*, n.27, 1999, p. 12.
23 *JM*, n.27, 1999, p. 5.
24 *JM*, n.37, 2001, p. 2.
25 *JM*, n.34, 2000, p. 9/*JM*, n.35, 2000, p. 12/*JM*, n.36, 2000, p. 15.
26 *JM*, n.25, 1998, p. 16.
27 *JM*, n.31, 1999, p. 2/*JM*, n.34, 2000, p. 9.

activist to be cited is Cristiano Torres, who is the only former Hansen's disease patient to have carried the Olympic torch.[28]

If all these stories show personal achievements, they also relate these achievements to social contributions. An article published in 2006 claims that the volunteers engaged in the movement should be thought of as performing an important social task.[29] Some articles emphasize that volunteering fosters the 'pleasure of feeling useful'[30] and 'valued'.[31] The fact that volunteer work is unpaid does not reduce its significance.[32] In displaying their accomplishments as activists, people can blend personal achievements and social contributions.

These cases suggest that it is very hard to establish a sharp distinction between personal achievements and social contributions. Despite clarifying different dimensions of struggles for esteem, Seglow's (2009) dichotomy seems misleading, as it does not consider the merging of these dimensions. It also seems problematic, because it deduces very specific effects from each dimension. According to Seglow (2009), the display of personal achievements would foster social competition, while claims of social contribution would advance solidarity. This does not seem to be a general rule.

In order to further clarify this point, I must move now to the other aforementioned way to claim one's personal achievements: the arts of everyday practices. Actions that could be thought of as ordinary may carry a great potential for esteem, as they help individuals to prove they are not useless:

> **José (Group 5):** Even if my hands are like these [shows hands severely affected by leprosy], I can thread a needle and sew a button.
>
> **Vera**: Can you still thread a needle?
>
> **José**: I can!
>
> **Vera**: And sew a button?
>
> **José**: Absolutely! [...] Do you see all these fences? [Pointing to fence around his house] I haven't paid a penny for that [...] I have done it myself!
>
> **Osmar**: Look at that! [...] This is incredible!

28 *JM*, n.39, 2004, p. 10.
29 *JM*, n.42, 2006, p. 12.
30 *JM*, n.39, 2004, p. 11.
31 *JM*, n.41, 2005, p. 12.
32 *JM*, n.37, 2001, p. 8.

> [Fuad Abdala was a] Tough and determined man, who has never given up, despite having been affected by leprosy and having lost his vision. The mutilations have not obstructed him from going to university, where he graduated in law. Excellent professional, example of kindness, he has always worked on a volunteer basis. Good father, he had eight kids, seven of them adopted. Good husband, he shared 50 years of his life with Palmira, his full time partner. And as a friend, he would always have a word of affection to everyone who approached him.[33]

The first conversation shows the happiness caused by the realization of tasks that, although simple, are extremely difficult for persons who have lost the sense of touch. José can sew buttons and make fences, which is regarded as 'incredible'. There is no claim to social contribution here, but simply the expression of one's personal merits. These small chores enable him to see himself as valuable. The second text is a fragment of an obituary published by Morhan's newsletter. It attempts to function as a life lesson. For those affected by leprosy, it is motivating as it evinces the possibility of overcoming obstacles. For others, it demonstrates accomplishments that contest stigma.

Although these statements clearly express personal achievements, it would be hard to say that they somehow stimulate social competition. In this regard, Seglow's (2009) argument that claims concerned with social contribution are the ones that foster solidarity seems problematic. There is no causal relation between the nature of a claim for esteem and its pragmatic effects. Claims of personal achievement and social contribution may foster either competition or solidarity, depending on other contextual elements.

To conclude, I would like to cite a last type of claim related to personal achievements which helps to show both problems of Seglow's (2009) proposition (that is, its sharp distinction between intertwined dimensions and its way of deducing effects from the nature of claims). In the data analysed, one of the most common personal achievements claimed by persons affected by leprosy is the capacity to take care of one's own family and raise one's children, as shown below:

> **Manuel (Group 1):** if I tell people I have been an intern patient – with more than fifty years of isolation – and I have raised a man for society… this will make them pay attention: 'This guy wasn't useless! He was sick, but he was a normal citizen'. If I tell people that Aparecida raised a lot of kids when segregated…
>
> **Aparecida:** Three! Two of them are nurses and my boy is a driver.
>
> **Isabel (Group 8):** I was married, and my first son is employed in the city!

These fragments express the pride of parenting. Manuel states that the fact of having raised his son, now 'a man for society', proves his life has been worth living. From

33 *JM*, n.40, 2004, p. 12.

his perspective, this seems to be his greatest achievement, evincing he 'wasn't useless!'. Again, it would be difficult to interpret this utterance as fostering social competition. It does not seem to ground any new dimension of misrecognition either. The expression of one's achievement here does not engender oppression or identity reification.

It is also important to note that Manuel's achievement is framed as social contribution. He has not only raised a man, but he has raised him 'for society'. That is why professions and employment are mentioned. Aparecida has raised two nurses and a driver. Isabel has a son employed in the city. Both of them are proud because they have managed to reintegrate their children. Both of them are proud because they have done something they believe to be good for society. Seglow (2009: 70) states that 'since parenting focuses on making children into secure, self-confident, autonomous and hence productive citizens, from society's point of view it looks more like a contribution than an achievement'. In the case of persons affected by leprosy, however, it complexly mixes both categories, as the activity of parenting has been managed in extremely adverse conditions.

Concluding Remarks

This article has sought to explore the relevance of social esteem in the framework of recognition, challenging the idea that struggles for esteem ground new forms of misrecognition. It presented Honneth's understanding of social esteem, emphasizing that he does not equate it to the positive evaluation of collective identities. Honneth's conception is centered on individuals and their possibility of being seen as estimable.

After presenting Honneth's definition and claiming that some of his critics do not do justice to his ideas, the article discussed the recent literature that points to the existence of different types of struggles for social esteem. Several scholars fear that claims steered by the display of personal achievements may lead to social competition. The article focused particularly on Seglow's (2009) argument about an internal tension in Honneth's proposals.

Based on these theoretical discussions, the article then presented a case study about the struggles for social esteem of persons affected by leprosy in Brazil. The analysis revealed that esteem is a central dimension of their claims. This finding corroborates the idea that struggles for esteem should not be equated to quests for the positive consideration of shared attributes. Persons affected by leprosy do not seek the affirmation of their difference. They struggle for social esteem through: 1) the contestation of stigma; 2) the claim of contributing to the accomplishment of social goals; and 3) the demonstration of personal achievements.

There are at least three implications that could be derived from the analysis of this case. The first one is that justice should not be restricted to the universal language of rights. The fear that struggles for social esteem may lead to new forms of oppression and misrecognition is itself dangerous. Restricting recognition to rights would imply misrecognizing a key dimension of the struggles of former leprosy patients.

These individuals are not demanding a right when they claim that they can help eliminate the disease or when they show their capacity to do incredible tasks. When they state that they have raised children for society or that they can sew a button with no hand sensibility, they are claiming they are not useless. In doing so, they challenge the degrading meanings that deprive them of the possibility of self-realization. In asserting their value, they also make clear that their personal achievements and social contributions are essential for the construction of their identities.

If justice is understood as grounded in self-realization, its conditions become dependent on the possibility of feeling useful. Such feeling cannot be granted nor assured *a priori*, but it can be easily inhibited when individuals only face demeaning and humiliating responses in their social interactions. By showing the importance of social esteem for self-realization, I thus claim that the possibility of being esteemed should be protected or promoted.

It must also be emphasized that social esteem is important for another reason: it plays a key role in empowering individuals to struggle against disrespect.[34] Individuals that are systematically stigmatized may internalize degrading meanings that end up limiting their capacity for agency. By seeing oneself as valuable, one can more easily challenge the situations and frameworks that are seen as unjust. When an individual shows her/his achievements and social contributions, s/he is simultaneously presenting herself or himself as a subject capable of confronting ingrained negative meanings and forms of misrecognition.

My argument, in sum, is that self-realization, cannot be assured only through universal rights. As recently highlighted by Cooke (2009: 79), 'contemporary politics must take seriously a concern for recognition that goes beyond a demand for recognition of universal qualities or capacities'. There is something in justice beyond general citizenship. This is the problem of Habermas' (1994; 1998) approach to recognition. According to Habermas: 'all that is required is the consistent actualization of the system of rights' (Habermas 1994: 113). In advocating that the language of rights may encompass recognition, Habermas leaves unexplored the non-universal dimension of selves. He argues that rights may be conceived of in ways that address the issue of cultural differences, but he does not seem to notice that the category of social esteem should not be reduced to struggles about cultural differences.

In the same direction, Robert Goodin once presented me with an intriguing question: 'what may the theory of recognition offer us that an extended theory of rights doesn't?'[35] At the basis of his question lies the premise that justice can

34 I am thankful to Ana Carolina Ogando for her support in the elaboration of this argument.

35 Personal conversation held in the Research School of Social Sciences (ANU), September 18th 2007.

be attained through the assurance of universal conditions of dignity. My analysis suggests, however, that the possibility of struggling to be seen as valuable due to one's contributions and achievements cannot be explained through the universal language of citizenship. The foundations for the construction of self-esteem are established in the specificities of individuals, allowing them to see themselves as important and needed. The crux of social esteem, its integrative function, and its impacts over practical self-realization cannot be grasped by the idea of citizenship, no matter how broadly it is conceived. And social esteem becomes important to justice precisely because the goal of justice is understood here as the promotion of the conditions for self-realization through moral grammars that are simultaneously reciprocal and inclusive.

The second implication of the analysis regards the distinction between struggles for esteem based on social contributions and those grounded on personal achievements. The case explored shows that social contributions and personal achievements may be interwoven. The distinction proposed by Seglow (2009) seems to indicate different facets of struggles for social esteem, more than a tension within Honneth's framework. From this perspective, it seems incorrect to derive direct consequences from types of claims. The demonstration of one's personal achievements does not necessarily lead to competition. In the same way, it is plausible to think that attempts to frame one's actions as social contributions may hurt social solidarities. The pragmatic effects of claims cannot be deduced from their nature, especially because it is often impossible to distinguish social contributions from personal achievements in struggles for esteem.

Finally, the third implication of the article relates to the fruitfulness of operationalizing Honneth's realms of recognition in empirical studies. The analysis of different cases and sorts of struggles can be very enlightening for a deeper understanding of the actual dynamics of recognition. Struggles for recognition take on different shapes in different contexts. The application of these concepts to empirical realities will help to clarify the nuances of recognition, as well as its strengths and shortcomings.

References

Alexander, J. 1996. 'Collective Action, Culture and Civil Society: Secularizing, Updating, Inverting, Revising and Displacing the Classical Model of Social Movements', in *Alain Touraine*. Edited by M. Diani and J. Clarke. London: Falmer Press, 205-34.

Bakirtzief, Z. 1994. 'Águas passadas que movem moinhos: as representações sociais da hanseníase'. Unpublished Masters Dissertation, Department of Social Psychology, PUC-SP.

Barnes, M., Newman, J. and Sullivan, H. 2006. 'Discursive Arenas: Deliberation and the Constitution of Identity in Public Participation at a Local Level', *Social Movement Studies*, 5(3), 193-207.

Boucher, G. 2004. 'The Struggle for Recognition'. Paper presented at the *Hegel and Ethical Politics Summer School*, February. Available from: http://www.ethicalpolitics.org/geoff-boucher/2004/recognition.htm [Accessed 5 October 2008].

Cooke, M. 2009. 'Beyond dignity and difference: revisiting the politics of recognition', *European Journal of Political Theory*, 8(1), 76-95.

Feldman, L.C. 2002. 'Redistribution, recognition, and the state: the irreducibly political dimension of injustice', *Political Theory*, 30(3), 410-40.

Fraser, N. 2000. 'Rethinking recognition'. *New Left Review* II (3), 107-20.

Fraser, N. 2001. 'Recognition without ethics?' *Theory, Culture & Society*, 18(2-3), 21-42.

Fraser, N. 2003. 'Social Justice in the age of identity politics: Redistribution, Recognition, and Participation', in N. Fraser and A. Honneth, *Redistribution or Recognition? A Political-Philosophical Exchange*. London/New York: Verso, 7-109.

Gould, T. 2005. *A Disease Apart: Leprosy in the Modern World*. New York: St. Martin's Press.

Gussow, Z. 1989. *Leprosy, Racism and Public Health*. Boulder, CO: Westview Press.

Habermas, J. 1994. 'Struggles for recognition in the democratic constitutional state', in *Multiculturalism: Examining the Politics of Recognition*, edited by A. Gutmann. Princeton: Princeton University Press, 107-48.

Habermas, J. 1998. *The Inclusion of the Other: Studies in Political Theory*. Cambridge, MA: MIT Press.

Hartmann, M. and Honneth, A. 2006. 'Paradoxes of Capitalism', *Constellations*, 13(1), 41-58.

Honneth, A. 1996. *The Struggle for Recognition: the Moral Grammar of Social Conflicts*. Cambridge, MA: MIT Press.

Honneth, A. 1997. 'Recognition and moral obligation', *Social Research*, 64(1), 16-35.

Honneth, A. 2001. 'Recognition or redistribution? Changing Perspectives on the Moral Order of Society', *Theory, Culture & Society*, 18(2-3), 43-55.

Honneth, A. 2003a. 'Redistribution as recognition: a response to Nancy Fraser', in N. Fraser and A. Honneth, *Redistribution or Recognition? A political-Philosophical exchange*. London and New York: Verso, 110-97.

Honneth, A. 2004. 'Organized self-realization: some paradoxes of individualization', *European Journal of Social Theory*, 7(4), 463-78.

Markell, P. 2003. *Bound by Recognition*. Princeton: Princeton University Press.

McBride, C. 2009. 'Demanding recognition: equality, respect, and esteem', *European Journal of Political Theory*, 8(1), 96-108.

McBride, C. and Seglow, J. 2009. 'Recognition: Philosophy and politics', *European Journal of Political Theory*, 8(1), 7-12.

Melucci, A. 1996. *Challenging Codes: Collective Action in the Information Age*. Cambridge: Cambridge University Press.

Mendonça, R.F. 2007. 'Hanseníase e mundo da vida: as diferentes facetas de um estigma milenar', *Eco-Pós*, 10(1), 120-47.

Mendonça, R.F. 2009a. *Reconhecimento e deliberação: as lutas das pessoas atingidas pela hanseníase em diferentes âmbitos interacionais*. Unpublished PhD thesis, Communication Science Program, FAFICH, Federal University of Minas Gerais.

Mendonça, R.F. 2009b. 'A dimensão intersubjetiva da auto-realização: em defesa da teoria do reconhecimento', *Revista Brasileira de Ciências Sociais*, 24(70), 143-54.

Mendonça, R.F. 2011. 'What if the realms of recognition contradict each other?'. Paper presented at the *Political Studies Association Conference*, London, 19-21 April.

Parkinson, J. 2003. 'The Legitimation of Deliberative Democracy' PhD thesis, Political Science Program, RSSS, Australian National University.

Petersen, A. and Willig, R. 2002. 'An Interview with Axel Honneth: The Role of Sociology in the Theory of Recognition', *European Journal of Social Theory*, 5(2), 265-77.

Seglow, J. 2009. 'Rights, contribution, achievement and the world: some thoughts on Honneth's recognitive ideal', *European Journal of Political Theory*, 8(1), 61-75.

Smith, N.H. 2009. 'Work and the struggle for recognition', *European Journal of Political Theory*, 8(1), 46-60.

Thompson, S. 2006. *The Political Theory of Recognition: A Critical Introduction*. Cambridge: Polity.

White, C. 2001. 'Cultural aspects of leprosy treatment in Rio de Janeiro, Brazil'. Unpublished PhD thesis, Department of Anthropology, Tulane University.

WHO. 2008. 'Global Leprosy Situation, beginning of 2008', *Weekly Epidemiological Record*, 83(33), 293-300.

WHO. 2009. Leprosy: The disease 2009 [online] *World Health Organization*. Available from: http://www.who.int/lep/leprosy/en/index.html [Accessed 03 February 2008].

WHO. 2010. 'Global Leprosy Situation, beginning of 2008', *Weekly Epidemiological Record*, 85(35), 337-48.

Conclusion

Simon Thompson and Majid Yar

In drawing this volume to a conclusion, it is worth reflecting again on the aims that we set out at the beginning. This book is intended to contribute to the ongoing and vibrant scholarly debate that has emerged around the theory and politics of recognition. A rich and diverse array of contributions has contributed to a strong revival of interest in the concept of recognition. It has become an increasingly important resource for theorizing and understanding politics, political action and political conflict. As such, it has come to command attention from scholars from all around the world and from across a range of disciplines. Yet we believe that there is a significant lacuna in the debates as they have thus far developed. Specifically, misrecognition – as both a theoretical concept and empirical phenomenon – has been relatively neglected. There has been a tendency to view it as a background issue, one that can be grasped simply as the *absence* or *lack* of recognition. Where it has been addressed, there has perhaps been a tendency to see it as a synonym of 'injustice', a phenomenon which does not warrant extensive elaboration, reflection or investigation in its own right. In assembling the contributions to this book, our hope has been to provide a corrective to this neglect of misrecognition as a meaningful and fruitful political and social category.

To say this is not to suggest that we propose in any way to supplant the theory of recognition with an alternative theory of misrecognition. Any such move would miss the fundamental point, namely that recognition and misrecognition are deeply intertwined and mutually constitutive. Equally, we did not aim to generate a systematic and inclusive framework for thinking about misrecognition: as with recognition, the manifold ways of conceptualizing misrecognition means that any attempt at such synthesis would do hermeneutic violence to the array of perspectives presented by the contributors to the book. At the same time, however, we did wish to subject misrecognition to careful and concerted reflection. This, we hope, has enabled us to address a range of important questions: how might an elaborated concept of misrecognition take shape? How exactly are the concepts of recognition and misrecognition related to one another? In what ways might the concept of misrecognition help enrich our understanding of the dynamics of particular political and social struggles? What role does misrecognition play in the emergence of such struggles? In tackling such questions, our aims have been twofold. Firstly, we have tried to help develop a theoretical vocabulary with which we might better articulate the dynamics of misrecognition, their underlying logic and configuration. Secondly, we have sought to demonstrate the practical value of the concept of misrecognition, its ability to help illuminate concrete social and political relations across a wide range of domains.

What, then, has been established in the contributions offered here? First, we would suggest, the authors in this volume have demonstrated that misrecognition comprises a distinctive phenomenon in its own right, which as such has its own roots and intersubjective logic. For example, Thompson and Hoggett demonstrate how psychic structures of affective ambivalence can be seen to lie at the root of misrecognition, thereby potentially 'derailing' the possibility of recognition. The psychic forces of hate, narcissism and envy drive misrecognition, and they must be overcome if paths to meaningful recognition are to be realized. The psychic dynamics of misrecognition are also addressed by Yar in his contribution. He seeks to establish, through an engagement with empirical research on crime, the ways in which the childhood experience of misrecognition (as emotional and physical abuse and neglect) reverberates through the life course, disposing the misrecognized to become themselves agents of further misrecognition. The fundamental importance of misrecognition is also excavated by Brace, whose contribution explores slavery as the ultimate expression of the denial of a person's humanity. Its moral significance, she suggests, far exceeds the notions of identity and authenticity that tend to condition debates around the politics of recognition.

A second significant line of argument concerns the ways in which misrecognition, far from being simply the regrettable absence of recognition, is itself constitutively implicated in the development of struggles for recognition. That is to say, the experience of misrecognition plays a critical role in activating social subjects' yearning and drive to overturn existing patterns of intersubjective relations. Ferrarese argues, in this vein, that *struggle* – born of the experience of 'resistance' from an 'enemy' who refuses one's claims – is the basis upon which one might acquire the status of a 'world changer'. Without the experience of misrecognition-as-resistance, struggles for emancipation cannot take coherent shape. A similar insight emerges from Meer's re-reading of W.E.B. Du Bois' concept of the 'double consciousness' experienced by African-Americans in a social and political context in which they are consistently misrecognized by a white majority. This 'double consciousness', which emerges directly from 'being an outcast and stranger', is in fact a form of 'gifted second sight': it enables the introduction into the world of new ways of thinking, feeling and experiencing, and as such has the potential to enrich society as a whole. Yet this rich resource for social transformation requires first the experience of misrecognition; without it, such a consciousness could not and would not take shape. Mendonça's case study of people affected by Hansen's Disease also points to the vital role of misrecognition in motivating political struggles. In particular, he shows how the experience of the stigmatization can inspire struggles for esteem. In these various ways, these authors confirm Honneth's claims for the motivating power of misrecognition for social and political struggles.

A third important insight which emerges from the contributions to the book is that the concept of misrecognition offers an important resource for understanding substantive domains of political and social experience. While theoretical and conceptual work is undertaken by many of the authors featured here, there is an equal importance attached to utilizing the lens of misrecognition to illuminate the differentiated experience of concrete social subjects. Hence several of the authors explore the logic, dynamics and consequences of misrecognition in relation to experiences as diverse as those of work, disability, racism, crime and disease. Thus, for example, Sayer cogently draws out the ways in which misrecognition inheres in the structural patterns of divisions of labour in our society. An integral element of the 'problem' of work in class-based societies is that, beyond the inequities of differential financial reward, consignment to particular kinds of labour denies workers meaningful opportunities to experience esteem and respect. Attempts, however well intentioned, to hide the differences in experience of workers from different social classes ultimately serve only to reproduce the misrecognition that is structurally embedded in the economic system. In his contribution on the politics and policies around disability, Calder elucidates what he perceives to be the limitations of misrecognition as an all-encompassing framework through which to grasp the phenomenon of injustice. He suggests that the tendency to focus upon the *cultural* dimensions of social experience unwittingly threatens to overlook the very real and material constraints and conditions which frame the lives of those with disabilities.

What emerges from the wide-ranging explorations offered here, then, is an enriched theoretical and analytical vocabulary with which we might better grasp the nature and significance of misrecognition. As we have already noted, this has not led to a single coherent theory of misrecognition, but rather towards a variegated understanding of how misrecognition might be better conceptualized, its import acknowledged, and its potential for the analysis of political problems and conflicts developed. Having said this, what if we did want 'a systematic and inclusive framework for thinking about misrecognition'? What work would we need to do to develop such a framework? What would it look like? In these final few paragraphs, we want to offer some thoughts on these questions. By doing so, we shall be sketching the outlines of an agenda for future research, at the level both of conceptual analysis and of empirical investigation. And, although we would not presume that any of the authors in this volume would fully endorse this agenda, it does emerge out of our reflections on their rich and varied contributions. We present our thoughts in the form of brief reflections on four questions.

First, what is misrecognition? We would argue that any satisfactory answer to this question needs to provide a clear account of the relationship of misrecognition to recognition, on the one hand, and to nonrecognition, on the other. While the first of these relationships has been extensively explored in this book, the second has received much less attention. In a footnote to his chapter, Yar proposes one way in which this distinction could be made: while misrecognition 'entails an act of recognition that is "distorted" or "incomplete"', nonrecognition 'entails an absolute refusal to acknowledge the existence of the other as a human subject' (this volume: 129). To develop this thought a little further, we would suggest that there are two elements to a relationship of recognition: (1) one party's acknowledgement of the other and (2) their attribution of positive status to that other. If this is so, then, in a relationship of nonrecognition, only the first of these two elements is in place. Although each party acknowledges the other's existence, neither attributes positive value to the other. Instead, each may despise or hate the other, or regard them as their mortal enemy. In a relationship of misrecognition, by contrast, although both elements are in place, the second somehow falls short or goes wrong. As Yar puts it, 'a subject is recognized in some sense or other, but not in a manner consistent with the requirements of a full and complete affirmation of a subject' (ibid.). Perhaps one party only acknowledges one aspect of the other's identity, but fails to recognize others. For example, feminists may claim that certain systems of patriarchal power only recognize stereotypically 'feminine' aspects of women's character. We would argue that gaining clarity about the relationships between recognition, misrecognition and nonrecognition will be vital for the future development of this field.

Second, are there limits to the scale of misrecognition? In this book, the idea of misrecognition has been applied both to direct personal relationships between significant others, and also to more mediated political relationships between the citizens of a state. In the introduction, we also mentioned in passing recent work which has attempted to apply the idea of recognition to matters of global justice. If these attempts are successful, it would seem to follow that the idea of misrecognition could also be applied at the global level. But is this right? Is misrecognition an idea which can be used to describe interpersonal relationships, relationships between citizens, and relationships between global actors? Some commentators are quite hopeful about the prospects for extending a recognitive framework of analysis up to the global level, even suggesting that love-as-recognition can be applied to matters of global justice. Volker Heins, for instance, explores the possibility of 'a universalistic love ethos' which would be the global extension of Honneth's conception of love (Heins 2008; cf. Thompson 2011). Others – including Honneth himself (2010) – are rather cautious about this prospect of applying ideas of recognition at a global level. Those taking this more cautious line may, for instance, argue that the nature of recognition, and therefore misrecognition, fundamentally changes as we move up the scale from family to state to global society. Or it may be argued that there strict limits to the scale of relationships of recognition and misrecognition. With the phenomenal rise in interest in matters of global justice in recent years, this is bound to be a matter on which political theorists of recognition will want to have their say.

Third, what is the relationship between misrecognition and other forms of injustice? Several of the authors in this volume have made reference to Fraser's work on three distinct facets of injustice. For her, actors may suffer from misrecognition, maldistribution or misrepresentation. They may not enjoy parity of participation because they suffer from status inequality, because they do not control sufficient resources, or because they lack adequate political voice. In developing this tripartite framework, Fraser wants to argue that political theorists of recognition, particularly those of a Hegelian bent, place too much emphasis on culture and identity, and not enough on the economic and political systems which may also be significant sites of injustice. This is Calder's point, who offers this paraphrase of Fraser's position: 'when it comes to social justice, misrecognition is not the only game in town' (this volume: 107). Does it follow that the other authors in this volume, by focusing strongly on misrecognition, fail to pay due attention to other forms of injustice? The answer to this question will depend on whether one endorses Fraser's contention that misrecognition is only one of three forms of injustice, or whether one accepts Honneth's assumption that, since recognition is 'the fundamental, overarching moral category' (2003: 2-3), it can encompass concerns with status, resources and voice. Perhaps the analyses of misrecognition offered in this book can cast fresh light on this well-known debate between these leading theorists of recognition.

Fourth, in what domains of social experience can the idea of misrecognition be fruitfully applied? In this volume, misrecognition has been used to analyse slavery (Brace), disability (Calder), criminality (Yar), class division (Sayer), and disease (Mendonça). As we mentioned in our introduction, it has also been deployed in studies of a wide variety of identity groups, social movements and political institutions. But does the idea of misrecognition remain the same in all of these cases? Or are there, for instance, distinctively cultural, social, economic and political forms of misrecognition? Do identity groups defined by 'race', ethnicity, nationality, language and religion have different experiences of misrecognition? Are different sorts of social institution afflicted by their own species of misrecognition? For instance, is that 'institutional racism' to be found in the police service different to that to be found in the health service? To date, most attempts to apply ideas of recognition and misrecognition to some particular case have focused on just one such case in isolation from all others. But all of the questions just posed, we would suggest, invite comparative analysis of the different forms that misrecognition may take in different spheres, groups and institutions. In closing this book, we have offered brief reflections on four questions that may be asked about misrecognition. Our hope is that, by doing so, we have demonstrated the fruitfulness of this idea, and have offered adequate encouragement to others to continue this conversation.

References

Heins, V. 2008. 'Realizing Honneth: Redistribution, Recognition, and Global Justice'. *Journal of Global Ethics*, 4, 141-53.

Honneth, A. 2003. Contributions to Nancy Fraser and Axel Honneth, *Redistribution or Recognition A Political-Philosophical Exchange*. London: Verso.

Honneth, A. 2010. Recognition between States. On the Moral Substrate of International Relations, represented at 'The Politics of Misrecognition' conference, University of Bristol, January 2010.

Thompson, S. 2011.'Recognition beyond the state' in Tony Burns and Simon Thompson (eds) *Global Justice and the Politics of Recognition*, London: Palgrave Macmillan.

Index